MYTHS, LIES, and
DOWNRIGHT STUPIDITY

ALSO BY JOHN STOSSEL

Give Me a Break: How I Exposed Hucksters,
Cheats, and Scam Artists and Became the Scourge of the Liberal Media . . .
(HarperCollins 2004)

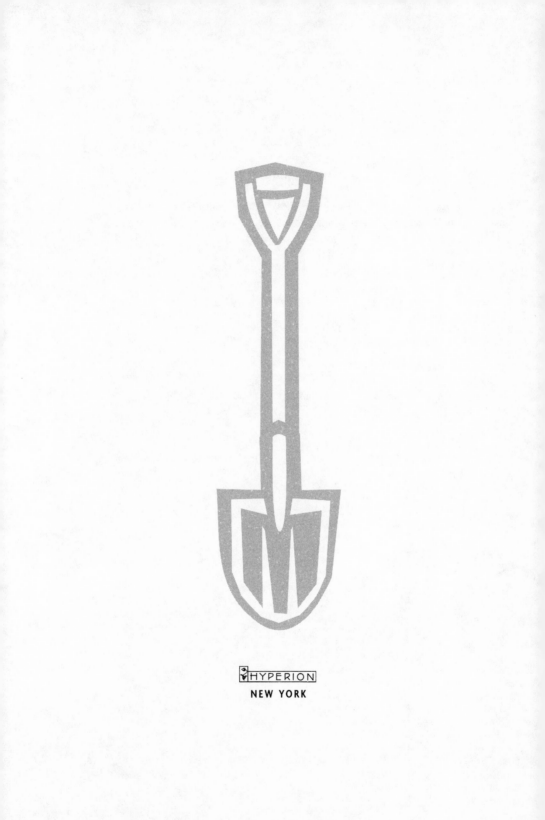

HYPERION

NEW YORK

MYTHS, LIES, and DOWNRIGHT STUPIDITY

Get Out the Shovel— Why Everything You Know Is Wrong

JOHN STOSSEL

Book design by Gretchen Achilles

Library of Congress Control Number: 2006922367

ISBN: 1-4013-0254-8

Hyperion books are available for special promotions and premiums. For details contact Michael Rentas, Assistant Director, Inventory Operations, Hyperion, 77 West 66th Street, 12th floor, New York, New York 10023, or call 212-456-0133.

FIRST EDITION

10 9 8 7 6 5 4 3 2 1

To you whom I cannot live without

CONTENTS

INTRODUCTION

MYTH-BUSTING IS fun. I wound up doing it by accident: Researching consumer stories, I discovered that much of what I thought to be true was nonsense.

On the other hand, "myth" doesn't necessarily mean "false"—it can also mean "a popular belief or tradition." Occasionally, just as we were ready to shovel the nonsense away, a myth would turn out to be true.

Usually, however, the shovel dug up lies and stupidity.

I hope that some of the lies behind the myths will make you as angry as they made me. Others may make you laugh. The later chapters will save you money, time, improve your sex life, reduce your anxiety, and even make you happier. This book is really the work of many of us at *20/20*. I wrote it, I put my spin on it, and I hold the shovel on the cover, but the shovels were really wielded by a hundred crack researchers. They dug through the nonsense and found the truth. I'm grateful to be able to take the fruits of their work and share them with you. Senior producer Martin Clancy, a talented writer and editor, was pivotal in making that happen.

Along the way, we met some very interesting people: scam artists, heroic seekers of truth, liars, and dimwits. In the following pages, you'll be able to eavesdrop on our conversations, so you can hear the truth—and the lies— just as I did. In fact, we're trying something new: If your appetite is whetted to actually see and hear some of what you are reading about, see the ABC Web links we provide in the endnotes. You'll get another perspective on the events and personalities I've had the chance to report on.

I have learned a great deal along the way. Who would have believed, for example, that walking on hot coals is actually painless? Or that you can swim in the "polluted" rivers around Manhattan and not get sick? Or that outsourcing is *good* for America?

Now I'd like to share my on-the-job education with you.

ACKNOWLEDGMENTS

I AM indebted to Becky Akers, Ted Balaker, Asher Levine, Alexander R. Cohen, Elizabeth Koch, Todd Seavey, and especially Andrew Sullivan for improving my writing. To my friends, Gerry Gold, Jim Floyd, Alan Myers, Joe Sibilia, Joe Simonetti, Mark and Miriam, Victor and Lois, and Lauren and Max for expanding my mind with their arguments. To David Boaz and Don Boudreaux for teaching me history and economics.

Much of the research for this book was done by *20/20* editors and producers Audrey Baker, Steve Brand, Joy Ciarcia-Levy, Melissa Cornick, Pat Dauer, Carla Delandri, Brian Ellis, Allan Esner, Rogene Fisher, Penny Fleming, Joel Herson, Colin Hill, Ruth Iwano, Sharon Kaufman, Janet Klein, Lisa Kraus, Tom Marcyes, Michael Mendelsohn, Bud Proctor, Ene Riisna, Glenn Ruppel, Joe Schanzer, Steve Schnee, Eric Strauss, Judy Tygard, Bonnie Vangilder, Susan Wagner, Rob Wallace, Dave Ward, and Ann Varney; I thank them for letting me steal the fruits of their work.

I thank Alyssa Apple, Ruth Curry, and my forward-thinking editor Gretchen Young for their guidance, and Andrea Rich, Richard Leibner, and Joni Evans for cheering me on.

Thank goodness for Bob Chitester, Rick Platt, and the others at www.intheclassroom.org who help me bring truths to high school students.

I thank the college students who dug out many of the truths in this book: Jennie Bragg, Alison Eddy, Elizabeth Harnier, Katie Packard, Amanda Pickens, Tracey Snyder, Rebecca Sosa, Steve Triana, and especially J.P. Polenz. If you are a college student and would like an internship, e-mail JohnStossel@abc.com

I am grateful to Ron Eustace, Michael Podgursky, Dr. William H. Schlesinger, Bradley Prescott, Stanley Coen, Dr. Michael Coe, Thomas Hazlett, Howie Rich, Joanna Schaffhausen, and Jerry Taylor, experts in their fields who contributed to this book without getting any citation in the text.

"Myths" wouldn't have been as reader friendly without *20/20* executive producer David Sloan, who suggested the Myth/Truth format, and it wouldn't have happened at all, had my assistant, Jennifer Cohen, not been persistent in pushing me to write this book.

And I couldn't have done any of this without Deborah Colloton, Mark Golden, Kristina Kendall, Frank Mastropolo, Patrick McMenamin, and Dori Rosenthal, the remarkably sane people who, under the management of Martin Phillips, compose what we call the "Stossel Unit" at *20/20*.

MYTHS, LIES, and
DOWNRIGHT STUPIDITY

CHAPTER ONE

CLUELESS MEDIA

Thomas Jefferson said he'd rather live in a country with a free press and no government, than in one with a government but no press. "The only security of all is in a free press," he wrote. "It is necessary, to keep the waters pure."

I couldn't agree more. Without media to tell us about the excesses of government, the risks of life, and the wonderful new ideas that emerge constantly from every cranny in America, our lives would be narrow, and our freedom diminished. The Fourth Estate both informs and protects us. "Where the press is free, and every man able to read," said Jefferson, "all is safe."

However, thirty-six years working in the media has left me much more skeptical of its product. Reporters are good at telling us what happened today: what buildings burned down, what army invaded, the size of the hurricane that's coming. Many reporters take astonishing risks to bring us this news. We owe them thanks.

But when it comes to science and economics, and putting life's risks in perspective, the media do a dismal job.

MYTH: The media will check it out and give you the objective truth.

TRUTH: Many in the media are scientifically clueless, and will scare you to death.

We don't do it on purpose. We just want to give you facts. But the people who bring us story ideas are alarmed. Then we get alarmed, and eager to rush that news to you.

We know that the scarier and more bizarre the story, the more likely it is that our bosses will give us more air time or a front-page slot. The scary story, justified or not, will get higher ratings and sell more papers. Fear sells. That's the reason for the insiders' joke about local newscasts: "If it bleeds, it leads."

Also, raising alarms makes us feel important.

If we bothered to keep digging until we found the better scientific experts, rather than the ones who send out press releases, we'd get the real story. But reporters rarely know whom to call. And if we did, many real scientists don't want to be bothered. Why get involved in a messy debate? It might upset someone in government and threaten the scientist's grant money. "I'd rather be left alone to do my work, and not have to babysit dumb reporters," one told me.

One real scientist, Dr. Bruce Ames of the University of California, Berkeley, did make the effort. He urged a skeptical reporter (me) to be more skeptical of pseudologic from pseudoscientists: "The number of storks in Europe has been going down for years, the birth rate's going down for years," Dr. Ames pointed out. "If you plot one against the other, it's a beautiful correlation. But it doesn't mean storks bring babies."

We've been swallowing the storks-bring-babies kind of logic for years. (My favorite version: I see fat people drinking diet soda; therefore diet soda must make people fat.) For instance, stories about pesticides making food carcinogenic would fill several pages of a Google search. To the scientifically illiterate, the stories are logical. After all, farmers keep using new pesticides, we consume them in the food we eat, and we keep hearing more people are getting cancer. It must be cause and effect! Get the shovel.

> **MYTH:** Pesticide residues in food cause cancer and other diseases.
>
> **TRUTH:** The residues are largely harmless.

Ames laughs at the claims of chemically induced cancers, and he should know—he's the one who invented the test that first frightened people about a lot of those chemicals. It's called the Ames Test, and its first use in the 1970s raised alarms by revealing there were carcinogens in hair dye, and in the flame retardants in children's pajamas. Ames helped get the chemicals banned.

Before the Ames Test, the traditional way to test a substance was to feed big doses of it to animals and wait to see if they got cancer or had babies with birth defects. But those tests took two to three years and cost $100,000. So Dr. Ames said, "Instead of testing animals, why not test bacteria? You can study a billion of them on just one Petri dish and you don't have to wait long for the next generation. Bacteria reproduce every twenty minutes."

The test proved successful. It was hailed as a major scientific breakthrough, and today, the Ames Test is one of the standards used to discover if a substance is carcinogenic.

But after getting the hair dye and the flame retardants banned, Dr. Ames and other scientists continued testing chemicals. "People started using our test," he told me, "and finding mutagens *everywhere*—in cups of coffee, on the outside of bread, and when you fry your hamburger!"

This made him wonder if his tests were too sensitive, and led him to question the very bans he'd advocated. A few years later, when I went to a supermarket with him, he certainly didn't send out any danger signals.

DR. AMES Practically everything in the supermarket, if you really looked at it at the parts per billion level, would have carcinogens. Vegetables are good for you, yet vegetables make toxic chemicals to keep off insects, so every vegetable is 5 percent of its weight in toxic chemicals. These are Nature's pesticides. Celery, alfalfa sprouts, and mushrooms are just chock-full of carcinogens.

STOSSEL Over there it says "Organic Produce." Is that better?

DR. AMES No, absolutely not, because the amount of pesticide residues— man-made pesticide residues—people are eating are actually trivial and very, very tiny amounts! We get more carcinogens in a cup of coffee than we do in all the pesticide residues you eat in a day.

In a cup of coffee? To put the risks in perspective, Ames and his staff analyzed the results of every cancer test done on rats and mice. By comparing the dose that gave the rodents cancer to the typical exposure people get, they came up with a ranking of the danger. Pesticides such as DDT and EDB came out much lower than herb tea, peanut butter, alcohol, and mushrooms. We moved over to the mushrooms as the cameras continued to roll, and Dr. Ames put his mouth where his convictions were.

DR. AMES One raw mushroom gives you much more carcinogens than any polluted water you're going to drink in a day.

STOSSEL So you're saying we shouldn't eat fresh produce?

DR. AMES No. Fresh produce is good for you! Here, I'll eat a raw mushroom even though it's full of carcinogens.

Dr. Ames is widely respected in the scientific community, but he is not on many journalists' electronic Rolodexes. He's the real deal, and no help at all if you're looking for screaming headlines.

MYTH: Radioactivity is deadly; keep it away from food!

TRUTH: Food irradiation saves lives.

A classic example of journalists falling for a stunningly stupid scientific scare—falling en masse and really hard—was the outcry over treating food with radiation.

The irradiation process would give consumers wonderful new options: strawberries that stay fresh three weeks, and chicken without the harmful levels of salmonella that the Centers for Disease Control and Prevention says kill six hundred Americans every year, and cause countless cases of food poisoning. (The last time you thought you had the flu, you may have really been sick from bacteria on chicken—this is no myth! Wash the counter, your hands, and everything that touches raw meat, because they are all crawling with potentially dangerous germs.)

But reporters and environmental activists don't worry much about the horrible toll from bacteria. For some reason, even when bacteria pose a far greater risk, the media obsess about chemicals and radiation. *Radiation!* Horrors! Three Mile Island! Jane Fonda! Nuclear bombs!

They don't worry much about bacteria because bacteria is *natural*. But radiation is natural too. We are exposed to natural radiation every minute of our lives: cosmic radiation from space, radiation from the ground, and radiation from radon in the air we breathe. Every year, the average U.S. citizen is exposed to natural radiation equal to about 360 dental X-rays.

The reporters and protesters probably didn't know that, but even if they did, they'd still be upset because irradiation plants propose passing radiation through *food*.

News stories featured Dr. Walter Burnstein, founder of a "consumer group" named Food & Water, saying, "This will be a public health disaster of the magnitude we have never seen before!" I have to admire the activists' skill in naming groups: *Food & Water*. What reporter could argue with a group with a name like that? They must be the good guys, right? I interviewed Dr. Burnstein and his "political organizer," Michael Colby.

> **MR. COLBY** If you look at the existing studies on humans and animals fed irradiated food, you will find testicular tumors, chromosomal abnormalities, kidney damage, and cancer and birth defects.
>
> **STOSSEL** Caused because somebody ate irradiated food?
>
> **MR. COLBY** Absolutely. Absolutely.
>
> **STOSSEL** [Food & Water claimed an Indian study had said that, but we called the author and she told us she didn't conclude that at all.] We just talked to her and she says she didn't say that! She never said those kids were developing cancer.
>
> **DR. BURNSTEIN** These are pure scientists and she doesn't want to make that break. We are taking it the extra inch. We're saying to people, "Don't—don't be put to sleep by people who work in test tubes— don't." I don't need proof that it goes to cancer. We already know it leads to cancer.

Reporters gave Burnstein and Colby's dubious claims so much credulous press coverage that politicians in Maine quickly banned food irradiation. New York and New Jersey followed suit. That spread fear to other states. I went to Mulberry, Florida, to report on a protest against Vindicator, a plant that proposed using radiation to kill germs on strawberries. When I got there, demonstrators were marching with picket signs, chanting, "Don't nuke our food! Don't nuke our food!" Their campaign persuaded the state of Florida to put a moratorium on Vindicator's opening.

> **DR. BURNSTEIN** Vindicator will go out of business, and not only Vindicator. That'll be the end of the entire irradiation industry . . . When we go to talk to people, we don't have to break their arms to convince them not to eat irradiated food. We just say, "Irradiated food," and people go, "What? Who wants the food irradiated?"

The fact that Dr. Burnstein was not a research scientist, but rather an osteopath with a family practice in New Jersey, didn't diminish the respect he got from the media. His protests drew headlines and TV coverage. Reporters knew radiation was bad for humans, and therefore bad for food.

One woman stood outside the Vindicator plant shouting angrily, "How much pollution are we going to put into our mouths?!"

"None," is the answer. People think food irradiation makes food radioactive, but it doesn't; the radiation just kills the bacteria, and passes right out of the food. That's why the FDA and USDA approved the process a long time ago. Spices have been irradiated for more than twenty years. Irradiation is *good* for us. If it were more common, all of us would suffer fewer instances of food poisoning and we could have fruits and vegetables that stay fresh weeks longer. But scaremongering has kept it from catching on.

Food & Water told people that the AMA and the World Health Organization did not approve of irradiation, but that was a lie. Both organizations did approve. WHO told us irradiation is as important as pasteurization.

Pasteurization also met public skepticism when it was introduced. Louis Pasteur discovered that heating milk would kill bacteria, but critics charged that pasteurization was "meddling with nature," and that it might change the properties of the food—or contaminate it. The U.S. dairy industry actually promoted raw milk as more acceptable than pasteurized milk. Only the persistence of scientists and medical experts allowed pasteurization to become standard practice. Irradiation might save as many lives, if the scaremongers would just get out of the way.

After three years of delays, the Vindicator plant finally was allowed to open. But fear of radiation has kept this good idea from spreading across America. Only a tiny fraction of American meat is irradiated today.

If 50 percent were irradiated, the CDC says nearly a million cases of bacterial infections could be avoided and 350 lives could be saved every year. 350 lives! Why isn't the press screaming about that? Because reporters and legislators look for danger in the wrong places.

Many reporters believe the activists because "*something* must be causing the cancer epidemic." Mysterious and unnatural additions to our environment are an easy suspect. After all, during the past fifty years, Americans have been exposed to chemicals and forms of pollution and radiation that humans have never experienced before. "No wonder there's so much more cancer!" say reporters. Get the shovel.

> **MYTH:** Chemical pollution is the cause of the cancer epidemic!
>
> **TRUTH:** There is no cancer epidemic.

You wouldn't know it from the media, but there has been no surge in cancers. The death rate due to cancer has been declining for more than ten years. You might argue that fewer die from cancer today simply because there are better treatments for the disease, but look at the cancer *incidence* rate.

The incidence of prostate and breast cancer is up, but that's only because there's more early detection. In the 1980s more men starting getting PSA tests, and more women had mammograms. Lung cancer increased in women because more women took up cigarettes, and skin cancer increased because of lunatic sunbathing. But overall cancer rates have not been rising, and lots of cancers, like stomach, uterine, and colorectal cancer, are on the decline.

We think there's a cancer epidemic because we hear more about cancer. Cancer is a disease of an aging population, and fortunately, more people now

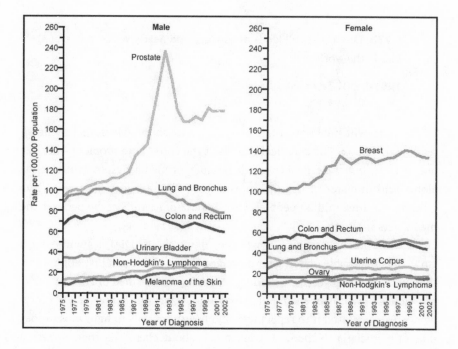

Annual Age-Adjusted Cancer Incidence Rates, National Cancer Institute, 2005.

live long enough to *get* cancer. More talk about it too. Many years ago people who got cancer were secretive about it.

The other big reason we think there is an epidemic is that the media, suspicious of chemicals, hype dubious risks.

Almost every week, there is another story about a potential menace. Reporters credulously accept the activists' scare stores: While I've been a reporter, I've been asked to do alarmist reports about hair dye, dry cleaning, coffee, chewing gum, saccharin, cyclamates, NutraSweet, nitrites, Red No. 2 dye, electric blankets, video display terminals, dental fillings, cellular phones, vaccines, potato chips, farmed salmon, Teflon, antiperspirants, and even rubber duckies.

I refused to do most of those stories, and now I have to ask, if the scares were valid, where are the bodies? If one-tenth of what the reporters suggested was happening did happen, there would be mass death. The opposite is true: Despite exposure to radiation and all those nasty new chemicals, Americans today live longer than ever.

The media hysteria may be nonsense, but our fear is real—and contagious. That can be deadly.

> **MYTH:** DDT causes all kinds of cancers, and nearly wiped out every bird in the world.
>
> **TRUTH:** DDT saves lives.

Malaria will kill more than one thousand children before you finish reading this book. The chemical DDT is at the core of the problem—not the use of DDT, but the *failure* to use it because of media hysteria. In Uganda alone, said minister of health Jim Muhwezi, "We are losing between two million and three million people a year." Think of it: *Millions* die because the media gets it wrong.

You are probably saying, *"What* is he talking about? DDT is awful!" But it isn't. DDT is capable of doing far more good than harm. You just don't know that, because some people, including reporters, are terrified of DDT.

Here's how it happened: Fifty years ago, Americans sprayed DDT everywhere. Farmers used it to repel bugs, and health officials to fight mosquitoes that carry malaria. Nobody worried much about chemicals then. It was a shock to watch the old videos my producer found: People at picnics just sat and kept eating while trucks sprayed thick white clouds of DDT on top of them. In fact, when the trucks came to spray, some people ran toward them—as if an ice cream truck had come—they were so happy to have mosquitoes repelled. Tons of DDT were sprayed on food and people.

Despite this overuse, there was no surge in cancer or any other human injury. Scientists found no evidence that spraying DDT seriously hurt people.

It did cause some harm: It threatened bird populations by thinning the shells of their eggs.

In 1962, the book *Silent Spring* by Rachel Carson made the damage famous and helped instill our fear of chemicals. The book raised some serious questions about the use of DDT, but the legitimate nature of those questions was lost in the media feeding frenzy that followed. DDT was a "Killer Chemical!" and the press was off on another fear campaign.

It turns out DDT itself wasn't the problem—the problem was that much too much was sprayed. That's often true with chemicals; it's the dose that matters. We need water, for example, but six feet of it will kill us.

In the 1950s we sprayed DDT indiscriminately, but it only takes a tiny amount to prevent the spread of malaria. If sprayed on walls of an African hut, a small amount will keep mosquitoes at bay for half a year. That makes it a wonderful malaria fighter. But today DDT is rarely used to fight malaria because environmentalists' demonization of it causes others to shun it.

That frustrates Dr. Amir Attaran, who researched the issue at Harvard University. "If it's a chemical, it must be bad," he told us. "If it's DDT, it must be awful. And that's fine if you're a rich white environmentalist. It's not so fine if you're a poor black kid who is about to lose his life from malaria." Uganda's health minister angrily asked us: "How many people do they want us to lose before we use DDT?"

Good question.

The U.S. government does spend your tax dollars trying to fight malaria in Africa, but it has not spent a penny on DDT. The money goes for things like mosquito netting over beds (even though not everyone in Africa even has a bed). The office that dispenses those funds, the Agency for International Development, acknowledges DDT is safe.

I went to the State Department to interview the USAID official in charge of international health. With a straight face, she denied that their no-funds-for-DDT policy had anything to do with being "environmentally correct." I felt like I was talking to a robot.

DR. ANNE PETERSON   I would recommend that if those who want to use [DDT for] indoor spraying, that they can and should. And it is definitely less harmful than dying and being exposed to malaria.

STOSSEL   But you won't pay for it?

DR. ANNE PETERSON   Currently we don't pay for it.

STOSSEL   This is pathetic. Millions of people are dying and you, to be politically correct, are saying, "No, we don't want to pay for DDT."

DR. ANNE PETERSON   I believe that the strategies we are using are as effective as spraying with DDT. And we are getting them out as far and as fast as we can. So, politically correct or not, I am very confident that what we are doing is the right strategy.

The right strategy? Dr. Attaran has a better perspective: "If I were to characterize what USAID does on malaria, I'd call it medical malpractice. I would call it murderous."

After my interview with Dr. Peterson, USAID said it has reconsidered its policy, and it may fund spraying of DDT.

We'll see. For now, millions die while USAID dithers.

The agency was simply responding to media hysteria. Media hysteria invites politicians to do the wrong thing. In this case, the result of the media getting it so wrong is millions of deaths.

Media attention also kills reputations, particularly when sensationalism and the herd mentality are in play. Serious subjects, worthy of careful examination, are often treated with a kind of journalistic shorthand that cheats readers and viewers, while ruining lives. In this next example, innocent children became unknowing pawns.

MYTH: "My teacher molested me." Kids wouldn't make up stuff like that!

TRUTH: Yes, they would.

This trendy media scare sent people to jail. Many were innocent of any crime, but they were convicted by the court of public opinion. The witnesses against them were children who testified to horrible events—events which, in many cases, never happened. But when the media express gets rolling, people get run over.

One victim was Kelly Michaels, a New Jersey preschool teacher convicted in 1988 of molesting twenty children in bizarre and sadistic ways. She spent five years in prison before an appeals court ruled that prosecutors had planted suggestions in the minds of the children who testified against her.

I don't blame the kids; I blame the prosecutors and the media. Reporters' imaginations and keyboards were fired up in 1983 by accusations of sodomy and satanic abuse at a California day-care center called the McMartin Preschool. The woman who started the barrage of charges was later discovered to be a paranoid schizophrenic. Her claims of devil-worship and sadism were outlandish on their face, but never mind: It was "good copy." Headlines blared, prosecutors roared, and seven people were charged in a total of 135 criminal counts.

It was nonsense. But the defendants had their lives ruined. The case against them was cooked up by therapists and social workers who planted suggestions in the minds of impressionable children, who then told horrendous tales to prosecutors. The prosecutors also listened to the drumbeats of the media, which stirred a different witches' brew for every news cycle.

Kids are highly impressionable. We know that, but psychology professor Stephen Ceci proved it in a study at Cornell University. He told me, "We are now discovering that if you put kids who were not abused through the same kind of highly leading, repetitive interview, some of those children will disclose events that seem credible but, in fact, are not borne out in actuality."

Ceci set up an experiment where he and his researchers asked kids silly questions like:

RESEARCHER Have you ever had your finger caught in a mousetrap and had to go to the hospital?
GIRL No.
RESEARCHER No?

At first, the kids say no. Then, once a week for the next ten weeks, the researchers ask the question again.

RESEARCHER You went to the hospital because your finger got caught in a mousetrap?
BOY And it—

RESEARCHER Did that happen?

BOY Uh-huh.

By week four or six or ten, about half of the kids say, "Yes, it happened." Many give such precise information that you'd think it *must* have happened.

RESEARCHER Did it hurt?

BOY Yeah.

RESEARCHER Yeah? Who took you to the hospital?

BOY My daddy, my mommy, my brother.

RESEARCHER Where in your house is the mousetrap?

BOY It's down in the basement.

RESEARCHER What is it next to in the basement?

BOY It's next to the firewood.

By the time I met that boy, weeks after the experiment was over, he still "remembered" convincing details about things that never happened.

STOSSEL Was there a time when you got your finger caught in a mousetrap and had to go to the hospital?

BOY Uh-huh.

STOSSEL Who went with you to the hospital?

BOY My mom and my dad and my brother Colin, but not the baby. He was in my mom's tummy.

What he told me was even more remarkable because just a few days before, his father discussed the experiment with him, explained that it was just a test, and that the mousetrap event never happened. The boy agreed—it was just in his imagination.

But when he talked to me, the boy denied the conversation with his father, and insisted the mousetrap story was true.

STOSSEL Did your father tell you something about the mousetrap finger story?

BOY No.

STOSSEL Is it true? Did it really happen?

BOY It wasn't a story. It really happened.

STOSSEL This really happened? You really got your finger caught? This really happened?

BOY Yeah.

Why would the boy lie to me? I said to Professor Ceci that I assumed he wasn't intentionally making up the story. Ceci said, "I think they've come to believe it. It is part of their belief system."

Some molestation "experts" thought they'd come closer to the truth by giving kids anatomically correct dolls. With dolls, the social workers wouldn't have to ask so many questions. They could just say, "Imagine you are the doll; what did the teacher touch?" Lawyers argued that kids "wouldn't make up" what had been done to the doll. But Ceci's colleague Dr. Maggie Bruck conducted tests that showed that they would.

Bruck had a pediatrician add some extra steps to his routine physical examination. He measured the child's wrists with a ribbon, he put a little label on the child's stomach, and he tickled the child's foot with a stick. Never did the doctor go *anywhere* near the child's private parts. Then, a few days after the exam, using an anatomically correct doll, Bruck and the child's father asked leading questions about the doctor's exam. We caught it on tape.

FATHER So what did he do?

GIRL He put a stick in my vagina.

FATHER He put a stick in your vagina?

GIRL Yeah.

[Then the girl claimed the doctor hammered the stick into her vagina. And she said the doctor examined her rectum.]

DR. BRUCK He was where?

GIRL In my hiney.

None of it was true. But when dolls were used, half the kids who'd never had their private parts touched claimed the doctor touched them. The tests made Dr. Bruck question her prior faith in the testimony of children. She told me she thinks dozens of innocent people are in jail.

Dr. Ceci told me their leading questions were mild compared to what the investigators asked: "What we do . . . doesn't come close, for example, to what was done in the Kelly Michaels case."

The appellate court decision that set Kelly Michaels free garnered just a smidgeon of the media attention her trial and conviction got. After she was freed, she told me about her nightmare.

MS. MICHAELS One day you're getting ready for work and making coffee, minding your business, trying to get along as best you can, being a reasonable, decent, honorable citizen, and the next minute you are an accused child molester with the most bizarre— I'd never even heard of such things even being done.

STOSSEL   They say you inserted objects, including Lego blocks, forks, spoons, serrated knives into their anuses, vaginas, penises—

MS. MICHAELS And a sword. It was in there.

STOSSEL —and a sword—

MS. MICHAELS Yeah.

STOSSEL —that you made children drink your urine, that you made kids take their clothes off and licked peanut butter off them. It's very hard to believe, yet the jury believed it and not you.

MS. MICHAELS No one was willing to doubt a child.

The media certainly wasn't. Professional skepticism took a holiday in the face of "good copy."

The media *like* bad news, and tend to believe it.

> **MYTH:** Divorce hurts women much more than men, and many men abandon their kids.
>
> **TRUTH:** Both men and women suffer after divorce, and lots of men want to give more to their kids.

The media (including the men, for psychological reasons involving guilt or other factors best left to Dr. Phil), see men as inviting, politically correct targets. When experts start trumpeting statistics that add up to "men are bad," reporters listen.

For years, I heard bad things about deadbeat dads. They were living it up, while their ex-wives and children had to scrape by. It's a recurring story, and the media regurgitates it regularly. It's also group slander.

In 1985, Lenore Weitzman, then a sociologist at Harvard, published data showing that men prosper after divorce, while women and children suffer terribly. Weitzman's report was appalling: Men's standard of living rose 42 percent after divorce, while women's declined by 73 percent. The media couldn't get enough of this exciting news. Those figures were cited not only in news stories, but in 348 social science articles, 250 law review articles, and 24 appeals court cases.

Around that time, government officials also reported that Census data showed that about half of the divorced fathers in America didn't pay child support they owed.

The evening newscasts and the papers featured both claims uncritically. The stories fit comfortably into the media's "save the victim" rut. But get the shovel: The stories didn't deserve the airtime or the headlines. A little reportorial digging would have burst the sanctimonious bubble.

Digging was finally done, but not by the media. Arizona State University psychologist Sanford Braver set out initially to examine the reasons for the shocking data. Why were those divorced fathers acting so irresponsibly? How could a dad abandon his child?

Braver was surprised to discover that the Weitzman figures were wrong, the result of a mathematical error. Weitzman later admitted she was wrong. She said a computer analyst had made a mistake—a mistake, in this case, heard around the world.

Braver conducted his own study of four hundred divorces, the biggest federally funded study ever done on divorced dads. His findings turned conventional wisdom, and all those media stories, on their heads. The 42 percent better for men, 73 percent worse for women data wasn't even close. "Our results," he said, "show that men and women come out almost exactly equally."

Braver then found that the Census data about deadbeat dads was way off too. The data came from questions asked of the custodial parent only. The custodial parent was almost always the mother. "Everything we knew about non-custodial fathers" in the Census report, Braver told me, "we knew from custodial mothers." Did some of the angry ex-wives lie? Probably, but we don't know, because the Census workers didn't bother to ask the fathers!

After my conversation with Braver, I went to Washington to meet with Dan Weinberg, the man who headed up that data collection for the Census Bureau. As often happens to me in Washington, I felt I was in another world:

STOSSEL So the Census worker says, how much in child support payments were you supposed to receive this year? And the woman remembers . . .

DAN WEINBERG Yes.

STOSSEL I just have a hard time believing that these people, many of whom are angry, are going to give honest answers.

DAN WEINBERG Actually—well, the anger may help them remember what they're supposed to receive.

STOSSEL Why not go to the man and ask, is it true?

DAN WEINBERG We would be violating the confidentiality of the custodial mother.

STOSSEL Is there *any* cross-check?

DAN WEINBERG No. We don't check any of it.

STOSSEL But wouldn't they lie just because they're mad at the man?

DAN WEINBERG People are basically honest.

The spirit of George Washington's cherry tree lives on along the Potomac. I too cannot tell a lie: The media both distort and oversimplify the issues of custody and child support. That reinforces the myth that many divorced dads never bother to see their children—the "runaway dads" so beloved by headline writers.

Some men are every bit as despicable as the media portray them, but Braver's study showed that the majority of divorced dads *do* try to see their kids. In many cases, "fathers were impeded in their efforts," Braver told me. "The mother just simply said, 'No, you can't see your kid.'"

We videotaped one such heartbreaking scene. A divorced father went to see his five kids for what he thought would be a full-day visit. He was entitled to that, under a court order, and the court also ordered the mother not to discourage the children from spending time with their father. But she clearly had poisoned his children's minds against him. The father stood just outside his ex-wife's house and begged his children, "Would you like to go out with me today?" "No," said one kid after another. Then the mother ordered the kids back into her house.

What comes through on the tape is the unbridled satisfaction of the mother and the helplessness of the father. But that's not the picture you get from the media. The media automatically cast divorced parents in the roles of villainous father and heroic mother. Many mothers are heroic, but so are many fathers. But a divorced mother as the villain? Heaven forbid! That would stand the world of media victimology on its head.

MYTH: Schools are violent.

TRUTH: Schools are pretty safe.

Media bad news bears love crime and violence. Turn on the television or pick up a tabloid, and you will be convinced that you have more to fear than ever before. Terrible things are happening, and everyone knows they're happening much more often. These stories are more candidates for the shovel. The gory pictures and the excited copy conceal the actual truth: America is safer than almost any country in human history.

The Columbine, Jonesboro, and Paducah school shootings during the late 1990s triggered a regular spate of stories about "spreading school violence." But school violence in America had been steadily decreasing. Violent crimes in schools dropped by half between 1992 and 2002, although reporting about school violence increased.

The shooting incidents were awful, but aberrations; more Americans die from lightning strikes than from school violence. More kids die in bathtubs. But the media had become obsessed with school violence. In the wake of Columbine, my network aired 383 stories about the tragedy. Sam Donaldson warned wary parents and students about "angry teens turning up in other towns." CBS News correspondent Bob McNamara called school shootings "an American nightmare that too many schools know too well."

But it wasn't a nightmare that schools knew well. In fact, students are probably safer in school than they are at home or at the mall. Crime statistics show that kids are twice as likely to be victims of violence *away* from school than they are in school.

The media hysteria encouraged people who run schools to do crazy things, like spend thousands of dollars on security cameras, and hire police officers to guard the doors. Some schools terrified students by running SWAT team drills; cops burst into classrooms and ordered kids down to the floor. The result? Kids in school felt less secure than ever before. Though school violence was down, studies show kids were more scared. "They can't learn under these conditions," says Dr. Frank Farley, former head of the American Psychological Association.

To listen to the media, Dr. Farley told me, you'd have to believe that Chicken Little was right: "The sky is truly falling. America is in terrible straits and our schools are a mess and they're violent. But they are *not* violent. I don't know why there is all this press coverage, other than the need for a story."

That's it. The media beast must be fed. Scares drive up circulation and ratings.

> **MYTH:** "Road rage" is an epidemic!
>
> **TRUTH:** It's not.

The inventor of the term "road rage" is unknown, but he or she has a lot to answer for. Not as much as the media does, though. In 1997, the American Automobile Association Traffic Safety Foundation issued a report on aggressive driving. *Newsweek* said we were being "driven to destruction," Stone Phillips on NBC said it was "a bigger problem than ever," and on ABC my colleague Barbara Walters said "the trend is frightening."

Others were scratching their heads. They didn't see what the media did. Robert Lichter, president of the Center for Media and Public Affairs at George Mason University, which studies media coverage, told me: "If road rage is something that's increasing, we should have more fatalities on the road. There should be more reports of reckless driving. But these things are going down."

So what was the evidence for all these stories? I went to the AAA Foundation, and confronted their chief spokeswoman about their claim that road rage had increased by 51 percent.

> **STEPHANIE FAUL** That's what it appeared to look like from our report. That's all I can tell you. We saw an increase in reported cases.
>
> **STOSSEL** Reported in the press?
>
> **STEPHANIE FAUL** Yes, reported in the press.
>
> **STOSSEL** It might be that reporters just started liking the alliteration, road rage?
>
> **STEPHANIE FAUL** Well, also they like the idea of violent death by strangers! It's a very common topic in the news reports.
>
> **STOSSEL** [quoting from her press release] "Reached epidemic proportions. A bigger problem than ever." Does the study justify that?
>
> **STEPHANIE FAUL** Well, yes and no.
>
> **STOSSEL** "A neglected epidemic."
>
> **STEPHANIE FAUL** Yeah, that's a—that's a bit strong.
>
> **STOSSEL** The impression from the reporting is that there's greater danger out there.
>
> **STEPHANIE FAUL** Yes. Because that's what sells papers, of course. I mean, you're in the media. You know that if you get people excited about an issue, that's what makes it appealing as a topic.

Get out the shovel! This is circular logic: The report was based on *media* mentions of aggressive driving. We in the media loved the catchy phrase "road rage" so much, we kept doing stories on it.

Robert Lichter suggested it all got started this way: "People were yelling at each other in their cars and making obscene gestures and even getting out of the car for years. Journalists just found a term for it. So last year, you went home and said, 'Somebody yelled at me from his car.' This year, you go home and say, 'I was a victim of road rage.'"

Then the AAA writes a report based on the spurt of stories—and new headlines are born. Media incest!

Once the media had a catchy phrase for it, road rage became an "epidemic."

> **MYTH:** Using your cell phone at the gas pump could cause an explosion.
>
> **TRUTH:** Don't tap dance either.

The media is alarmed:

CELL FONE FIREBALL (*New York Daily News*)
BUYING GAS? DON'T TOUCH THAT PHONE! (*Toronto Star*)

The facts are more reassuring. Cell phones are a source of static electricity, and anything that supplies a spark—however minuscule—can ignite a fire if the spark is near fuel vapors. If you are pumping gas yourself, with a cell phone in your hand that rings at the wrong time, theoretically you might be in danger. But there is no evidence that cell phones are causing fires.

Still, the media keeps pumping out the stories. In 2004, the *Poughkeepsie* [N.Y.] *Journal* ran this headline:

CELL PHONE RING STARTS FIRE AT GAS STATION

The story quoted the local fire chief, Pat Koch, as saying gas vapors were ignited by the ringing of a cell phone. But—hold the presses and get the shovel!—just days later, Koch changed his tune: "After further investigation . . . I have concluded that the source of ignition was from some source other than the cell phone . . . most likely static discharge from the motorist himself." To its credit, the *Poughkeepsie Journal* gave its follow-up story as much play as the original. The media rarely do that.

The University of Oklahoma actually has a "Center for the Study of Wireless Electromagnetic Compatibility," which researches the effects of electronic devices on our lives. The center examined incident reports and scientific data, and concluded that there was "virtually no evidence to suggest that cell phones pose a hazard at gas stations." The researchers went even further: "The historical evidence," it said, "does not support the need for further research."

Any static electricity, any spark-producing activity, is dangerous near vapors. So rubbing your rear end against a cloth car seat on a dry winter day is more risky than using your cell phone near the fumes. Don't dance near the pumps with metal taps on your shoes either!

MYTH: We have less free time.

TRUTH: We have more.

- "We're fried by work, frazzled by the lack of time."—Newsweek, *March 9, 1995.*

- "Life couldn't get any busier."—The Advocate *(Baton Rouge, Louisiana), May 19, 2005.*

- "Can your life get any busier?"—Saint Paul Pioneer Press, *September 20, 2004.*

- "Life is becoming busier for many Americans."—Times-Picayune *(New Orleans, Louisiana), May 28, 2000.*

Victimhood again. Reporters love reporting that life is getting worse. News stories tell us we're "running ourselves ragged," and that Americans "have no free time." Pick up a magazine and read all about it: not enough time for romance, for relaxation, for our kids. Busy, busy, busy—less time than ever before. Except, it's not true.

When I went looking for real data, some scientific measure of how we spend our time, all paths led to the University of Maryland. There, sociologist John Robinson records how people spend their days. Beginning in 1965, he's had people fill out diaries so he could calculate how much free time people really have.

STOSSEL I assume since 1965, we've lost free time.

JOHN ROBINSON It's not the case. There is a discrepancy between what people say and what they report when they keep a time diary.

His time diaries show that since 1965, we've gained almost an hour more free time per day. Researchers say it's because Americans today work fewer hours, marry later, have fewer kids, retire earlier, and have better tools, like washing machines and microwaves.

The idea that we work harder than our ancestors is pure nonsense. Until 1890, half of all Americans worked in agriculture. People romanticize farms, but the old-fashioned family farm meant backbreaking labor under a broiling sun. Work began at dawn and continued past dark. Work in mines and factories was worse. Modern jobs are much easier. Our ancestors would be agog to see how much time we spend playing golf, watching TV (an average three to four hours per day), and going to our kids' soccer games, while complaining about how much we work.

But don't tell that to any magazine editors you know; you wouldn't want to ruin a perfectly good thing for them. The free-time myth is good for circulation.

MYTH: Gas prices are going through the roof.

TRUTH: Gasoline is a bargain.

The media periodically get upset about "record" gas prices.

"The price of gasoline has risen again to a record high!" said one newscaster in 2004. "The high prices are making it harder for some to keep their heads above water," said another.

Drivers assume what they see at the pump confirms what they've heard on TV. One told me the prices are "scary." A woman said gas was "going up and up and up, and it's the most expensive it's ever been." And she was on a bike.

The media were saying that gas prices were at record highs for one simple, simple-minded reason: They are economically illiterate, so they didn't account for inflation. That makes the numbers look bigger than the costs actually are. Such reporting is silly. Not adjusting for inflation would mean that the movies *Meet the Fockers* and *Rush Hour 2* outgrossed *Gone With the Wind*.

It's not as if the reporters would have to work at doing calculations to figure this out. Not only are there instant inflation calculators on the Web, but the U.S. Department of Energy accounts for inflation in its annual report of gas prices. At the time I'm writing this, the average price of gasoline in the U.S. is $2.26 per gallon. Once you account for inflation, that means gas today is sixty-seven cents a gallon cheaper than it was in 1922, and sixty-nine cents cheaper than in 1981. True, after Hurricane Katrina the price did reach an average of $2.87 per gallon—but that still is lower than the record average set in March 1981 of $3.12 per gallon.

By failing to account for inflation, the media have some Americans so alarmed that they can't think straight. "What costs more," I asked customers at a gas station, "gasoline or bottled water?" The answer I got from almost everyone was gasoline.

At that very gas station, water was for sale at $1.29 for a twenty-four-ounce bottle. That's $6.88 per gallon, three times what the station charged for gasoline.

It gets sillier. I asked gas station customers, "What costs more, gasoline or ice cream?" Again, most people said gasoline cost more. But at $3.39 a pint, "premium" ice cream costs about $27.00 a gallon.

We should marvel at how cheap gasoline is—what a bargain we get from oil companies. After all, it's easy to bottle water, but think about what it takes to produce and deliver gasoline. Oil has to be sucked out of the ground, sometimes from deep beneath an ocean. To get to the oil, the drills often have to bend and dig sideways through as much as five miles of earth. What they find then has to be delivered through long pipelines or shipped in monstrously expensive ships, then converted into three or more different formulas of gasoline and transported in trucks that cost more than $100,000 each. Then your local gas station must spend a fortune on safety devices to make sure you don't blow yourself up. At $2.26 a gallon (about forty-six cents of which goes to taxes), gas is miraculously cheap!

But what we heard from the clueless media was, "Gas prices are at record highs!"

> **MYTH:** We are running out of oil fast.
>
> **TRUTH:** Not so fast!

"It's going to be a catastrophe!"

When they're not complaining about the price of gas, doomsayers would have us believe that we are burning oil at an "unsustainable" rate.

Camera-hungry politicians know that predicting doom gets them TV face time. "It's inevitable that this is just the beginning of this gasoline crisis!" Senator Charles Schumer told me, as Hurricane Rita approached landfall in 2005. The New York Democrat is notorious for his hunger for media coverage. (A Washington joke: Where is the most dangerous place to be? Between Chuck and a camera.) Schumer told me that after Rita hit, the price of gas would rise to "five dollars a gallon."

He was eager to spend your money to cure his panic. Schumer wants a new "Manhattan Project" that would use huge amounts of tax money to fund "independent energy sources." I reminded him that the last time government tried that, it wasted billions on the totally failed synfuels project. That was a $20 billion Carter administration plan to develop a cheap way to make synthetic natural gas from coal. Schumer said that synfuels was a failure because "political leaders" chose it, but this time Congress would have "nonpoliticians" decide which projects to fund.

Sure they would.

If nonpoliticians are going to decide which projects to fund, why do we need Chuck Schumer? We already have a system in which nonpoliticians decide what projects to fund. It's called "the market."

If the price of a barrel of oil stays high, lots of entrepreneurs will scramble for ways to supply cheaper energy. They'll come up with alternative energy sources or better ways to suck oil out of the ground. At fifty dollars a barrel, it's even profitable to recover oil that's stuck in the tar sands in Alberta, Canada. Peter Huber and Mark Mills point out in their book *The Bottomless Well* that those tar sands alone contain enough oil to meet our needs for a hundred years.

But the media don't pay much attention to that. *Not* running out of oil is not a very interesting story.

> **MYTH:** A full moon makes people crazy.
>
> **TRUTH:** I was crazy enough to report that.

We media people routinely and mindlessly corroborate myths about science and nature. People already believe that a full moon influences people in weird, negative ways, and reporters are quick to confirm it. Here are samples of what the clueless media has said about the full moon:

- "The moon's effects are legendary . . . Few of us can escape the power of the moon."—*Hugh Downs, 20/20, November 8, 1984.*

- "Spokane County sheriff's deputies have no need to check their lunar tables to know when it's a full moon out there."—*Spokesman-Review, October 19, 2005.*

- "A Florida researcher studied murders in Dade County, and found more murders were committed during full moons than any other time. So tonight, watch out."—*John Stossel*

Yes, I confess: I actually said that on *Good Morning America* years ago. The Dade County study seemed plausible—people might drink, party, and therefore murder more people when the moon was full. It was only much later that I discovered the study was flawed. Michael Shermer, editor of *Skeptic* magazine, embarrassed me by explaining that "Researchers went back, reanalyzed the data, and discovered that there's nothing unusual going on."

Shermer said thirty-six other studies prove there is *no* full-moon effect, but people still believe there is one because our memories play tricks on us. Our brains look for patterns, and when we find one, it sticks. We remember something unusual that happened on a full moon.

"We don't remember the unusual things that happen on all the other times because we're not looking for them," Shermer told me. "These things go on all the time, and there's no full moon, they're not looking for it, they don't remember it. We remember the hits, we forget the misses." (See also Chapter 9, The Power of Belief.)

Next time you see the "more violence during full moon" headline—get the shovel.

MYTH: We're drowning in garbage!

TRUTH: There's plenty of room.

- "New York City produces 20,000 tons of solid waste every day and the Sanitation Department is running out of places to put it. It argues in a new report that the only place left is the sky."—*The New York Times, April 21, 1984.*

- "We're going to be drowning in garbage."—*William K. Reilly (former EPA administrator), from Newsday, February 1, 1989.*

- "A World Drowning in Litter."—*BBC News, March 4, 2002.*

This myth got jump-started with a real-life incident that took on a life of its own. In 1987, a barge full of New York trash was supposed to be shipped to a landfill in Louisiana. But on the way to Louisiana, the shipper tried to save money by dumping his trash in North Carolina. Suspicious local officials turned him away, and called the media. The complaints of "We don't want New York's garbage!" got so much publicity that by the time the "garbage barge" reached its original destination, the Louisiana dump wouldn't accept it anymore. That brought more publicity.

Television news crews rushed to the scene. Before you could say "Fabricate a crisis to raise money," activists around the country had added "the garbage crisis" to their agenda. Said Cynthia Pollock of the Worldwatch Institute, "We are now approaching an emergency situation!" That got more publicity.

But it wasn't true.

The EPA says that, although some cities have to ship garbage to other states, overall landfill capacity is actually increasing. Dump operators keep finding new ways to pack the trash tighter, to make it decompose faster, and pile it higher.

Some landfill owners actually compete for our trash; they make money off it by putting grass on top of it and building ski slopes and golf courses.

And America has huge amounts of open space. Not that we are going to fill it all with garbage—all of America's garbage for the next five hundred years would fit into one landfill one hundred yards high. And it wouldn't even be the size of one of Ted Turner's ranches.

The fact that we have plenty of room—gets no publicity.

> **MYTH:** The world is too crowded.
>
> **TRUTH:** That's garbage too.

We've heard this one for decades. News articles warn of "the population bomb," a "tidal wave of humanity," and plead "No more babies." Clueless alarmists like Ted Turner warn, "There's lots of problems all over the world caused by too many people." It's true that the world population today is more than six billion people, but who says that's *too many*?

We could take the entire world population, move everyone into the state of Texas, and the population density there would still be less than that of New York City. I said that to Turner, who then looked at me as if I'd unwrapped a dead fish.

> **TED TURNER**   It is a catastrophe that's just a time bomb that's waiting to happen.
>
> **STOSSEL**   But people are our greatest wealth. More people is a good thing.
>
> **TED TURNER**   Up to a point. Up to a point. And you, as a newsman, should damn well know that. Eventually you stand around in a desert with nothing to eat.

That's absurd. The media runs pictures of starving masses in Africa and blames that on overpopulation. One writer, worrying about Niger, said that we must "reduce birth rates drastically, otherwise permanent famine . . . will be the norm." But Niger's population density is nine persons per square kilometer, minuscule compared to population densities in wealthy countries like the USA (28), Japan (340), the Netherlands (484), and Hong Kong (6,621). The number of people isn't the problem.

Famine is caused by things like civil wars and government corruption that interfere with the distribution of food. Sudan had famine when government militia forces stripped the land of cattle and grain. In Niger, 2.5 million people are starving because food production is managed by the state. The absence of property rights, price controls, and other cruel socialist experiments under way in Malawi, Mozambique, Swaziland, and Lesotho are starving millions more. In Zimbabwe, it's Robert Mugabe's kleptocracy that's doing the damage.

The number of people isn't the problem. Improved technology now allows people to grow more food on less land. The UN says the world *overproduces* food today.

More than 125,000 babies will be born before you finish reading this book, but they're not a burden, they're a blessing. They're more brains that might cure cancer, more hands to build things, and more voices to bring us beautiful music.

The clueless media, in pursuit of the scare *du jour*, do us a nasty disservice by focusing on the wrong things. Because of the constant parade of frightening stories, huge amounts of money and energy are spent on minuscule risks. In the meantime, millions die of malaria, thousands die from bacteria, teachers are jailed, fathers are kept from their kids, and most everyone is frightened needlessly.

There are real problems in the world. The media ought to focus on *them*.

CHAPTER TWO

HE AND SHE

I abhor sexism as much as the next man. Or woman. Rules that prohibit women from doing things that men do are just wrong. I acknowledge that even in 2006, the world is still riddled with sexism. When I read books to my baby daughter, I had to constantly change "hes" to "shes" because almost all the powerful characters were male: The Cat in the Hat. Batman. Mickey Mouse. Goofy. Even on *Sesame Street*: Bert, Ernie, Grover, Cookie Monster, Mr. Snuffleupagus—all the major protagonists were men (Zoe and Rosita came later). I'm not sure what Big Bird is, but my daughter called him "he."

It's still a sexist world.

But does that mean the solutions proposed by the dictatorial left and monster government will make things better? No.

> **MYTH:** The EEOC (Equal Employment Opportunity Commission) will make America less sexist.
>
> **TRUTH:** The EEOC will torment people and enrich lawyers.

Been to Sears lately? If you buy something there, you should know that some of your dollar went to pay for years of litigation between Sears and the EEOC. The EEOC sued Sears because more men than women held jobs selling things like lawn mowers and appliances. Since the salespeople were paid a commission, they made more selling those expensive appliances. The disparate employment numbers themselves were proof, said the government, that Sears discriminated against women.

Sears denied discriminating: "We asked women to do those jobs. It's just that few women want to sell things like lawn mowers."

Is that too politically incorrect a concept for government lawyers to get? Men and women do have different interests. Go to any Wal-Mart and you'll see women looking at clothes, men in the hardware department. It's just the way most of us are. More men selling lawn mowers and more women selling cosmetics does not imply evil discrimination that requires armies of lawyers from the State.

The EEOC was unable to produce any women who would complain that they'd been discriminated against, so Sears finally won the suit. The twenty million dollars the litigation cost was passed on to us customers.

Local "equality police" are just as intrusive. In New Jersey, the busybodies got upset about "ladies' night." Bars often offer women free drinks or cheap food to get more women in the door. In 2005, the New Jersey Department of Law and Public Safety ruled that ladies' night is "unlawful discrimination."

Not that men were complaining. At New Jersey's Gaslight bar, women get free food on Tuesdays. Men like that. It brings more women into the bar. One customer told us, "It's a great way to meet people."

But one man who does object is John F. Banzhaf III. Banzhaf has been dubbed the "Father of Potty Parity"—a title he bears proudly. It refers to his threats against public buildings that don't install more women's toilets than men's. Banzhaf sues because women take longer in the bathroom, so a building with an equal number of men's and ladies' rooms may have longer lines at the ladies' room. It doesn't matter that the building owner didn't intend to discriminate, says Banzhaf, "anything that has the 'effect or consequence' of [advantaging] one gender over the other is illegal whether or not the result is intended."

Wouldn't you love someone like him to have control over your life?

You never know who Banzhaf will sue next. He teaches public interest law at George Washington University, where he encourages his students to sue people. It's a "good class project," he says. The defendants then have to dig deep to hire their own attorneys, but that doesn't seem to bother Banzhaf. What does bother him, he says, is sexism: His students sued and got ladies' nights banned in Washington, DC.

Banzhaf said, "You can't charge men more than women. It's the law."

He's right. It *is* against the law—which ought to make us think about how many bad laws we have. Ladies' night is a long and useful tradition, but activists have managed to get it banned in more than a dozen states.

Bar owners said that ladies' night isn't about discrimination. It's about giving customers what they want. Frank Sementa, who owns D'Jais, in Belmar, NJ, said that in his bar there were "always more men than women." Ladies' nights equal out the ratio of men to women—and his customers like that.

Men *and* women like it? Too bad: The regulators are here. Bar owner Christos Mourtos, faced with the ruling against him by New Jersey's antidiscrimination bureaucracy, ended a twenty-five-year custom of ladies' nights at his bar. He doesn't understand how the bureaucrats could call ladies' nights discrimination against men, because men like it.

And of course he's right. The bars aren't oppressing men; they're giving them what they want. Men like to go to bars where there are women, and women often need a little price incentive to get them to go to a bar. But New Jersey civil rights chief J. Frank Vespa-Papaleo dismissed that argument: "Places of public accommodation must achieve their commercial objectives without running afoul" of discrimination law, he ruled. A "governmental or social policy objective," he noted, might have been a different story.

Oh. Now I get it. When the government wants to get something done, the principle of non-discrimination—which the Constitution of the United States guarantees as protection against *government* action—may be trumped. But when you or I want to exercise our rights of free association and private property—which the Constitution is also supposed to protect—we have to yield.

The equality police know best.

And since public officials are spending your money, not their own, they go to great lengths to obtain "equality." In 1994, the city of Milwaukee said every medical investigator must wear a tie. We interviewed Patricia Martin as she was trying to knot her tie, and she was fit to be tied: "I feel like I'm dressed in a Halloween costume," she said, "and I'm trying to look like a man."

It's Patricia's job to go to crime scenes and collect forensic evidence. The dress code was imposed when her boss, Jeffrey Jentzen, decided his investigators—men and women—must dress more professionally. And that meant men would have to wear jackets and ties.

"Not fair," said the men, "it's discriminatory." Their union filed a grievance, and won.

So Jentzen decreed, *"Everyone* must wear ties."

Then the women hired lawyers; they demanded they be paid damages for being forced to wear a tie. When one lawyer sues, at least two lawyers get work; the medical examiner's office hired one of Milwaukee's most expensive law firms to defend the necktie policy. One of their lawyers, Jim Scott, seemed a little ashamed of the lawsuit. He told us, "Before we're done, we'll spend *tens of thousands* of dollars."

Taxpayer dollars at work! I interviewed medical examiner Jentzen.

STOSSEL Do you always wear a tie?

JENTZEN I always wear a tie.

STOSSEL *[I pulled out a photo]* This is you at the Jeffrey Dahmer crime scene, you're not wearing a tie.

JENTZEN That picture was taken in, uh, 1991 and, you're right I don't have a tie in that crime scene.

STOSSEL But you said it's required for professional conduct.

JENTZEN As of 1994, it is, yes.

STOSSEL Your lawyer says this is costing taxpayers tens of thousands of dollars. Is this worth it?

JENTZEN I think the answer is yes.

I think the answer is . . . get the shovel!

A week after my "Give Me a Break" story on the necktie policy aired, Milwaukee's medical examiner's office reversed the policy. However, the ending was not all happy. Patricia Martin was later fired—as retaliation, she says, for participating in our story.

> **MYTH:** Feminist lawyers' lawsuits fight sexism.
>
> **TRUTH:** Feminist lawyers' lawsuits make other lawyers richer.

You pay for the feminists' lawsuits if you or your kids take SAT tests. Boys have done better on these tests, especially in math, so lawyers from the ACLU say the test must be biased against girls, and that denies girls their fair share of National Merit Scholarships. ACLU attorneys failed to point out any specific defect in the tests, but they had plenty of proposals on how to give girls a leg up: rewrite the exams, add points to girls' scores, divide the scholarships evenly between the sexes regardless of merit, and/or add millions more dollars in scholarships each year for women.

"Different" is something they won't stand for. So far, the SATs have been reformatted and a female-friendly written examination has been added, but attorneys are still complaining. Lawyers and equality police won't be happy until variance in gender, socio-economic backgrounds, and race are eliminated in every aspect of life.

Activist lawyer Gloria Allred told me that we need *more* equality lawsuits. She and Banzhaf sued clothing stores that charge men less for alterations, and dry cleaners that charge more to clean women's blouses. The terrified dry cleaners quickly changed their policy, though privately they told me they *should* charge women more, because cleaning women's clothes takes more time. Blouses come in many different fabrics, shapes, and sizes, which require different machines and different settings, while men's shirts can usually be cleaned on one machine. The dry cleaners also told us, "Women demand more." They have a more acute sense of touch and vision. "They see the spot—men don't even know there is one." There actually is a difference between men and women.

When I suggested to Gloria Allred that dry cleaners might be practicing smart business rather than sexism, she said I was wrong: "I can smell sexism more than you can."

Oh, yes, and the equality lawyers smell sexism all the time. One year, John Banzhaf's students filed *human rights* complaints against hair salons that charged more to cut women's hair. Human rights violations?! Charging women more for haircuts is a common-sense adjustment to a real sex difference: Taking care of women's hair takes more time. Not always, but often enough that it's prudent to have different prices. The salons don't price their work to hurt women; they price it based on how much time they spend with female customers. If they did charge women "unfair" prices, the free market would punish them—women wouldn't go to those salons.

By contrast, if idiot governments demand equal prices, women *will* be hurt—because some salons will avoid serving them at all. And when Banzhaf's law students sue, men *and* women are penalized, because the salons have to hire their own attorneys and pass the costs on to their customers. The attorneys cost as much as a thousand haircuts.

But Banzhaf and his eager students see only good in his lawsuits.

STOSSEL Now the salons [have to] hire a lawyer.

JOHN BANZHAF The salons could hire lawyers, and either together or separately try to fight us in a hearing, but our law in the District is so clear, it says you cannot justify a different price for men and women even if you can show that it costs you more.

STOSSEL Even if it is true that it takes longer to cut women's hair, it's still illegal?!

YASMINE TIRADO (one of his law students) Pretty much, it's plain and simple. You cannot charge more for the same service.

STOSSEL No exceptions?

YASMINE TIRADO Not unless you run out of business.

STOSSEL But then the only way to prove it would be to go out of business!

YASMINE TIRADO That's what the statute says.

That's busybody lawyer logic: We will force your business to fit our vision of the world . . . even if it drives you *out* of business.

MYTH: Aside from physical differences, men and women are pretty much the same.

TRUTH: There are differences—plenty of them.

When I went to Princeton, my professors taught me that sexism is the reason that more men succeed in science, business, and sports. Think about it, they said: For years, piggish men forbade women to work, vote, or own property. Those laws are gone, but their evil effects are not. Blatant sex discrimination still keeps some women from succeeding.

Since men and women are equal, said the gender equality crowd, it's not natural for women to spend more time nurturing, or for more men to pursue sports. The disproportion is a cultural artifact, and we will achieve total equality if we just stop being sexist. I believed the hype, but it was nonsense, and now plenty of evidence says it's nonsense.

June Reinisch, former director of the Kinsey Institute at Indiana University, was one of many researchers who told us that some gender differences are clearly innate. Even newborns behave differently, she told me: "Males [react] more than females. If you give a little puff of air on their abdomen, they [are] much more likely to startle than females." Female infants, she told me, have a distinctly rhythmic way of using their mouths: "They suck on their tongues, they move their lips and so forth, more than males do."

These infants are not conforming to society's preconceived gender roles—they were born different.

This is not a bad thing. It doesn't mean that a woman cannot be a CEO or an engineer and that a man cannot nurture kids or teach school. It just means more men may like engineering and more women may want to stay home with the kids. More men may be willing to sacrifice family for money, and women may have better verbal skills.

Difference doesn't mean one is *better*. Considering men's strength and spatial skills, it's all right that most architects and athletes are men (as long as the government doesn't forbid women to participate). And because of women's superior verbal and people skills (there's plenty of research supporting that), it's okay that most teachers, psychologists, pharmacists, and real estate agents are women. Let's allow everyone to do what he or she does best.

It's better to act on the basis of what *is* true, rather than someone's idea of what *should* be true. And the truth is, we are different.

"*No!*" say the gender equality feminists.

The cultural establishment is so determined to see women as a class of persecuted victims under constant threat of subjugation that they refuse to acknowledge any difference between the sexes, or to open their minds to the evidence of gender differences. They don't even want them *talked about*.

When Lawrence Summers, the president of Harvard, spoke at an academic conference on women and minorities, he suggested fewer women than men attain top positions in science because of discrimination, the demands of family life, or innate differences between women and men. He called for more research.

The fury! A professor of biology from MIT walked out. The *New York Times* ran endless stories on how upset women were about Summers's remarks. Harvard faculty members denounced Summers for saying what he said. Summers then apologized. *Several* times, he apologized for what he said.

This is disgusting, suffocating, censorship-by-intimidation. And it's sad when the president of America's oldest institution of higher learning endorses the intimidation by apologizing.

I understand how he felt. I've spent my career in the mainstream media. When everyone around you believes, say, that we *obviously* need national health care, that capitalism does more harm than good, that a glass ceiling keeps women from advancing, etc., it's hard to keep fighting about it. It's easier to just shut up.

But university presidents shouldn't shut up. And Summers certainly shouldn't have apologized.

Outside of academia and elite fussbudget circles, gender differences are simply fact.

It's why in child custody cases, judges favor mothers. They assume a mother's custody is usually best for the children. Evolution, experience, and multiple studies suggest that women put in more parenting time and more often define their relationships through intimacy and care. Now that men are complaining that women are unfairly favored in custody battles, we have an odd partnership: men's rights advocates agreeing with feminists like Gloria Steinem, who say men and women are exactly equal.

I assumed that Steinem, who was once one of my heroes, wouldn't deny all the new gender science. I assumed that she would acknowledge that there are some differences. I was wrong. When I sat down with her, it was a chilly interview. After she denied that men have more interest in combat and sports, that men are more aggressive and break more laws, I tried the flip side, suggesting the women have biological advantages.

STOSSEL Aren't women, in general, better nurturers?

GLORIA STEINEM No! Next question.

How absurd to just deny it.

It's even more destructive to use the power of government to try to force the differences to disappear. Gloria Allred told me, where there are differences, she will sue until women "win."

STOSSEL Maybe women are biologically different! Why sue me because of that? We're all paying for your lawsuits!

GLORIA ALLRED Women have a right to be angry, they have a right to go to court to vindicate their rights, they have a right to get elected to public office, to make the public policy so they will not be deprived of their rights!

STOSSEL And if *they don't get elected,* you're going to file a suit demanding they *be* elected?

GLORIA ALLRED I think we should do each and every act which is necessary and appropriate to protect our rights and the rights of our daughters.

Wow. I want my daughter's rights protected too, but election results must be gender-equal? She should sue if women lose elections?

The equality lawyers want to coerce people to behave the way they and the social engineers say we should. They're entitled to promote their dumb ideas. But it's unfortunate that because they have law degrees, they get to use force. So we have to help pay for their vision.

These days, that vision has little to do with equality of opportunity and everything to do with equality of results. Women are pushed to do the exact same things men do, whether they want to or not.

Take sports.

> **MYTH:** Title IX makes competitive sports more fair for girls.
>
> **TRUTH:** Title IX helps lawyers and hurts boys.

Watching sports, I usually see more men. On the field, and in the bleachers too. Donna Lopiano, head of the Women's Sports Foundation, told me that the reason is years of sex discrimination.

STOSSEL Just as many women want to do sports as men?

DONNA LOPIANO Yes.

STOSSEL No doubt in your mind?

DONNA LOPIANO No doubt in my mind.

STOSSEL Women are just as interested in running around, bumping into people as we men are?

DONNA LOPIANO If you build it, they will come.

To make sure they build it, Congress passed a law: "Title IX." It sounds so reasonable: "No person in the United States shall, on the basis of sex, be subjected to discrimination under any education program." Who could argue with that? The well-intended law was supposed to give girls the message that they are just as valued as boys on the playing field.

But, as usual, the law had unfortunate consequences. When Brown University tried to save money by cutting four teams—two men's and two women's—the gymnasts sued. "Women should be treated equally," Eileen Rocchio, a former Brown University gymnast, told us, "and the numbers at Brown are not equal!"

Under Title IX, the ratio of female athletes is supposed to match the ratio of female students. But the requirement caused Brown administrators big problems: No matter how hard they begged women to try out for teams— no matter how much they talked up fencing, ice hockey, and women's basketball—fewer women than men wanted to play. Brown is a suffocatingly politically correct school, more obsessed with equality than most, and even *there* the gender equity game stalled for lack of interest. Penalty! Violation!

It didn't matter that Brown expanded women's athletics teams so much that it had more women's sports teams than most any school in America. What mattered was that more athletes were male. Can't have that, can we? After the Title IX suit was filed, Brown was ordered to start three new women's teams. "Other schools will take note of that," said Eileen Rocchio.

They'd better, or the lawyers will take *all* their money.

It's expensive to start new teams. Add the usual start-up costs— uniforms, equipment, a court or field on which to play—to the Title IX investigations and private lawsuits, and where does that leave college athletics? Increasingly, complying with proportionality mandates means avoiding expensive litigation by dropping men's sports. Princeton and Notre Dame cut varsity wrestling. Providence cut men's baseball, tennis, and golf. UCLA cut its men's swimming and diving program—the one that's brought America sixteen Olympic gold medals.

"This isn't good for young men," wrestling coach Leo Kocher of the National Coalition for Athletics Equity told me. "We're perpetrating an awful thing against the men. We're saying we're punishing you because you have more interest in sports than women. And that's wrong. In the last five years, we've lost 10 percent of our male athletes. That's 20,000 males."

The unintended—and unfair—effects of Title IX aren't limited to universities. The equality police sued high schools too. At Merritt Island High in Florida, the boys' baseball field was nicer than the girls' softball field. The boys' field had lights, bleachers, a concession stand and scoreboard. But this was not because the school spent more on boys. The school gave the exact same amount to each team, but the boys got sponsors to chip in to improve their field. Parents of the boys volunteered to build the concession stand and bleachers.

Then they worked on the grass. "Weekends and at night, they come out here," Harold Bistline, the school board's attorney told me, "and they get out on their hands and knees, and they weed this baseball field." But even though the boys and their parents did the extra work, a court told the school board that under Title IX, the boys were *still* not allowed to have a better field.

Civil rights lawyer Lisa Tietig filed a lawsuit to force the school board to limit what parents give.

LISA TIETIG They have an obligation to regulate those private donations so that they're given fairly. Now if that means . . .

STOSSEL The school board has to tell parents who they can give to?

LISA TIETIG They can say, "You can donate that money, but you can't use it until the girls have an equal amount."

STOSSEL And this is a good thing?

LISA TIETIG Sure. Sure, it's the only way that we're going to get equality in the athletic fields.

The bewildered school board proposed a solution: They would unplug the boys' scoreboard, shut down the concession stand, and rope off the bleachers so no one could sit there. That would take away the good things the boys and their parents had volunteered to do. That would make things "equal." What a waste.

But that didn't bother the civil rights lawyer. "They have an obligation to do this," said Lisa Tietig. "It's the law, and it doesn't matter whether they have money."

That's lawyer reasoning: It doesn't matter whether the school has the money. I did notice, however, that the lawyer seemed pretty eager to get money for herself. Lawyers with robes (judges, we call them) ruled that attorneys deserve extra pay if they win civil rights suits. It's supposed to be an incentive to encourage lawyers to do their "public service." That meant if Lisa Tietig won, she could collect, not her usual $150 an hour fee, but $900 per hour.

STOSSEL So you have an incentive to keep finding those inequities and suing?

LISA TIETIG Sure, that's built into the law.

STOSSEL And that's a good thing?

LISA TIETIG Sure.

Good for her. Not so good for schoolchildren.

A judge sided with attorney Tietig. The fields must be gender equal, no matter where the money comes from. Even the *signs* have to be equal. Merritt High baseball coach Chuck Goldfarb discovered that the hard way.

COACH GOLDFARB I got a sponsor to put "Home of the Mustangs" up there with a horse swinging a bat. The ruling was that it was not gender equal.

STOSSEL The judge ordered it painted over. Looks pretty stupid—blank.

COACH GOLDFARB Looks real stupid. I mean, it's a blank sign. It looks like a movie screen. We could have a drive-in theater out here now.

It would be funny if it weren't so expensive. Tietig sued ten Merritt Island high schools. Every dollar spent on lawsuits means less for the fields. They could have built many baseball fields for what they forked over to lawyers.

It's great that activists have made more people aware of gender discrimination, and encouraged women to pursue athletics. We now have record numbers of girls filling up soccer fields and basketball courts. I coach a women's volleyball team, and I once coached girls' soccer. I want my daughter to have every opportunity my son has.

But so does every parent. We didn't need Title IX and lawyer bullies to force schools to offer more sports to girls. That would have happened anyway, as parents, teachers and school administrators became aware of gender discrimination and moved to fix it.

Demanding equal participation is absurd. No matter what the feminists say, fewer girls than boys will want to play sports. It's not fair to hurt boys and punish taxpayers by trying to force perfect equality.

Men and women are different. As Leo Kocher told me, "If you're going to define discrimination as unequal numbers of males and females, then we've got nothing but discrimination all over this society because men and women do not pursue everything in the exact same numbers."

In schools, girls usually dominate the chorus, student government, and the yearbook. Dance classes don't get an equal number of boys, even when they try to recruit them. If we accept the activists' argument that any inequality must be caused by discrimination, then the suits will go on until the lawyers take all our money. And all our freedom.

> **MYTH:** Women earn less doing the same work.
>
> **TRUTH:** Women earn less because they want different things.

The politicians stood in front of the Capitol, playing to the cameras, shouting about the "victimization of women":

SENATOR TOM HARKIN (D-IA) Who cleans our hotel rooms and our motel rooms? Women!

SENATOR HILLARY CLINTON (D-NY) We need to make sure that employers treat men and women equally!

Senators Clinton and Harkin were complaining about the "wage gap," the fact that on average, a woman makes 78.5 cents for every dollar earned by a man. The politicians on the lawn said the gap is caused by sexism. "No matter how hard women work, or whatever they achieve in terms of advancement in their own professions and degrees," shouted Congresswoman Rosa DeLauro (D-CT), "they will not be compensated equitably."

Most people believe this. After that demonstration, I went on the *Tony Danza Show* and I asked his studio audience: "In the same job, doing the same work, who will be paid more, a woman or a man?"

"The man!" they screamed.

If it's true, then employers are practicing shameful sexism.

But does this even make sense? If employers knew that women would do the exact same job for less money, they'd hire only women. It would be moronic to hire a man.

Warren Farrell finally figured that out. Decades ago, Farrell was the rare man who, with Gloria Steinem and other women, went to feminist protests. He's the only man to have been elected three times to the board of the National Organization for Women. He told me, "I used to wear a '59 cent' pin to protest the fact that men earned a dollar for each 59 cents [now it's 78.5 cents] that women earned for the same work."

But then he had his "eureka" moment.

WARREN FARRELL I asked myself one day if men are earning a dollar, maybe I'll go out and start an all-female firm and I'll be able to produce products for fifty-nine cents, that male firms are producing for a dollar—

STOSSEL You'd get rich!

WARREN FARRELL I'd get rich! [So I thought] there's something wrong with the statistic.

Farrell then spent about fifteen years going over U.S. Census data and other studies. He found that the wage gap exists not because of sexism, but because more men are willing to do certain kinds of jobs. He illustrates this when making speeches.

He asks people to stand up if they work more than forty hours a week, or, "if you worked in a field that exposed you to the wind, the rain, and the snow for at least two years of your life . . ." He goes on to list some of the nastier and more dangerous jobs.

Again and again more men stand. "*That's* why men earn more," says Farrell. We take jobs that are more likely to require longer hours, longer commuting times, safety risks, and frequent travel. Those jobs pay more because they take more time, and fewer people want to do them.

It's not sexism, he said, it's just supply and demand. Women make less because they want different things.

>**WARREN FARRELL** The women themselves say they're far more likely to care about flexibility. The men say: I'm far more likely to care about money. Women say: Do I need more money, or do I need more time? And women are intelligent enough to say, I need more time. And so women lead balanced lives. Men should be learning from women!

It was time for the confrontation. That's often the most interesting part of a TV story—that moment when you bring someone facts that don't mesh with what they've said, and hear how they respond. Who would I confront for this story? Much of the country believed the wage gap was all about sexism, so who should speak for them? Senator Clinton said no, so I asked Martha Burke, chair of the National Council of Women's Organizations. She's written a book about discrimination, and led the noisy protests against sexism at the Georgia golf club that hosts the Masters. I assumed the logic of Farrell's argument would give her pause. I was wrong:

>**STOSSEL** If a woman does equal work for 25 percent less money, why would any employer ever hire a man?
>
>**MARTHA BURKE** Because they *like* to hire men, John. They like to hire people like themselves and they darn sure like to promote people like themselves. There's still a feeling in this country, A, that men own the jobs, and B, that men are automatically better at jobs.

Get the shovel. Employers like men so much that they're willing to lose 25 percent for every person they hire? Ridiculous.

Let's move on to other gender myths.

MYTH: Women are worse drivers than men.

TRUTH: Men are worse.

Women have a bad reputation when it comes to driving. Headlines like "Bad Driving 'Linked to Hormones'" fan the fire, sparking jokes like Q: *Why was Helen Keller a bad driver?* A: *Because she was a woman.* But researchers with the Social Issues Resource Center beg to differ. Their 2002 report analyzed a stack of studies on male and female driving differences and came to a bold conclusion: "In all studies and analyses, without exception, men have been shown to have a higher rate of crashes than women."

Men, the report claims, drive faster than women and have less regard for traffic laws: They speed, drive drunk, run stop signs, and therefore crash twice as often as women do. In the U.S., men cause 71 percent of all road fatalities, a figure that's remained constant since 1975.

But don't men drive many more miles than women do? Wouldn't that account for some of the difference? It's true that males account for 62 percent of all miles driven, vs. 38 percent for females, but even after miles are clocked and driving hours are factored in, men *still* get in way more fatal accidents. Check out the graph below.

The good news is that the trend of fatal crashes for both men and women has been steadily decreasing.

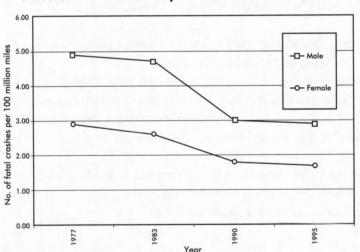

Drivers in fatal crashes per 100 million miles, 1977–95

Why are men so accident-prone? Blame it on the Stone Age. Those hunter-gatherer genes that helped us feed our families are still active today, and are apparently wreaking havoc on our streets. World Health Organization reports find that men are more aggressive than women in general: A greater number of men die from falls, drowning, poisoning, and a host of other probably avoidable accidents. The WHO 2002 report makes no bones about its perspective: " 'Masculinity' may be hazardous to health."

MYTH: Girls feel the most pressure to have sex.

TRUTH: Boys say it isn't so.

It's an image we've all grown up with: The boys are aggressors and girls are reluctant prey. If it was ever that way, it isn't today.

Now it's boys, more than girls, who feel pushed into having sex. My colleague Deborah Roberts recently interviewed several high school students from New Jersey who confirmed a surprising survey from the Kaiser Foundation: 33 percent of teen boys feel pressure to have sex, compared to only 23 percent of girls.

HIGH SCHOOL BOY Like, guys who were experienced with having sex, they'd be, like, going to younger kids, like, "Well, I have sex like, all of the time."

DEBORAH ROBERTS So, does that make you feel the pressure to have sex, because you don't want to own up to not having done it?

HIGH SCHOOL BOY [It] gets me nervous like, knowing that I'm at this age and I haven't—done it yet. And, like, everyone else has so, like, maybe, like, I feel like I should be doing it.

2ND HIGH SCHOOL BOY When you're with somebody, there's a lot of pressure from your friends. Like, all right now you're with her, how long is it going to take you? What are you waiting for?

Boys aren't necessarily the unabashed sexual predators we'd always assumed. Often, when they pressure girls, it's only because they feel pressure themselves.

> **MYTH:** Having sex during pregnancy is harmful to the baby.
>
> **TRUTH:** Only in your mind.

Concern about the consequences of sexual activity during pregnancy is as natural as it is widespread. "What about the baby?" people worry. Of the couples who responded to a survey we commissioned, 80 percent said that they thought about the baby in some way when they were having sex. 40 percent feared they might do serious harm to the baby. The biggest fear was miscarriage. Men worried twice as much as women.

Relax. My *20/20* coanchor, Elizabeth Vargas, sat down for a reassuring conversation with Dr. Jacques Moritz, chief of gynecology at New York's St. Luke's Roosevelt Hospital.

> DR. JACQUES MORITZ There's no evidence that sex is going to cause a miscarriage, that's for sure.
>
> ELIZABETH VARGAS But mothers-to-be are often told to avoid physical exertion. You're not supposed to get your heart rate over 140. Some women stop running, they stop flying. You would think that sex could have negative impact, on a fetus or a baby.
>
> DR. JACQUES MORITZ Flying is okay, running is okay with limitations. All those things are okay, and definitely sex. So, you should enjoy it. Many times, women's hormones go up. Their desire to have sex goes up. But unfortunately, many times, in the same relationship, the men's desire goes down.

Ironically, men back off at the very time their partner's desire is high. The experts' advice: Don't worry about the baby—go for it.

> **MYTH:** In sex, size doesn't matter to women.
>
> **TRUTH:** Size matters.

In the 1960s, even the most insecure American male found reassurance in the conclusion by sex researchers Masters and Johnson that a man's penis size has little or no correlation to his partner's enjoyment of sex because the elastic walls of the vagina adjust to the size of the man. We did an online poll on ABCNews.com about it recently, and 56 percent of the respondents—both men and women—said they agreed that size didn't matter.

But that's not true for many women, say today's top researchers in the field of sexology. "Men have been assured that size doesn't matter; women have been told that they only have feeling in the first two inches of their vagina," Dr. Joy Davidson, a clinical psychologist and sex therapist, told us. "We've all been sold a bill of goods about sex, and it's time to tell the truth. The reason size matters is very simply that women do have nerve endings deep inside the vagina."

Evolutionary anthropologist Helen Fisher says girth matters more than length. "It's the thickness of the penis that distends the muscles around the vaginal canal and can create pressure on the female genitals that can add to her joy."

Height matters to women too. *20/20* once put short and tall men in line-ups behind a two-way mirror, and then invited groups of women to choose a date. They always chose the taller guys.

Listening to their comments made me cringe. We told them that one man, who stood just five foot three, was a doctor, a best-selling author, and a champion skier who'd just built his own ski house. "He's still too short!" said the women.

Another man was only five feet tall. He was handsome and well dressed. But the women weren't interested. We said he was a millionaire. He still got turned down. I asked the women what it would take to make them want to date him. "Maybe the only thing you could say is the others are murderers," was the response.

Size, all kinds of size, *matters*.

MYTH: Men cheat much more than women.

TRUTH: You'd be surprised.

The notion that men are philandering pigs has been popular for centuries. There is evolutionary logic behind it. Anthropologist Helen Fisher points out that, for millions of years, a woman knew that her children were more likely to survive if she could find a man who would stay with her. He would protect her and her children. Women who succeeded in finding such men were more likely to pass on their genes to future generations. By contrast, men were more likely to pass on their genes if they had sex with lots of women and fathered many children. Even today, we're told, women seek emotional stability and men seek sex—right?

Only sometimes. The most comprehensive study of infidelity shows that about 80 percent of women remain faithful to their husbands during marriage, while 65 to 85 percent of men remain faithful to their wives. That's pretty close. Cheating isn't just a guy thing.

Of course, cheating is secretive. But a small portion of the population openly endorses multiple partners, or multiple *wives*.

MYTH: Polygamy is cruel to women.

TRUTH: The women aren't complaining.

A joy of working for *20/20* is that I get to go places I wouldn't normally go, and as a result, I keep learning that what I thought I knew is wrong.

Once I went to Lake Powell, Utah, where I met sixty-one-year-old Alex Joseph. He said he was living the good life, and much of what made it good was the fact that he had eight wives. Joseph was a Mormon and a polygamist. He took to heart the guidance of the first Mormon prophet, Joseph Smith, who believed that the Old Testament sanctioned polygamy. Smith himself was said to have had twenty-seven wives.

Alex Joseph had twenty children and at least twenty-seven grandchildren. "If you don't like children, there's no reason to do it," he told me. "If you don't like the company of women, there's no reason to do it."

I like children and the company of women. But I can't imagine having eight wives. Besides, what's in it for the wives?

I expected the women to be sad and quiet, pressed into marriage by dictatorial fathers, husbands, or ministers. I also thought they'd be jealous of the other wives. Instead, I found cheerful women who talked gaily about how much they liked their "sister-wives," and how happy they were to have them helping with the children and housework. Each sister-wife had her own room, home, or trailer, and their husband would take turns—spending a night with one, and then another.

It was a complete brain-twister for me. The wives didn't see it as having to share a husband; to them polygamy meant joining a bigger, more nurturing and supportive family. It meant *more* emotional stability, not less. Some of the women seemed to like their sister-wives more than their husbands.

But what about the law? Aren't multiple wives illegal in America? Yes. The Mormon church itself stopped advocating polygamy more than a hundred years ago, in response to public pressure and a Supreme Court decision against it. Nevertheless, polygamy is still practiced fairly openly in parts of Utah and northern Arizona.

Joseph and his wives argued that since none of his wives felt she was a victim of a "crime," what they did as a family was none of the government's business. One of his wives, Boudicca Joseph, told me, "What right does the state have to dictate morality?"

They didn't have to work hard to convince me. What my reporting keeps teaching me is that laws that punish adults for "victimless crimes"— gambling, drug use, prostitution, etc.—do much more harm that good. Bans make things worse by creating black markets, where things get ugly fast. Drug dealers form gangs to protect their illegal loot; police take bribes from dealers. Arresting prostitutes drives prostitution underground, where there's more disease and violence.

In fact, one reason the government might have been reluctant to arrest Joseph was what happened the last time there was a crackdown on polygamy.

In 1953, the state of Arizona sent carloads of armed police into the polygamous community of Short Creek. They were going to "save the children." Calling polygamy a cancer, they arrested every man and woman they found. Authorities put 263 Mormon children in state homes or foster care. At first, the media sided with authorities, reporting that police had "rescued" children from a dangerous cult. But the reporters' enthusiasm faded as they watched crying children being separated from their equally distressed mothers.

After the crackdown, the children languished in state homes and foster care for two years, and public opinion began to change. The press suggested that the government had hurt more children than it helped. Authorities eventually returned the children to their parents. Today, Short Creek, now called Colorado City, is home to many polygamous families. Police leave them alone.

Even the prosecutor of Lake Powell thought the government had no business limiting marriage to two people. She told me she wouldn't send Alex Joseph to jail even if the state ordered her to: "I will not prosecute victimless crimes," she said. "I'll just tell them 'Too bad.'"

The prosecutor's judgment might have been clouded by the fact that she happened to be one of Joseph's wives. Which wife was she? I asked.

ELIZABETH JOSEPH   Let's see, what am I? [she started counting on her fingers] Ting, ting, ting, ting, ting. He had five when I married him, including my two best friends . . .

By the time Alex Joseph died in 1998 he was married to a real estate broker, a park ranger, a contractor, a midwife, a radio producer, the town prosecutor (that's Elizabeth), and two homemakers. Most still live near one another and consider themselves sister-wives.

The Church of Latter-Day Saints and Utah officials point out that polygamy is illegal, but officials leave practicing communities alone.

CHAPTER THREE

BASHING BUSINESS

O ne reason I became a consumer reporter was that I assumed business was fraught with cheating and deceit. Many consumer reporters believe that. Legislators and lawyers believe it too. It's intuitive to despise business.

Even the rich hate business. When the steel industry stood up to President Kennedy's efforts to dictate its prices in 1962, the President—the wealthy son of one of the wealthiest men in America—exclaimed, "My father always told me that all businessmen were sons of bitches, but I never believed it till now."

MYTH: Businesses rip us off.

TRUTH: Most don't.

Okay, some do.

Enron, WorldCom, and Tyco became famous for it.

I won Emmy awards exposing cheaters, like milk producers who conspired to keep prices high, RJ Reynolds Tobacco when it handed out Camel cigarettes to kids, and vocational schools that promised jobs that did not exist.

But I eventually noticed that most cheating is pretty trivial, that the vast majority of businesses don't cheat, and that the cheaters rarely get away with it for long.

> **MYTH:** Government must make rules to protect us from business.
>
> **TRUTH:** Competition protects us, if government gets out of the way.

It took me a long time to learn that regulations can't protect consumers better than open competition, and in fact, they often harm us. My learning curve was steep. After all, I worked in newsrooms where "consumer victimization" was a religion and government its messiah. But after fifteen years of watching government regulators make problems worse, I came to understand that we didn't need a battalion of bureaucrats and parasitic lawyers policing business. The competition of the market does that by itself. Word gets out. Angry customers complain to their family and friends; consumer reporters like me blow the whistle on inferior products and shoddy service. Companies with bad reputations lose customers. In a free society, cheaters don't thrive.

Once I learned more about economics, I saw how foolish I'd been. Government uses force to achieve its ends. If you choose not to do what government dictates, men with guns can put you in jail. Businesses, by contrast, cannot use force, no matter how big they are. So all business transactions are voluntary—no trade is made unless both parties think they benefit. In 1776, economist Adam Smith brilliantly realized that the businessman's self-centered motivation gets strangers to cooperate in producing a multitude of good things: "He intends only his own gain, and he is in this, as in many other cases, led by an invisible hand to promote an end which was no part of his intention."

Few of us appreciate the power of that invisible hand. I don't give my pencil a second thought, and yet I could spend years trying to produce one without turning out anything as good as the worst pencil available today. Leonard Read of the Foundation for Economic Education opened my mind to this idea when I read his essay "I, Pencil." Here is a shortened version:

I, Pencil, simple though I appear to be, merit your wonder and awe . . . not a single person on the face of this earth knows how to make me.

My family tree begins with what in fact is a tree, a cedar of straight grain that grows in Northern California. Contemplate all the saws and trucks and rope and the countless other gear used in carting the cedar logs to the railroad siding. Think of all the persons and the numberless skills that went into their fabrication: the mining of ore, the making of steel and its refinement into saws, axes, motors; the growing of hemp and bringing it through all the stages to heavy and strong rope; the logging camps with their beds and mess halls, the cookery and the raising of all the foods. Why, untold thousands of persons had a hand in every cup of coffee the loggers drink!

The logs are shipped to a mill. Can you imagine the individuals who make flat cars and rails and railroad engines? These legions are among my antecedents.

My "lead" [is] graphite mined in Ceylon. Consider these miners and those who make their many tools and the makers of the paper sacks in which the graphite is shipped and those who make the string that ties the sacks and those who put them aboard ships and those who make the ships.

Millions of human beings have had a hand in my creation, no one of whom even knows more than a very few of the others.

Neither the worker in the oil field nor the chemist nor the digger of graphite or clay nor any who mans or makes the ships or trains or trucks nor the president of the company performs his singular task because he wants me. Indeed, there are some among this vast multitude who never saw a pencil nor would they know how to use one.

There is still a fact more astounding: the absence of a master mind, of anyone forcibly directing these countless actions which bring me into being. No trace of such a person can be found. Instead, we find the Invisible Hand at work.

I, Pencil, am a complex combination of miracles: a tree, zinc, copper, graphite. But to these miracles which manifest themselves in Nature an even more extraordinary miracle has been added: the configuration of creative human energies—millions of tiny know-hows configurating naturally and spontaneously.

People assume someone needs to be "in charge" to achieve those miracles, but no one is in charge. What philosopher Frederick Hayek called "spontaneous order" makes it happen.

Without any central authority or master planner, the invisible hand quietly flips the switches that turn markets on. Competition brings us good stuff that keeps getting better—better cars, phones, shoes, medicines. Yet we take this for granted and demand more. We complain if the supermarket's 30,000 items don't include a flavor we want.

In newsrooms where I've worked, it's trendy to sneer at people in business. "They're selfish, greedy, tacky. We are the artists, the thinkers, the people who care about others. We demand that government regulate business to keep the greedy bastards from ripping us off, hurting the poor, despoiling the earth . . ." In Hollywood, the villain is more likely to be a businessman than a terrorist. The media elite firmly believe: Business is bad.

To be fair, antipathy toward business existed before the media amplified it. There's something instinctive about resenting the people who trade for profit. Workers hate their employers, who pay them, but love the government, even though it takes 40 percent of their money and squanders it.

It's an idea as old as it is irrational. In feudal times, people hated the "bourgeoisie." It wasn't just because they envied their wealth, says economist Thomas Sowell. People revered royalty, no matter how absurdly rich they were, but resented middle-class merchants who sold them what they needed. Anger at the merchant's profit, suggests Sowell, is the grist for racial and ethnic hatred that has led to mass slaughters. Everywhere there is hatred of "middleman minorities": The Chinese in Southeast Asia, the Lebanese in the Middle East, the Jews in Eastern Europe, Indians and Pakistanis in Africa, and Koreans in America's Black ghettos. These groups improve their customers' lives in many ways, yet often their customers come to hate them for it.

Some folks simply loathe profit and commerce. They want to "fix" it by making it "kinder." One way they think they can do that is by insisting that authorities guarantee "fair" prices.

> **MYTH:** Price controls protect consumers.
>
> **TRUTH:** Price controls create shortages and terrible hardship.

Price controls make perfect sense to people who know little about economics: "Since business owners are greedy and quick to take advantage of their customers' ignorance or desperation to 'gouge' them, it would be fairer to limit what those selfish people can charge! The only losers would be those nasty capitalists who make 'excess' profit. Price controls would save everyone money! Why not impose them?"

Because price controls don't work.

They've been tried many, many times, but they've *never* worked, if by "worked" we mean made life better for consumers. Instead, price controls create shortages and cause all kinds of harm, from starvation in Communist countries to long gas lines in the United States. Yet this bad idea doesn't die.

Even after starving Russian mothers sent their children into the fields to kill mice for food, and even after the Soviet Union collapsed under the weight of central planning and price controls, many of our leaders still insist that *their* central planning and price controls will work.

I've covered their schemes, big and small. I'll start with the small:

My former senator, Alfonse D'Amato, was upset about your friendly neighborhood robot, the ATM. I put ATMs up there with microwave popcorn on the list of great inventions. How did I ever survive without cash machines?

I'm old enough to remember when getting cash meant standing in a long line and then convincing a teller that you were you. There was *always* a line. You could only withdraw money between nine a.m. and three p.m. at your own bank. Today I can wander out in my sweatpants at two a.m. and get cash on the corner. I like getting cash whenever I want it, and I'm willing to pay $1.50 for that convenience.

But if D'Amato and other self-appointed do-gooders had their way, I wouldn't have that choice. D'Amato proclaimed ATM fees "wrong" and "immoral." At the time, he was not just another congressional blowhard, but chairman of the Senate Banking Committee, and he planned to outlaw the fees. He branded them "absolutely unacceptable—a great scam."

D'Amato went on TV to denounce the "usury" of ATM fees. He claimed, "They cost the average consumer, some reports indicate, a hundred fifty dollars a year more."

"A hundred fifty dollars?" I asked him.

He stammered, "That's—well, begin to think of it. Think of how many transactions that would take."

His staff got the figure from a newspaper article. The real cost was a third of that. But the senator decided to "solve" this nonexistent problem anyway. He was eager to pander to constituents who didn't like the fees.

We had no trouble finding voters who agreed with D'Amato. They told us they shouldn't have to pay to withdraw *their own money.* As one ATM user said, "There wasn't a service charge to put it in, so why should there be one to take it out?"

Why? Because ATM machines aren't free! We interviewed Barbara Stillman, a woman who started a cash-machine business. She owned one ATM and serviced four others. The machine she owned cost her fifteen thousand dollars (some cost fifty thousand). Her initial outlay of fifteen thousand dollars was just the beginning. She had to service the machines and put her own cash in them (the banks reimbursed her four days later). Stillman drove to some of her machines, but had to pay hundreds of dollars to fly to her busiest ATM; it was on Block Island, just off the coast of Rhode Island. Tourists there used her ATM, even though they hated paying Stillman's whopping fee of four dollars. One vacationer complained, "Four dollars is an excessive charge to get money. But we're on vacation, so we do it."

Four dollars was the highest fee we found, and her service charge would certainly have become illegal if Senator D'Amato had his way. That would have taught the greedy Stillman a lesson. Of course, it also would have hurt her customers because it would have put her out of business. Why should the Barbara Stillmans of this world take risks if they can't take profits?

Here's what she told us: "When I'm loading a machine, I could be robbed. If somebody stole the machine, that's a risk. I have no incentive at all to go over there and risk my life flying on an airplane, and why would I want to risk that for nothing?"

In fact, a few years later, she decided "the risk wasn't worth even four dollars per customer." She quit the business.

Most cash machines are owned by banks, but banks have costs too. Politicians can pretend that banks can afford to dispense cash for free, but it isn't so.

We don't need "consumer advocates" like Al D'Amato to keep businesses from charging too much. In a free society, competition holds prices down, and in the cash business, there's plenty of competition. If Stillman's four-dollar fee earns her too fat a profit, competitors will swarm in. They'll court her customers by offering cash for less. On Block Island, in fact, competition has driven the price down to about $2.50. That's how capitalism works. If Stillman charged an "unfair" fee, the free market would correct it without any help from the United States Congress.

When I confronted my senator about his plan, I didn't hide my exasperation.

STOSSEL   It's freedom! People are willingly paying this surcharge, and we're getting more machines.

ALFONSE D'AMATO   It's absolutely not freedom. They don't have a choice. What choice does a person have?

STOSSEL   You make it sound like ATMs are like heroin, and—

ALFONSE D'AMATO   That's true.

STOSSEL [Heroin!?] Aren't you pandering here?

ALFONSE D'AMATO No, I don't think so. Someone's got to stand up for the little guy.

Get out the shovel! D'Amato was *hurting* the little guy. And eventually, the little guys voted him out. Bye, Al.

D'Amato's proposal was the subject of my first "Give Me a Break" column for *20/20,* and I hope I contributed to its defeat. Consumers don't need price controls.

Controlling prices has repeatedly robbed us of convenience and of new products and services. At least inconvenience usually isn't fatal, but it will be fatal if the economically illiterate succeed in imposing price controls on the product they are most eager to regulate: prescription drugs.

> **MYTH:** Drug companies are evil price gougers.
>
> **TRUTH:** The higher the price of drugs, the more good drugs we get.

People hate drug companies. Seeing that Lipitor can cost fourteen hundred dollars a year, or that a medication for cancer patients costs four thousand dollars a month, people say that big drug companies are evil, and that "We need price controls!"

Politicians respond reflexively: Drug companies are "the robber-barons of the American health care system," shouted Senator David Pryor of Arkansas on the floor of Congress.

On the other side of the Capitol, Congressman Peter DeFazio of Oregon wagged a strident finger at his House colleagues. "You will be held to account at the next elections by the tens of millions of Americans who can't afford their pharmaceutical drugs!"

Grab the shovel. That's the nauseating sound of politicians pandering. Do they ever think about how we get these wonderful drugs?

Drugs don't just suddenly appear. Thousands of researchers work tirelessly to develop them. Most attempts fail. But the few successes repay the costs of the failures. Imagine what life was like before the polio vaccine: Thousands spent hours in iron lungs trying to breathe.

People complain about the high cost of vaccinations. But *treating* polio costs billions more than preventing it.

A lifetime vaccination against polio sets you back about twenty dollars. Compare that to the lifelong costs of iron lungs, medical care, and lost wages—to say nothing of the physical and emotional suffering.

The drug companies keep bringing us new miracles. Tour de France winner Lance Armstrong says he's alive only because of his chemotherapy drugs. "If I had this illness twenty years ago," he said, "I wouldn't have lived six months."

Armstrong's testicular cancer treatment cost a lot—around fifteen thousand dollars. But it didn't just spring providentially from some laboratory beaker. It was the product of extensive, and very expensive, research by a pharmaceutical company—a kind of scientific crapshoot in which there are very few winners. Of every five thousand chemical compounds that researchers discover, only one reaches the pharmacist's shelf.

My older, smarter brother Tom knows this firsthand. He's an example of drug company failure. (I love calling Tom a failure because he got better grades in school and was Mom's favorite.) His work illustrates the risks drug companies take.

Tom is codirector of the Hematology Division at Boston's Brigham and Women's Hospital. For thirty years, he did basic research, some of which led to discoveries with practical applications. One was licensed to Biogen Idec, a biotech company, after he convinced them that it might help people with cystic fibrosis breathe more easily.

Biogen Idec financed a regimen of tests that cost twenty million dollars. Unfortunately Tom's discovery didn't work against cystic fibrosis. Biogen's twenty million dollars was a complete loss. Tom thinks the drug might help people with another disease, so there will be new tests and millions more in expenses. Odds are that Tom's discovery will fail those tests too.

Even if the drug does pass through the gamut of tests, it will cost his benefactor hundreds of millions more to get the drug to market. The Tufts Center for the Study of Drug Development says the average cost of developing a new drug is a staggering 802 million dollars. Then, even when a new drug is approved, odds are that it will never turn a profit. Less than a third of marketed drugs have enough commercial success to recover the cost of their research and development.

The hated pharmaceutical companies make big profits, but I *want* them to make big profits because they have to make huge investments, suffer lots of failures, and go through ten to fifteen years of testing before they can bring me the drugs that might save my life or alleviate my pain.

But if you talk to people waiting for their prescriptions at a pharmacy, you don't hear appreciation for all the dollars the drug companies invested; what you hear are complaints about prices. "It makes me mad," one lady told us, "doesn't it make you mad?"

Drug companies do some things that ought to make us mad. Some spend millions on "drug-detail" men, salesmen who lavish doctors with gifts and vacations in order to get them to prescribe that company's drug. ABC's Brian Ross used hidden cameras to videotape them giving away steaks, neckties, flower arrangements, and rooms at the Waldorf-Astoria Hotel. Drug companies also spend a fortune on TV ads that over-promise. They pay their CEOs exorbitant salaries.

But that's capitalism! Like free speech, it brings good and bad. I forgive the bad because it's far outweighed by the good.

Pharmaceutical companies' critics jump all over them for spending about four billion dollars a year advertising to consumers. But that four billion dollars is dwarfed by the nearly *fifty billion* dollars that they spend developing new drugs.

But most people just want those big, bad drug companies punished. Sixty-five percent of people surveyed want government regulation of drug prices. It's the same old story: People see high prices, assume they're being gouged, and foolishly believe that government can save the day.

> **MYTH:** The U.S., lacking price limits on drugs, cruelly harms the poor and the sick.
>
> **TRUTH:** Price controls harm the poor and the sick.

It is true that the U.S. is the only industrialized country that does not impose price controls on drugs. But that is a *good* thing. If price controls were instituted for drugs in the U.S., far fewer drugs would be invented.

When price controls were introduced in Canada in the late 1960s, drug research there dropped by more than half. If the United States—which makes up 45 percent of the world's pharmaceutical market—suddenly decided to institute price controls, amazing drugs would be lost.

Do people consider that when they demand that the government set lower prices? Rarely. AIDS activist Mark Milano disrupted candidates' speeches during the 2000 political campaign by screaming about the cost of AIDS drugs. He said price controls were the only humane solution.

So I invited him in to talk about it.

MARK MILANO *[He's hopping mad here, smug in the moral superiority of his position]* We're the only country that is paying these exorbitant prices.

STOSSEL *[True, but it lets me bait the hook]* What country has a good system?

MARK MILANO *[His face goes blank for a moment, then brightens as he says]* I would say New Zealand has a great system.

STOSSEL *[Now I can reel him in]* How many new drugs come out of New Zealand?

MARK MILANO *[Another pause, and now he looks uncomfortable]* It's true that most researchers focus here in America and in—in Europe. Japan does a tremendous amount of drug research.

STOSSEL Well, how many new drugs came out of Japan?

MARK MILANO *[Now he looks very uncomfortable]* It's hard to pin down exactly where a new drug comes—but some do come from Japan and—and other countries. There have been drugs that have . . .

STOSSEL But most come from America! Do you think that's an accident?

MARK MILANO I don't think it has to do with the fact that we have no price controls, no. Anyway, most of the new drugs coming out come from the federal government.

Again, Milano is talking nonsense. He's passionate about AIDS drugs, but of the fifty-six drugs that were available for AIDS when I interviewed Milano, the National Institutes of Health said it could take credit for only five. The vast majority of new drugs come from greedy private companies.

The critics and politicians want it both ways. They never acknowledge that the investor-owned drug companies drive medical progress, and that taking away financial incentives takes away new medicines.

If they succeed in protecting us by lowering drug prices, they'll "protect" us from the very innovation we need. Their ideas should be quarantined before they infect anyone else.

MYTH: Price "gouging" is evil.

TRUTH: "Gouging" saves lives.

Politicians trot out price controls, and their aliases, anti-gouging and anti-profiteering laws, again and again. Every time there's a hurricane, you know that once the winds die down, a politician will rant about "gouging." You can also bet the media will cheer him on.

After Hurricane Katrina devastated the Gulf Coast in 2005, there were shortages of water, batteries, gasoline, chain saws, etc. Some merchants quickly raised their prices, and politicians and the media raged about that. They wanted "profiteers" punished.

If you're a politician trying to score points by cracking down on mean, greedy people, anti-gouging rules are good for your career. But if you're one of the consumers the law supposedly protects, you won't fare as well.

George Mason University economist Donald J. Boudreaux says that price increases "perform the vital task of economic triage." Consider this scenario: You return home after a cataclysmic storm to find the power is out. You desperately need batteries. You find a store that's open. The owner thinks it's immoral to take advantage of your distress; he wouldn't dream of charging you a dime more than he charged last week. Unfortunately, you can't buy a battery from this compassionate guy because he sold out three days ago. Panicked families grabbed extras to stock up, leaving none for you.

You continue on your quest and finally stumble across that dreaded monster, the price gouger. He now offers a pack of batteries that cost five dollars last week for the "outrageous" price of thirty dollars. You pay him in order to survive the disaster. You resent the gouger, but if he hadn't charged thirty dollars, he'd have been out of batteries too. His "exploitation" saved the day.

It works that way because people look out for their own interests. Before you got to that dealer, other customers did. At five dollars, they stocked up on batteries. They bought *more* than they needed—they got extras for themselves and a relative, until the store ran out. Raising the price puts the brakes on their buying and makes sure batteries and chain saws go to those who really need them. That was not the seller's intention, but it's certainly the result. In addition, raising the price makes new batteries appear. Word gets out: "Big profits to be made on batteries!" Suppliers rush batteries to the scene of the disaster, and the price quickly drops back to five dollars, or less.

Motives matter little. As Adam Smith wrote, "It is not from the benevolence of the butcher, the brewer, or the baker, that we can expect our dinner, but from their regard to their own interest."

Consider the store owner's perspective: If he won't make a big profit, why should he open his store at all? Staying in a disaster area is dangerous. It means leaving his family to wait on strangers. Without extra profit, why go to all that trouble and risk?

It's the price gougers who supply the batteries and water, ship the gasoline, fix the roof, and rebuild the cities. Gouging saves lives.

Right after Hurricane Katrina, I wrote a newspaper column about that simple truth. People got upset.

"You, sir, are scum. Plain and simple, you are scum. How dare you say that the price gougers are saving lives."

". . . the single stupidest, most offensive thing I have ever read. I hope you lose your job over this, you soulless cretin."

E-mail after e-mail from people who hate the very mechanism that makes their lives better: capitalism.

After Hurricane Katrina, there was overwhelming demand for carpentry work. The area's own population of carpenters wasn't enough.

If this were a totalitarian country, the government might just order a bunch of tradesmen to go to New Orleans. But in a free society, tradesmen from other areas must be persuaded to leave their homes and families, their employers and customers, and drive from, say, Chicago to New Orleans. If they can't earn more money in Louisiana than Illinois, why make the trip?

Some carpenters may be motivated by a desire to be heroic, but we can't expect heroes to fill the need, week after week; most will travel there for the same reason most Americans go to work: to make money. Any tradesman who treks to a disaster area must get higher pay than he would get in his hometown, or he won't go. Limit him to what his New Orleans colleagues charged before the storm, and even a would-be hero may say, "The heck with it."

On the other hand, if he charges enough to justify his venture, he's likely to be condemned morally or legally by the very people he's trying to help. They just don't understand basic economics. If price controls forbid prices to rise, tradesmen will be content to stay at home, and New Orleans will take years longer to rebuild.

When Hurricane Andrew hit Florida in 1992, the state's attorney general, Bob Butterworth, was outraged by the "unconscionable" gouging. "I don't see any difference between the looters who go through the rubble in the trailer parks and the business people who cash in on this disaster by gouging customers," he said.

Florida passed laws that punish price gougers with fines of up to twenty-five thousand dollars and made it a third-degree felony for out-of-state contractors to work without a license. Florida law dictates that penalties be increased if those contractors work during a disaster, which of course is when hurricane victims need them most.

In 2004, Hurricanes Charley, Frances, Ivan, and Jeanne all hit Florida. The extensive damage required droves of tradesmen to do repairs, but because of all the consumer "protection" rules, Florida's recovery was slow and difficult.

Florida became known as the "Blue Roof State" because of the thousands of blue plastic tarps that covered damaged roofs for close to a year. The demand for roofers was so severe that some hurricane victims had to wait up to five weeks just to get an estimate for a roof job.

The recovery could have been much faster if only Florida had gotten rid of its ridiculous restrictions. Let the market work, and services that were in short supply become available.

Some regulators say that's not fair to the poor "because poor people can't afford those sudden price spikes that you free-marketers so cavalierly support!"

But such paternalism doesn't help the poor. Poor people need batteries too, and $30 batteries are better than no batteries at all. The poor may have to pool their resources and share the flashlight and radio with neighbors, but some supplies are always better than none.

If the free market is allowed to work its magic, the opportunity to profit will bring so many new suppliers to the disaster site that prices will quickly return to pre-disaster levels. Or even lower. Sometimes the new competitors invent even cheaper ways to do things.

Everyone benefits—the poor *and* the rich—when the politicians don't "protect" us with price controls.

MYTH: A higher minimum wage helps workers.

TRUTH: A higher minimum wage helps some workers, but hurts more.

Wage controls are just as stupid and counterproductive as price controls.

Several years ago, the city council of Santa Monica, California, decided to make the town a workers' paradise. It passed a union-backed law requiring that everyone must be paid at least double the federal minimum wage, or about $12.25 an hour. Activist and minister Sandy Richards told me, "We're making a decision [that] it's not okay to pay people such a low wage that they can't even survive."

Sounds great—until you try it. "I just can't believe how crazy our city council is," Patty Phillips, proprietor of Patty's Pizza, told us. "They don't get it. They don't care. I'd like to know which one of them ever had a job or ever had to make a payroll?"

Patty was angry about the "living wage" law even though her business would not have had to obey it because she took in less than five million dollars a year. But Patty wanted Patty's Pizza to grow. If it did, the living-wage rule would kick in, and she would have to raise her prices so much, she might go *out* of business.

I talked with Jeff King, who owns two restaurants in Santa Monica. "The living wage will lead to layoffs," he said. "It'll dry up the entry-level job for just the people they're trying to help."

That's what Santa Monica's economically ignorant politicians don't get: Just as price controls discourage production, wage controls discourage hiring. The poorest workers are hurt most. When you fix wages above the market rate, the rate freely set by the give-and-take of supply and demand, you temporarily help experienced workers by giving them an artificial raise. But you also take away all incentive to hire an "entry-level" worker.

Jeff King was once one of those: He started in the restaurant industry's traditional entry-level position, dishwasher. So did Jeff's chief chef, Carlos Martinez. Martinez's first job paid less than four dollars an hour. He worked his way up, first to cook, then line cook, then chef. He moved from restaurant to restaurant, getting more money and promotions. Now he makes twenty-seven dollars an hour. The system works—until the do-gooders decide to "fix" it.

They may want to do good, but they have no clue. That was obvious when I talked with activists for the wage law:

MADELINE JANIS-APARICIO The living wage is not going to cause layoffs.

STOSSEL Boy . . . you must be smart. You can micromanage all these businesses. [They stared at me in silence] What conceit! You know best—rather than supply and demand.

DENNIS ZANE That is a preposterous and insulting remark. In fact, we're discussing here a question of simple fairness. There are workers working for low wages, poverty wages.

VIVIAN ROTHSTEIN It's totally legitimate to set standards of wages, standards of health, standards of development. And that's what local government is about.

MADELINE JANIS-APARICIO Policy makers always have to make those kinds of decisions.

JOHN STOSSEL Policy makers?

MADELINE JANIS-APARICIO Right. Policy makers need to define lines.

JOHN STOSSEL *[How do they know where the "correct" line is?]* If thirteen dollars is good, why not twenty dollars? *[Why not fifty?]*

SANDY RICHARDS We didn't feel like you could lay a hit like that—we want it to be reasonable. These very prosperous businesses can absorb these higher wages without even skipping a beat.

How arrogant is that? How can activists and politicians, most of whom have never built a business, presume to know what a business can "absorb"? What happens in real life, of course, is that businesses stop hiring the unskilled.

Wages aren't just money. They are signals that guide people to where they should work and show employers how to expand. If wages are seven dollars an hour at one restaurant, but nine dollars an hour across the street, Carlos Martinez may move across the street—and up the ladder. Jeff King might open another restaurant in a town where wages are lower. These freely floating signals deliver capital to the places where it will take root and grow. That makes America prosperous.

Russell Roberts, an economics professor at George Mason University, makes it a practice when he gives lectures to "educated" groups to ask them what proportion of the workforce earns the minimum wage. These are congressional staffers, law professors, and journalists. The typical answer is 20 percent of the workforce. The correct answer is less than 3 percent. "It's always a good reality check for people," he says. "People need to realize that competition for workers keeps wages up, not legislation."

The "seen" benefits of a higher minimum wage are obvious—some people make more money. That's nice. They will thank the politicians.

The insidious ways that people are hurt are harder to see, but much more widespread.

There's the company that closes because it can't afford to pay the higher wages. There's the company that decides to produce its product with fewer workers. There's the company that never expands. And above all, there's the business that never opens—never hires people. Those people who were never hired don't complain—they wouldn't know whom to blame—they don't even know that they were harmed. They are the unseen victims.

Here's the good news: Voters repealed Santa Monica's "living wage" law just a year after the city council adopted it. Common sense prevailed. But the bad news: at least 122 other living-wage ordinances have passed. Politicians in Washington, DC, demand all workers be paid $6.60 an hour. In Santa Fe it's $8.50, and in San Francisco, $8.62. Policy makers love to pretend that they're Santa Claus, but they're not Santa, and they have closed their minds to the unseen consequences of their laws.

> **MYTH:** Outsourcing is a "crisis." It takes jobs from Americans.
>
> **TRUTH:** Outsourcing creates American jobs.

Unions are furious about outsourcing. They say that it's a "crisis," and that we have to stop "our" jobs from leaving America and punish companies that "export American jobs." When unions are upset about something, politicians are quick to respond. While running for president, John Kerry complained about "Benedict Arnold" CEOs who "take American jobs overseas." Republicans didn't argue with him.

When the chairman of the president's Council of Economic Advisers, Gregory Mankiw, said that outsourcing "is probably a plus for the economy," Republican congressman Don Manzullo said he should be fired. House Speaker Dennis Hastert also complained, and Mankiw quickly wrote a letter of apology. In Washington, sound economics takes a backseat to pandering.

While everyone was complaining about diabolical outsourcing, we asked America's largest labor organization for its best examples of outsourced workers. The AFL-CIO sent us to Shirley and Ronnie Barnard. They worked at a Levi's factory in Powell, Tennessee, until Levi's transferred those jobs to Mexico, closing its Tennessee plants. Shirley was near tears as she told us how terrible outsourcing is. "You've done something for twenty years, got up, went to work every day, and then all of a sudden you don't have anyplace to go and nobody needs you anymore. You don't have a job."

The media were quick to cover the layoffs. They rushed to Tennessee and interviewed crying, unhappy workers. They covered the AFL-CIO's "Show Us the Jobs" tour, where Shirley and a series of other workers told heartbreaking stories of how greedy employers had abused them.

Lou Dobbs feels their pain. The CNN anchor made complaints about outsourcing a trademark of his show. When politicians and unions are mad about something, the mainstream media join in.

MYTH: If the mainstream media say it's a big problem, it is.

TRUTH: If it has to do with economics, the mainstream media frequently get it wrong.

I asked Lou Dobbs about outsourcing: "Companies just shouldn't do it?" "Absolutely not," he answered.

"Because of cheap labor, we're destroying our middle class," Dobbs continued. "That is just stupid. Being stupid is un-American."

Wait a second. It's *restricting* outsourcing that would be stupid and un-American!

Why? First, because outsourcing creates opportunity for miserably poor, hard-working people in India and other third-world countries. That's a good thing, and hardly un-American.

Second, outsourcing saves us money. Most clothing we buy is made overseas. Lou Dobbs sees that as a terrible thing.

LOU DOBBS *[in anchorman tones]* This country cannot even clothe itself. Ninety-six percent of our apparel is imported!

STOSSEL But that's okay! *[He looked shocked when I said that.]* We have more choices for less money.

LOU DOBBS When was the last time you bought a suit of clothes? Because if your prices went down, I would be shocked.

This man went to Harvard? The graph below shows the drop in clothing prices, adjusted for inflation. As outsourcing increased, clothing has gotten cheaper.

CPI Graph for Clothing

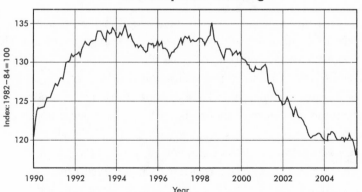

Lots of toys and TVs are now made overseas. Look at the price drops there.

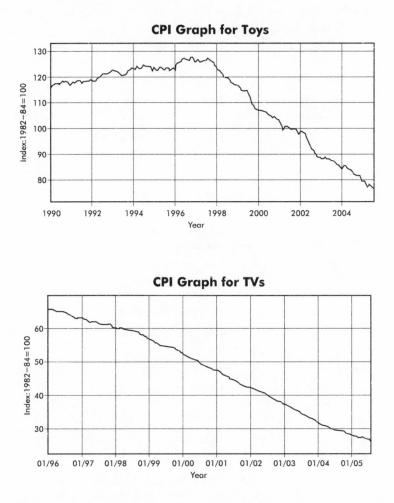

Okay, saving money is great for consumers, but what about workers? What about all those jobs going overseas? It's been reported that close to 500,000 jobs have been outsourced since 2000.

These statistics are scary, but misleading.

Just because a person in India does a job an American once did doesn't mean that more Americans are unemployed. We watched fifty people in India do programming work that was formerly done in California at a company called Collabnet, run by Bill Portelli. Portelli shipped the jobs to India when he discovered Indian engineers cost less than half what American engineers cost. I asked him whether that cheats Americans out of jobs, and he laughed.

"If I hadn't hired the people in India, I would have had to lay people off. Basically, I've created jobs in America! I've built better products, created jobs, been able to raise salaries."

Portelli hired more Americans because outsourcing saved him enough money to expand operations in California. If he hadn't outsourced, he might have gone broke. I said this to Dobbs, and my jaw dropped at his answer. "Then he probably should be out of business! Because the fact of the matter is, either his business would be successful with American workers or it's not going to be successful at all."

Get the shovel! A company should fail rather than outsource?

The benefits of outsourcing were made still clearer when we spoke again with Shirley, the AFL-CIO's example of an outsourcing "victim." She struggled after she lost her Levi's job. But then she found another job, which pays more than her old one. Work at Levi's was noisy and physically difficult; her new job is in an air-conditioned office. She told us, "It's a whole lot easier. Oh, I love my job now!"

Shirley told us that other Levi's workers also found new work. "Some of them have really got excellent jobs," she said, "jobs that they would never have even left Levi's for if the plant hadn't closed. This kind of forced them to make a decision what they wanted to do, and they're really happy at what they do."

Shirley, the AFL-CIO's poster child for the evils of outsourcing, was actually giving us examples of the often invisible benefits of outsourcing. Some of her fired coworkers got *better* jobs. Companies, free to save money by having some work done abroad, created more jobs in America.

Outsourcing is hard on the people who are laid off, and layoffs are very visible. The media are quick to cover them. Reporting on layoffs is an easy assignment. The victims are in one location, at the plant on the last day of work. Show up with a microphone, and people stand in line to share their anger. Everyone can see their pain.

The people who gain work because of outsourcing are harder to see. The media rarely even notice them. But the unseen is more important, because there are more gains than losses. Since 1992, America has lost 391 million jobs. But Brink Lindsey of the libertarian Cato Institute opened my eyes by pointing out that, during those same years America *created* 411 million jobs! Twenty million more than we lost. The media have a tough time covering that because those jobs are created quietly, in a thousand places.

The Levi's plant that closed is being converted into a college. The jobs of the construction crews building it and all those who will teach and do other work there one day won't be mentioned on the evening news. But they're a product of outsourcing too.

What Lou Dobbs won't tell you—maybe because he doesn't know—is that the big outsourcers are big job creators. A study by the Tuck School of Business at Dartmouth found that companies that sent jobs abroad ended up hiring twice as many workers at home. Senator Kerry's "CEO Benedict Arnolds" are not traitors, they're heroes.

Outsourcing is not a crisis. The crisis will come if we try to stop it.

MYTH: The new jobs being created are inferior.

TRUTH: Most are better than the old ones.

Unions claim the new jobs are low-paid "hamburger-flipping McJobs." But it's not true. If it were true, the average American wage would be dropping. It isn't. Even adjusted for inflation, the average American wage has jumped 6 percent in the last 10 years.

Most of the new jobs are good jobs: According to the Bureau of Labor Statistics, two-thirds of the thirty fastest growing occupations in the U.S. require highly skilled workers and provide more than the average national wage. Some of the fastest growing occupations include environmental engineers, software engineers, and service jobs in health care and education.

Lou Dobbs, politicians, and others in the media suggest service jobs are inferior. They weep over the loss of jobs in manufacturing.

DOBBS This country has lost the ability to feed and to clothe itself, to build its own automobiles, to provide its appliances, its electronics, its computers! CNN 8/19/04

GOV. ED RENDELL, PENNSYLVANIA We are losing manufacturing jobs. We're hemorrhaging them. We have to stop that. We cannot be a country whose economy is based on tourism and service industry and producing CDs. MSNBC 12/4/03

REP. BERNIE SANDERS (I), VERMONT The middle class of America is shrinking! . . . New jobs being projected will be low wage, poor benefit jobs. CNN 2/9/05

REP. TIM RYAN (D), OHIO Manufacturing is hemorrhaging all over the country. CNN 4/7/05

LISA SYLVESTER, CNN CORRESPONDENT The United States has been hemorrhaging manufacturing jobs. CNN 2/9/05

"Hemorrhaging" this and "hemorrhaging" that. Are they repeating somebody's talking points? Their complaints are silly. As *The Economist* says, "Manufacturing jobs disappear because economies are healthy, not sick."

The economically illiterate believe there's something better about manufacturing jobs—that only manufacturing builds a stronger America. Nonsense.

Any job where workers earn money is a good job. When it comes to our own kids, we understand this truth. The jobs that we want our kids to hold are in the service sector—we want them to be doctors, lawyers, architects, and engineers. How many of us long for our children to work in assembly plants?

In the 1800s most American workers worked on farms, while today fewer than 2 percent do. If all those teachers, nurses, biologists, massage therapists, etc. had to return to agriculture, Americans would be poorer, not better off.

MYTH: Sweatshops exploit people.

TRUTH: Sweatshops help people.

People are *very* upset about "sweatshops." At first glance, they seem to have a good argument: "If you're going to employ people overseas, at least don't exploit slave labor in sweatshops!"

Protests against sweatshops have disrupted college campuses and meetings of the World Trade Organization. Ardent activists, pandering politicians, and even Hollywood actors rail against the "injustice" of foreign factories that pay just a fraction of American wages.

We videotaped protesters parading around with signs saying "Worker Justice." Who could argue with that? No one wants worker *in*justice. But these slogans are as meaningless as the phrases "social justice" and "sustainable development." Who's for "*un*sustainable development?" Worse, the protesters' theories about "worker justice" hurt the poor people they claim to defend.

"I wish these people would begin to think with their brains rather than with their hearts," Bibek Debroy told me. He's an economist who lives in India.

"I don't understand the expression 'sweatshops,'" Debroy said. "There's nothing wrong with sweat. Sweat is good! Sweat is what most people in the developing world, including India, do all the time!"

That sweat not only puts food on the table, it puts roofs over the tables. The clothing factories the protesters call sweatshops are exactly the kind of businesses that helped people in now thriving places like South Korea, Taiwan, and Hong Kong escape poverty.

In poor countries, the factories the well-fed American protesters revile routinely pay twice what local factories pay, and triple what people can earn doing much harder and more dangerous work in the fields.

"Exploiting people?" snorts Kenyan trade expert June Arunga. "Nobody in my country thinks about companies exploiting them. When there's a new company opening a factory, people are excited about it." They use those jobs as a step up the economic ladder.

"Most of them work for these companies for a while, then go off and start their own businesses. It's a win-win situation for everyone."

Arunga rolls her eyes at the college protesters. "They have no idea of what they're talking about. They are comparing that to what they have in their rich homes."

My interviews with Debroy and Arunga still echoed in my head when I sat down with some die-hard protesters, members of United Students Against Sweatshops. We had taped USAS's protest at Harvard. Their cause was so fashionable that Senator Ted Kennedy and actors Matt Damon and Ben Affleck showed up to support it.

The students were certain of the moral superiority of the anti-sweatshop campaign. I started with what Debroy and Arunga had told me.

> **STOSSEL** They called people like you "rich, ignorant, and clueless."
>
> **MANDIE YANASAK** *[Emerson College]* The image that we have as being rich and clueless and just idealist college students is a false one. Do I have a vision of how I want the world to be? Sure, of course I do. I want the world to be one where people don't have to struggle to feed their children.
>
> **LINDSAY-MARISOL ENYART** *[University of New Mexico]* Workers are forced to migrate into the city or into places where factories like these exist.
> *["Forced?" Who is forcing them? Force is something only governments can impose. To get an employee to come to work for them, businesses must offer*

workers something better than they had before. In the Third World, people
choose low paying work because their other choices are worse. The activists
miss the force-vs.-voluntary distinction every time. They make the same error
when they say Nike or The Gap exploit "slave" labor. Calling sweatshops
"slave" labor insults the victims of real slavery. Sorry for the diatribe. I got
carried away. Back to the interview.]

STOSSEL Who's forcing them? They travel to the factory. They chose to work there!

LINDSAY-MARISOL ENYART [shocked at my insensitivity] I mean, you would prefer eating to not eating.

STOSSEL But if you insist on higher wages, some of these factories will close. You're going to put people out of work.

MANDIE YANASAK We're not trying to close down sweatshops.

STOSSEL Yes, you are. I mean, you say you're not, but that's the result of your protests. Some places will close, they'll go where the wages are lower.

MANDIE YANASAK The goal is to raise the wages across the board.

That's the goal, but a minimum wage or restrictions on sweatshops won't achieve it.

Like most do-gooder anti-market nonsense, the sweatshop protests have unintended consequences: American complaints about child labor persuaded factories in Bangladesh to stop hiring adolescents. The result, according to UNICEF, was that many young girls became prostitutes instead. Smug Americans have an idealistic vision of the perfect world, but they don't recognize the harm that they do by trying to impose their ideals. The perfect is the enemy of the good.

MYTH: Business believes in free markets.

TRUTH: Most businesspeople couldn't care less about free markets, and will stifle competition if it serves their interest.

While fatuous rich kids try to dictate to the third world's poor, where are the capitalists? Why aren't they defending their fellow businessmen? Why aren't they shouting about the glories of the free market instead of leaving it to me?

Because capitalists rarely think about the principles that brought them success. Worse—when market competition becomes a nuisance—they try to kill it: They conspire to restrain trade. Adam Smith saw that years ago when he wrote: "People of the same trade seldom meet together, even for merriment and diversion, but the conversation ends in a conspiracy against the public, or in some contrivance to raise prices."

Vigorous competition makes it hard to raise prices. If GM and Toyota collude and set high prices for new cars, Ford and Honda will clean their clocks by offering cars for less. It's even harder to collude in industries with low start-up costs. If every established taxi company raises taxi fares, new entrepreneurs offering cheaper rides will grab the business. In a free market, businesses can't kill competition because they can't use force. So what do some of them do? They turn to their friends in government. Politicians get to use force.

The Internet has revolutionized the marketplace. It's harder for your local merchant to overcharge you when, just by surfing the Web, you can find the same item elsewhere for less. The Internet also saves you money because it eliminates middlemen.

So if you are an expensive middleman, or selling something with big markups, the Internet is bad news for you. You'll need to innovate—rise above the new competition by offering extra perks, or personal services, or faster delivery.

Or you could get your political buddies to pass legislation limiting Internet sales. That's what car dealers did.

Internet car-buying services now let you shop for prices and options without ever leaving home. Debbie Kassay tried a company called Carorder.com. She clicked on the manufacturer and model, and it offered her a bargain on a Mitsubishi Gallant.

Debbie went to the Internet because she hates the hassle of visiting car dealerships in person. So do lots of people. But as much as you dislike dealerships, Detroit dislikes your bypassing them even more. It insists you buy your car from a dealer. And today, you can purchase a car online *only* if a dealer is involved. And guess what: The dealer then gets a cut. Even though Debbie's dealer didn't negotiate the price, help her choose options, or explain features of the car to her, she was forced to pay him as though he had.

How did the auto industry create a loophole in Internet commerce big enough to drive an SUV through? Political clout. Detroit and its dealers wield enough influence in state capitals to make direct sales of cars on the Internet illegal. The automotive industry often fights government regulation, but when it can use government for its own ends, it does.

Here's what the spokesman for the National Automobile Dealers' Association had to say about that:

> **DAVID HYATT** [dead-serious] If the manufacturer sells directly over the Internet, it leaves the dealer in an unfair competitive situation.
>
> **STOSSEL** Unfair to whom?
>
> **DAVID HYATT** Their own dealer. The—if—if that were allowed to happen in the long term, it would, in fact, put dealerships out of business.
>
> **STOSSEL** So what? The Internet put lots of middlemen out of business. Consumers like it. I don't want to buy from the dealership.
>
> **DAVID HYATT** [pregnant pause, then] The key is that there is a very healthy system in place.

Healthy for his car dealers, anyway.

Liquor wholesalers also were upset when they discovered wine lovers were ordering their favorite Merlots and Chardonnays over the Internet. Can't have that! In twenty-four states, government protected these expensive middlemen by prohibiting direct-to-consumer wine shipments from out of state. If a wine enthusiast from Chicago hankered for his favorite California Pinot Noir, he'd have to go to an Illinois store and pay a hefty mark-up.

But when Virginia vintner Juanita Swedenburg couldn't ship a case of her award-winning Chardonnay to New York, the Institute for Justice, a libertarian public interest law firm, helped her fight the law. In 2004, the U.S. Supreme Court broke up the liquor wholesalers' cozy racket.

But real estate agents are still using their political clout to protect their 6 percent commissions.

In 2001 and 2002, California's Department of Real Estate, run by (surprise) a real estate broker, sent warning letters to some "for sale by owner" websites, demanding that they comply with licensing laws for brokers. This was ridiculous. The websites are the equivalent of classified ads; they just list available homes. Forcing the website to get brokers' licenses would just increase costs for home sellers. Fortunately, in 2004, a federal court held the Department of Real Estate's demand unconstitutional.

Discount brokers also threaten brokers' 6% commission. They offer services at lower rates, like a flat fee of $250 to host a two-hour open house, or $499 to review the contract paperwork.

So traditional brokers have persuaded politicians in many states to pass "minimum service" laws that force discount brokers to offer more services (and thereby force consumers to pay higher fees).

When I confronted David Lereah, chief economist for the National Association of Realtors, about that, he said, "Not everyone is providing the adequate amount of services to protect the consumer."

Excuse me, but if I want a Realtor to protect my interests, I'll hire one. But if I think I'm better off selling my home with less help than they want to sell me, that should be my choice.

Part of being a free person is deciding for yourself what's in your interest. That doesn't mean you can't get expert help, but it does mean you get to decide when, how much, and from whom. If realtors or car dealers think Internet sales and discount brokerages are bad options, they should make their case through advertising. They shouldn't try to get their cronies in government to outlaw competition.

That genius Adam Smith understood this years ago:

"To widen the market and to narrow the competition is always the interest of the dealers . . . The proposal of any new law or regulation of commerce . . . ought always to be listened to with great precaution, and ought never to be adopted, till after having been long and carefully examined, not only with the most scrupulous, but with the most suspicious attention. It comes from an order of men whose interest is never exactly the same with that of the public."

It's so sad. Businesspeople rarely defend free markets. Professors at fancy universities vilify markets. Reporters sneer at them. There is such hatred of capitalism and profit that Americans even pass laws that kill people.

> **MYTH:** Selling body parts is immoral, and should be illegal.
>
> **FACT:** There's nothing immoral about saving lives.

Most Americans believe it is immoral, if not absolutely disgusting, to buy and sell parts of people.

And yet Americans *need* other people's body parts, especially kidneys. More than sixty thousand people whose kidneys have failed are waiting for transplants now. Many survive by enduring hours hooked up to dialysis machines.

The dialysis machines are technological wonders. They clean your blood, pinch-hitting for diseased kidneys. But they cannot do it as well as a kidney, and dialysis is painful, exhausting, and tedious. Expensive too: The government spent eighteen billion dollars treating dialysis patients in 2001 alone.

So sixty thousand Americans pray for kidneys. Some will get them from friends and family who donate organs. More will receive them from strangers who die in accidents. But accidents and altruists don't provide enough kidneys. More than six thousand husbands, fathers, wives, mothers, sons, and daughters die every year waiting for an organ transplant. Seventeen deaths a day.

Some dialysis patients are desperate. Ed Lavatelli told us, when it came to a new kidney, price was no object. "I would pay whatever I had to, really. If I had to borrow it, I'd borrow it because it's indescribable to be a person with kidney failure. It really is."

Tragically, Ed's agony was needless because plenty of people were willing to help him. Ruth Sparrow of St. Petersburg, Florida, wanted money, so she ran a newspaper ad saying: "Kidney, runs good, $30,000 or best offer."

She got a couple of serious calls, she said, but then the newspaper refused to run her ad again and warned her that she might be arrested.

When a human kidney was offered on the auction site eBay, bidding reached nearly six million dollars before eBay put a stop to it.

Why did eBay halt a successful auction? Why weren't desperate people allowed to use money as a motivator? Why shouldn't someone with two healthy organs be allowed to put one on the market?

Because other people *hate* the idea. Back in 1984 when Al Gore was a congressman, he sponsored a law making the sale of organs a crime, punishable by five years in a federal penitentiary. Congress couldn't contain its enthusiasm; the bill passed 396 to 6. Nearly all countries have now outlawed the buying and selling of organs, and every association of medical ethics has condemned the practice. Some call the idea of organ sales a new form of cannibalism.

So giving someone a kidney is a good deed, but selling the same kidney is a felony. A patient on the kidney waiting list named Margaret Harris asked a good question: "If I make a deal with you, why is it the government's business?"

I told her, "They feel that they have to set a moral tone for what's right and wrong."

"Why?" she asked. "Who are they protecting?"

Not Margaret Harris. She died waiting for both an answer and a kidney. She was one of about six thousand patients who left grieving families that year because not enough kidneys were available.

I talked with Steve Rivkin, who joined a waiting list for kidneys when it was *thirty thousand* names long. "I don't think that there's anything wrong with paying money for a kidney transplant," he told me. "I just want a kidney that works!" Steve was going for dialysis treatments three times a week, five hours a session. He hated it.

Steve got sympathy, but no help, from Dr. Brian Pereira, former president of the National Kidney Foundation.

> **DR. BRIAN PEREIRA** I empathize with this patient's need for a kidney that works. The good news is that this person can continue on dialysis under the current system, which functions extremely well.
>
> **STOSSEL** What? Seventeen deaths a day is "extremely well"?
>
> **DR. PEREIRA** Seventeen deaths a day is a statistic that we need to understand in the light of what could happen on the down side. The fact that the current situation is desperate doesn't justify an unwise policy decision.

Grab that shovel! The Kidney Foundation believes that poor people would be vulnerable to "exploitation" if there were an open market for kidneys. But how are they exploited?

In some poor countries, where people are more pressed for money and less impressed with pseudo-principles, some sell their kidneys. I found pictures of men from the Philippines who'd exchanged one of theirs for just a thousand dollars. They posed on a beach, showing their scars. Such pictures make wealthy Americans say, "Look how these poor people were exploited! They risked their lives for just a thousand dollars."

But what gives us the right to decide for them? You or I might not have done it, but *no one forced them*. They're poor, and they wanted the thousand dollars more than they wanted two kidneys. To say the poor are too desperate to resist a dangerous temptation is patronizing. Whatever his income, everyone has free will.

On my TV report about organ selling, British philosopher Janet Radcliffe Richards sneered at the idea that we must ban the sale of organs to protect the poor. "This seems to me just about as bad an exploitation of the poor by the rich as you could get. . . . What's the difference between giving a kidney if you're poor and selling it if you're poor? The difference is that you get some money, and you're not quite as poor."

Steve Rivkin went online to try to save his life. The dirty little secret of the organ transplant world is that while marketing organs may be illegal, it happens all the time. Several websites help buyers and sellers of body parts find each other.

Steve posted an ad, and soon people from all over the world were calling to sell him a kidney. "There were some sad stories out there," Steve told me. "One couple had gone bankrupt. He just was looking for a way to pay everything off, start over fresh, and move on . . . it's a fair exchange, you know, you're talking about two desperate people."

One desperate for a kidney, the second for money.

But Big Brother will not allow them to make a voluntary trade.

DR. BRIAN PEREIRA No barter, no sale of organs. That's where we have to step in.

STOSSEL Who's "we"?

DR. BRIAN PEREIRA The government, the professional societies who help the government make the right policies.

That conceit—that the government and "professional societies" must decide for all of us—kills people. Government and professional societies have no right to decide that suffering people should continue suffering, and dying, because some people are offended by other adults' voluntary choices. It all comes down to one simple question: Who owns your body, you or the government?

Bringing money to the process doesn't make the exchange of an organ evil. As Steve Rivkin told us before he died, money is what makes transplants happen. "The doctors make money, the hospitals make money, the organ procurement organizations make money. Everybody gets something except for the donor!"

If you think it's immoral to sell an organ, fine, don't do it. But sick people shouldn't have to die because some people despise free markets.

Considering the blessings the free market makes possible—our longer, healthier lives, our unprecedented amounts of leisure, food so abundant that we worry about obesity rather than malnutrition—it seems churlish that people complain about capitalism. We ought to embrace it, not curse it. Like an unappreciated mother, the market is overwhelmingly good to us even when we hate and hinder it.

For too long, I didn't realize the market is our best friend. Instead, I thought it was government. What a mistake! Government's ceaseless war against the free market makes everyone's life harder.

CHAPTER FOUR

MONSTER GOVERNMENT

rowing up, I believed that government was a good thing, like Mommy and Daddy: It helped and protected us. It took me a while to understand that government could become *too much* of a good thing: patronizing, overprotective, and destructive to our liberty.

We have strayed from the path of what Thomas Jefferson, in his first Inaugural Address, called "a wise and frugal government," one that "shall restrain men from injuring one another, which shall leave them otherwise free to regulate their own pursuits."

We need government to restrain us from injuring each other, defend us against attack, protect the environment, and do *very* few other things. *Limited* government is a wonderful thing. But our government has grown from the founders' genius vision to a monster that sustains itself with constantly increasing taxes, endless meddling, and ever-greater intrusion into what was once private life.

Politicians claim their laws and programs will solve problems. The media are quick to cover the problems and explain how a new law should fix them. That's the "seen" benefit. The media are less good at covering the "unseen," the unintended consequences of the law. There are always many, and they soon become an excuse to pass even more laws.

Nobel Prize winner Ronald Coase put it this way: "If a federal program were established to give financial assistance to Boy Scouts to enable them to help old ladies cross busy intersections, we could be sure that not all the money would go to Boy Scouts, that some of those they helped would be neither old nor ladies, that part of the program would be devoted to preventing old ladies from crossing busy intersections, and that many of them would be killed because they would now cross at places where, unsupervised, they were at least permitted to cross." Then government would pass new rules further restricting old ladies' movements.

This is why government itself has become a clear and present danger.

Smokey the Bear's rules for fire safety should apply to government: Keep it small, keep it in a confined area, and keep an eye on it.

MYTH: Republicans shrink government.

TRUTH: Republicans say they will, but they don't.

Years ago, interviewing economist Walter Williams for an ABC News program called "Greed," I was perplexed when Williams said "a thief is more moral than a congressman; when a thief steals your money, he doesn't demand you thank him."

I thought that was silly hyperbole, but watching Congress spend, I see that Dr. Williams was right, and I was naïve. Government confiscates huge amounts of our money—even more than we know about. Then Congress spends much of it on self-promotion—and asks us to thank them for it.

When the Democrats held power, I confronted the king of pork, Senator Robert Byrd, about spending our money on "Honorable Robert Byrd Highway"–type projects in West Virginia. His answer in our interview was as arrogant as he was: "I would think that the national media could rise above the temptation of being clever, decrepitarian critics who twaddlize, just as what you're doing right here."

"Twaddlizing?" I asked.

"Trivializing serious matters," he explained.

I persisted, "Is there no limit? Are you not at all embarrassed about how much *you* got?"

Byrd glared at me in silence, and finally demanded, angrily, "Are you embarrassed when you think you're working for the good of the country? Does that embarrass you?"

The Republicans promised to change the culture. When they ran for office, they said they'd shrink The State. They even used the same words. On one of my TV specials, *John Stossel Goes to Washington*, I ran split-screen clips of Ronald Reagan and George Bush Sr. saying in unison, as if they were singing a duet: "Government is too big and spends too much."

Democrats sold panic. "Don't vote for them! They're going to take away your favorite programs!" They needn't have worried. The Republicans got elected, but if the Democrats' goal was to expand the government, they were the real winners.

President Reagan at least slowed the growth of the State. He vetoed seventy-eight bills passed by the spendthrifts in Congress, but President George W. Bush has vetoed nothing and spent money even faster than the Democrats did. Republicans sometimes say that spending is up only because of the war, but even if you take out defense and homeland security, discretionary spending has still increased 40 percent since Bush took office. Spending at the Department of Labor is up 29 percent; at the Energy Department, 33 percent; Agriculture, 41 percent; and at the Department of Education, spending is up 135 percent. Some of those agencies shouldn't exist at all. In the 1980s, the Republicans said they wanted to eliminate the Department of Education. They should have. Its budget is up *169 percent* since 1995.

Even Republicans who once criticized Democrats for overspending are doing disgusting things now that they are in power. When the Democrats controlled Congress, Alaska congressman Don Young told them, "Any of you think that 1 percent can't be cut out of any part of your budget, you haven't been here that long. And most of you have been here that long!"

Good for him, but now that his party can get its hands on your money, he's the biggest pig of all. He heads the Transportation Committee, and got his fellow representatives to vote him 450 million dollars to build two bridges to little-populated parts of Alaska.

One of these two "bridges to nowhere" was particularly egregious because it would connect Ketchikan, Alaska, to a nearly uninhabited island. Yet it would be monstrous—replacing a short ferry ride with a bridge higher than the Brooklyn Bridge and almost as long as the Golden Gate. Even some in Ketchikan laugh about it. One told us, "Short view is, I don't see a need for it. The long view . . . I still don't see a need for it."

Congressman Young says his pork is justified because his bridges will "create jobs." Get the shovel. Politicians always say "job creation" to justify pork, but it's political deceit. Yes, the hundreds of millions of dollars will create some temporary construction jobs, and benefit Ketchikan. That's the "seen" benefit. But the millions of dollars would create more jobs if they weren't taken from taxpayers in the first place. They'd go to shoe stores, bowling alleys, medical research projects, and thousands of other better uses to which free people put their money rather than spending it on bridges to nowhere. If government pork "created" jobs, Congress might as well pay people to dig holes and then fiil them up. I suspect Congressman Young will suggest that soon—as long as the holes are dug in his state.

In 2005, after Hurricane Katrina had devastated the Gulf Coast, Oklahoma senator Tom Coburn tried to redirect the Alaska pork, and use the money to rebuild the I-10 bridge over Louisiana's Lake Pontchartrain, badly damaged by the storm.

"No!" screamed his colleagues. Alaska's other big porker, Senator Ted Stevens, had a little tantrum. He stood on the Senate floor and said if his state's loot was cut, he'd resign and "be taken out of here on a stretcher!"

Good! Senator Stevens, please go. I'll help carry the stretcher.

Unfortunately, Congress has an unwritten code: "Don't threaten the other congressmen's swag." The Senate reprimanded *Coburn* by voting against his proposal 82 to 15.

Alaska's other senator, Lisa Murkowski, said it would be "offensive" not to spend your money on the bridge in her state. When she first became a senator, I asked her if Republicans believed in smaller government. She said they did, but then, perhaps because she was still new at the game (her father, who'd become governor, had just appointed her to fill his own Senate seat) and was not yet a professional obfuscator, she was unusually candid: "We want smaller government. But, boy, I sure want more highways and more stuff, whatever the stuff is."

I'll say. Alaska gets much more pork per resident than other states. "Oh, you need to come up," she said. "You would realize it's not pork. It's all necessity. . . . People look at Alaska and say, 'Well, gee, they're getting all this money,' but we still have communities that are not tied in to sewer and water. There are certain basic things that you've got to have."

But my children shouldn't have to pay for them. If people want to live in remote areas of Alaska, they can pay for their own "stuff," through state or local taxes, or better yet, through private businesses. Why should all Americans pay to run sewer lines through the vast, frozen spaces of Alaska? Because Alaska has no money?

Don't believe it. Alaska has so much revenue from oil production, it has no state income tax or sales tax. Instead, it writes each of its citizens a check every year from something called the Alaska Permanent Fund.

The Alaska congressional delegation is as crafty as it is determined. When criticism of their bridges started attracting too much media attention, they ostentatiously had them "eliminated" in a conference committee report. That is, the bridges were not mentioned specifically in the final bill—but the

452 million dollars earmarked for "Alaska projects" remained intact! This one deserves a golden shovel for sheer chutzpah.

Stevens, Murkowski, and Representative Don Young—who once told critics of the Bridge to Nowhere that they could "kiss his ear"—are not unique. Republican politicians talk about limited government, but the longer they are in power, the more they vote to spend.

> **MYTH:** Vote for me; I'll cut the waste.
>
> **TRUTH:** Not on this planet.

Politicians talk about cutting "waste," but they don't do it. They can't do it.

Efficiency is not something government can achieve. Civil service rules forbid firing bad workers and rewarding good ones. Even if those destructive rules were repealed, government work still lacks the focus and drive that competition for profit and survival bring. In fact, if you can name one thing government does more efficiently than the private sector, I'll send you a check for a thousand dollars. Wasting money, creating red tape, etc., don't count (libertarians, save your e-mails)—if the private sector's goal was to waste money, it would waste money even faster than government.

The federal government only fires about one in three thousand workers each year for poor performance. This is stunningly low.

Private companies slash thousands of jobs even when they're profitable. It's the "creative destruction" that lets them stay profitable. Jack Welch, revered as a great manager because he turned GE into a 300-billion-dollar corporation, says if an organization is to stay vital, it should get rid of about 10 percent of its workers every year. He says, "We tell people in the bottom ten, look, you got a year. Find yourself somewhere to go. And they do!"

That sounds cruel, but the result is not. The departure of the 10 percent creates opportunity for other workers. And the fired workers often find jobs that are a better match for their talents. The "bottom 10 percent" were often miserable in their old jobs. They hang on because change is daunting, and searching for a new job is frightening. But after the layoffs happen, many find they are better off. "Being fired was the best thing that happened to me!" is a comment I've heard from many.

When Capital Cities Corporation bought ABC, I was anxious about Capital Cities' reputation for cost-cutting. I was right to be anxious. My bosses were ordered to cut ABC's staff by 1,800 people. I was appalled. "How can we maintain the quality of *20/20*," I asked angrily, "if we don't have a lighting specialist, and if we have to limit the editing time?"

My complaints were ignored, and I was surprised to find we could do the work with fewer people. Then Disney bought Cap Cities, and there were more layoffs. Again we found new ways to do things. We never would have done it without the pressure.

Government agencies never face that kind of pressure. Occasionally a manager proposes minor cuts, and then comes the outrage: Cutbacks? "No!" scream the special interests, or whatever you want to call the partnership of the bureaucrats and the people who receive their largesse. Without competition forcing hard choices, government managers cave.

So government only grows. Thomas Jefferson said it's "the natural progress of things" for government to grow, and "liberty to yield." Even when government programs have horrible, unintended consequences—even when they harm more people than they help—government can't stop.

> **MYTH:** Farm subsidies guarantee us an ample food supply.
>
> **TRUTH:** Food would be just as plentiful without subsidies.

Congress gives billions of your tax dollars to farmers. Watching President Bush sign the Farm Security and Rural Investment Act, I marveled at the way a dozen members of Congress gathered around him, trying to squeeze closer so they'd be seen applauding in the photo op.

Farm subsidies are popular with politicians because Big Agriculture lobbies hard, and many farm states are swing states. In addition, farms are romantic. No one wants to lose the family farm. And people believe that without subsidies, we wouldn't have a reliable food supply.

But what a totally insane myth that is.

Hundreds of the "farmers" that get your tax money through farm subsidies live in New York City. Only a few, like Mike Sonnenfeldt, were willing to face our cameras to talk about it.

Sonnenfeldt is in the real estate business. He lives a few blocks from me in an elegant apartment building that's also home to Steven Spielberg and Steve Martin. Sonnenfeldt collects cotton subsidies.

STOSSEL Why do you collect cotton subsidies?

MIKE SONNENFELDT I have no idea.

STOSSEL How can you not know?

MIKE SONNENFELDT Because I bought a piece of property that got traded for a piece of property and I'm not sure exactly even why I get it.

That's often how it works. Once government handouts start, they rarely stop, no matter how ridiculous they get. Ted Turner has gotten $491,179 in farm subsidies, David Rockefeller has gotten $524,167, and Enron's Ken Lay got $22,486.

To be fair, most farm subsidy money goes to real farms, although mostly to big agri-businesses, not the "family farm" the politicians drool over.

I interviewed the owners of one such family farm. Fred and Larry Starrh grow cotton in California. Over seven years, they had collected 3.5 million dollars of your money.

They were offended when I called them "welfare queens."

FRED STARRH I take umbrage with that remark.

Fred and Larry actually liked me until that point. They watched *20/20* and said they were fans—I think that's why they agreed to be interviewed. They said they believe in limited government, but still believe they deserve your money because cotton farmers have "special needs." It's hard to think of the Starrhs as needy, since they have a huge 12,000-acre spread in Shafter, California. But they say their costs have increased faster than prices. Subsidies are just a small part of their income, but they say without them, they can't make a profit.

To that I say, "So what?" Not making a profit doesn't entitle them to our money. Most businesses that can't make a profit simply go out of business. Woolworth closed. So did TWA. So do 20,000 restaurants every year. It's the freedom to fail that's helped make America as prosperous as it is, because it frees people to do more productive things. "About ten percent of U.S. firms go out of business each year due to mismanagement, obsolete products, and other reasons," notes Chris Edwards in his book, *Downsizing the Federal Government*. "Other data shows that more than half of new businesses disappear within four years of being established."

But that's never allowed to happen on subsidized farms. When Fred and Larry can't make a profit, you pay for their handouts.

FRED STARRH I don't look at it as a handout whatsoever. I absolutely refuse to accept that.

STOSSEL But it's, it's welfare. The government is giving . . .

FRED STARRH I look at it as a way to maintain a viable agriculture in this country.

But that's the myth. Government officials, ignorant about markets, seem to believe that nothing happens unless government provides it. But subsidies don't maintain viable agriculture. Most crops don't get subsidies. Potatoes, almonds, peaches, asparagus, carrots, lettuce, onions, tomatoes, and at least fifty other crops get no subsidies. There's no shortage of any of those foods. Farmers who grow them manage to thrive without feeding off taxpayers.

In 1984 New Zealand eliminated farm subsidies cold turkey. The changes met fierce resistance, but Edwards reports that "farm productivity, profitability, and output have soared since the reforms." The Federated Farmers of New Zealand say that the experience "thoroughly debunked the myth that the farming sector cannot prosper without government subsidies."

Yet Fred and Larry say farming "can't survive" without subsidies.

FRED STARRH You don't wanna let agriculture fall on its ear.

STOSSEL I don't think agriculture would fall on its ear. *You* would fall on your ear. Peach farmers and plum farmers, they don't get this welfare. They make money. Why do you need it?

LARRY STARRH If I can't grow my six thousand acres of cotton because the subsidy's gone, where am I gonna go with that acreage? Do I just idle it?

STOSSEL I don't know. Where do I go if our ratings go down? That's life.

FRED STARRH Well, we disagree with you 110 percent. And we are right, and you are wrong.

Without billions of dollars in handouts, Fred and Larry told me American cotton would disappear.

FRED STARRH It would go to China. It would go to India. It would go to Pakistan.

STOSSEL Good! [That surprised them]. Let's get cheap cotton from those places and stop throwing millions of dollars at you!

LARRY STARRH Is that what you want?

STOSSEL Yes! If you can't make a profit, then you don't deserve to keep doing what you're doing.

FRED STARRH Well, I totally disagree with you, John. And the legislature is with us at this point, so we're winning, and you're losing.

He's right. They are winning, and you and I are paying for it.

Around 1900, America had six million farms, and the Agriculture Department employed 3,000 people. Today there are only two million farms, but the Department employs 100,000 people. At this rate, soon there will be more bureaucrats than farmers.

Subsidies are like a heroin fix. They feel good, but they lead to more subsidies. Cotton subsidies raise the price of cotton. That makes clothing manufacturers want to buy foreign cotton—but since that would hurt American farmers, government restricts imports. This wrecks the lives of poor farmers worldwide, because they can't sell their cotton in America. To make up for that, Congress then spends billions more on foreign aid, and then billions more on another subsidy to American manufacturers so they can afford to buy the expensive American cotton. One bad policy on top of another.

In 1954, congressmen argued it was crucial to national security that America have enough wool to make soldiers' uniforms. Today most military uniforms aren't even made of wool, but no matter, the Agriculture Department still pays hundreds of millions to sheep and goat ranchers. Subsidies have gone even to "farmers" like my ABC colleague Sam Donaldson, because he and his wife raised sheep and goats on their New Mexico ranch. Donaldson calls the payments "a horrible mess" (he's sold the livestock and no longer collects subsidies), but he compares them to the home mortgage deduction, saying, "As long as the law is on the books, it's appropriate to take advantage of it." I can't argue with that reasoning: I once collected federal flood insurance for a storm-damaged beach house.

If it's right to call the women collecting welfare payments "welfare queens," then it's appropriate to call the Starrhs, Sam Donaldson, and me welfare queens too.

The Starrhs find the title of welfare queen offensive. "Change it to king. Welfare kings. Because 'queens' is bad in California," joked Larry Starrh. "Call me SpongeBob, please."

A "sponge" he is, to the tune of nearly 3.5 million dollars of your money. Is there a shovel handy?

In September 2005, President Bush shocked the heck out of me by announcing to the UN that "the United States is ready to eliminate all tariffs, subsidies, and other barriers to free flow of goods and services as other nations do the same."

But I won't hold my breath waiting for it to happen.

> **MYTH:** We need government to give us PBS.
>
> **TRUTH:** No, we don't.

I enjoy PBS, but like farm supports, PBS is welfare for the well-off. It's billed as the provider of *Sesame Street* and other popular children's programming, but PBS shows skew upscale. Compared to other Americans, PBS viewers are 44 percent more likely to make more than $150,000 a year.

It hardly seems fair that the government forces you to buy that channel for me. If I want to see opera, I should pay for it myself. Why should you be taxed to pump *La Bohème* into my living room? It barely made sense in 1967, when most Americans only had the Big Three broadcast networks, but now there are hundreds of channels. If there's a demand for opera or BBC drama, the market will provide it.

PBS is justly famous for programs like *Sesame Street*. But popular programs are just that—popular. That means they have other ways to get money. People already give so much money to PBS that today it only gets 15 percent of its funds from the federal government. David Boaz, author of *Libertarianism: A Primer,* points out that "businesses and nonprofits deal with 15 percent revenue losses all the time. If NPR and PBS lost all their federal money, they wouldn't disappear."

Whenever anyone suggests cutting the PBS budget, people say, "They're trying to kill *Sesame Street*!" But *Sesame Street* is big business and would survive in any environment. Children's programming does not need taxpayer subsidies. *Reason* magazine's Jacob Sullum points out, "Noggin, which is more 'commercial-free' than PBS stations, carries twelve hours of kids' shows (including two different versions of *Sesame Street*) every day. Parent-acceptable children's programming can also be seen on Nickelodeon, the Disney Channel, and ABC Family."

Some people, who apparently have never watched *20/20* or *60 Minutes,* claim we won't have tough journalism on TV unless government funds it. Only PBS will do "honest" documentaries, they say, because PBS isn't dependent on corporate support. Thirty years ago, Ralph Nader proclaimed that consumer reporting would never appear on commercial TV. It would only thrive on public TV, he said, because commercial stations would defer to advertisers.

Today, it's clear that Nader was totally wrong (as he is so often). The opposite is true: PBS carries almost no consumer reporting, probably because the bureaucrats who run it are too nervous about offending *anyone*. By contrast, there is plenty of consumer reporting on commercial TV. I criticized my employers' most valued customers for years. For heaping abuse on the people who paid us, I was given promotions.

Why? Because viewers want tough news—even news hostile to big advertisers. Commercial television provides it because even if some sponsors boycott, the loss is made up by the money *other* sponsors are willing to spend to reach the viewers the consumer-friendly reports attract. The free market serves its customers, and in the TV business, the customers are viewers.

PBS, on the other hand, is broadcasting by bureaucracy. This is a bad idea. We need separation of news and state. "We wouldn't want the federal government to publish a national newspaper," writes Boaz. "Why should we have a government television network and a government radio network? If anything should be kept separate from government and politics, it's the news and public affairs programming that Americans watch. When government brings us the news—with all the inevitable bias and spin—the government is putting its thumb on the scales of democracy. It's time for that to stop."

It won't stop. When government starts, it never stops.

> **MYTH:** Government helps the needy.
>
> **TRUTH:** Government hurts the needy by vomiting the public's money everywhere.

After the 9/11 attacks, Congress passed a compassionate piece of legislation called the Supplemental Terrorist Relief Act. It was to give low-interest loans to small businesses disrupted by the attacks, allowing them to rebuild. The loans were supposed to help hotels, retailers, and small service businesses in lower Manhattan.

But as usual, the government passed your money out *everywhere*. Terrorist Relief Act loans went to Dunkin' Donuts shops in Connecticut, Pennsylvania, Georgia, Vermont, and Ohio. The manager of the Essex Junction,

Vermont, Dunkin' Donuts defended his loan, saying 9/11 affected his business. "Instead of getting probably a large coffee and a couple of doughnuts," Tony Silva said, his customers got "a small coffee and a doughnut."

The Patriot Act was supposed to provide federal funding to states to equip the fire, police, and EMS officers who serve at the front lines of a terrorist attack. But the congressmen who wrote the law apparently believed that patriotism starts at home. Money was allocated under a complicated formula where each state, regardless of its size or location, got an equal slice of the pie before risk was even considered.

One result is that the police and fire departments in Casper, Wyoming (population 49,644), can talk to one another, and to their hospitals and EMS units, on a brand-new communications system. New York City (population 8,000,000) is still waiting for a similar system. Colchester, Vermont, got $58,000 for a rescue vehicle capable of boring through concrete to search for victims in collapsed buildings. Colchester has a population of 18,000 souls and a severe shortage of big buildings.

It gets worse. Government health insurance requires states to pay for men's erections. I'm all for men having good sex lives, but why would government subsidize *that*?

Our bloated government just cannot stop vomiting out the money. For years, Medicaid has been spending millions of dollars on Viagra and other erectile dysfunction drugs. The Clinton administration told states they had to pay, because the law requires that Medicaid pay for any FDA-approved drug deemed medically necessary. Bush administration officials kept the policy. They wouldn't agree to a television interview about it.

Doctors are so addicted to government funding that even insane and embarrassing subsidies are passionately defended. "Erectile dysfunction is not fun, it's a disease," said Dr. Steven Lamb, who appears often on ABC. "It needs to be treated. It needs to be paid for."

I gave him a hard time about it. "Sex is a government entitlement now? Do you ever think about budgeting? What the taxpayer pays?"

"What we're trained in is to be your advocate," he said. "I do not take costs into account."

Of course not. Government-funded medical insurance invites doctors to declare endless "needs"—knowing someone else will bear the cost.

Eventually there was outrage. Not, sadly, merely because people woke up and realized that government shouldn't fund Viagra. No, only when money was needed for Hurricane Katrina relief, and it was revealed that the government was giving Viagra to child molesters, did Congress allow

Medicare and Medicaid to stop paying for erections. Congress *allowed* it. Some states are still paying.

But there you have it: Government programs can be cut! All it took was natural disaster and a truly insane and embarrassing subsidy.

MYTH: You know what taxes you pay.

TRUTH: You don't have a clue.

Government is better at sneaking into your wallet than even the most talented pickpocket. You don't even realize the money is gone.

A major part of the taxes we all pay is essentially invisible. The employer contribution of the payroll tax that funds Social Security and Medicare is not shown on any pay stub, but the burden of it ultimately is passed on to workers in the form of lower wages, hidden prices, and reduced investment. Thirty-seven percent of federal taxes are hidden. The consequence of this is that the public does not perceive the true (high) cost of the government, and as a result, demands more government services.

Thanks to the miracle of new technology and a marketplace white-hot with competition, the cost of making a phone call has gotten cheaper. A three-minute cross-country call that once cost two dollars now costs twenty cents. So why is the bill so high?

Because government takes more. Look closely at your bill: "Federal Universal Service Fee," "State Deaf Relay Charge," "Municipal License Tax," "State Gross Receipts Tax," "Emergency 911 Fee," "Excise Tax," "State Fees."

Those are all stealth taxes on top of your talk. When I went to confront someone from the cell phone industry about them, I was surprised to learn that their spokesman was Steve Largent. Largent is an ex-congressman who was once an amazing short-guy NFL player who caught passes for the Seattle Seahawks. Now he has to catch flak from people like me. When I asked him why we have to pay so much more than the "$39 a month" claimed in their ads, Largent said, "It's not our fault. Most of the charges are fees that *government,* not the phone company, adds to your bill."

He's right. If a greedy politician wants more of your money, he could raise your income or property taxes, but you'd notice and get mad. Maybe you'd vote him out. How do they raise taxes without people seeing it? Require companies to add them. Nebraska taxes add 25 percent to your cell phone bill. Add up the local, state, and federal taxes and that's an extra 8 to 34 percent to your monthly phone bills.

The politicians do it to hotels, taxis, and car rental companies too. Travelocity says renting a car at an airport costs an average 26 percent more because of sneak taxes. It's clever, because it gets you to blame Hertz or Verizon instead of the money-hungry politicians.

Even talk isn't cheap when politicians get their hands on it.

> **MYTH:** "I humbly ask for your vote..."
>
> **TRUTH:** Nothing humble about it.

In Edwin O'Connor's salt-of-the-earth novel *The Last Hurrah,* the manipulative Mayor Skeffington blunts the opposition of a powerful patrician family by seducing one of its lesser lights into public service. He does an ego dance on the young heir's head, dangling the trappings of being fire commissioner: red helmet, red limousine complete with siren and flashing red lights, shiny gold badge. The candidate is ensnared, the family politically co-opted, because Skeffington cannily understood the magnetic power of ego massage.

It is a tool as powerful as pork, and takes on special potency when wielded by skilled craftsmen in the United States Congress. A big instrument of their work is a publication falsely entitled the *Congressional Record.*

When the members of the House and Senate quit work for the day, lights continue to burn in a building on nearby North Capitol Street. It's the Government Printing Office, and while the rest of Washington sleeps, the GPO makes history, or rather, prints history. Since 1873, every night that Congress has been in session, the GPO has printed "the record" of what was said. Stenographers in the House and Senate take down every historic word and ship it off to the Printing Office. The Printing Office stays open all night so they can be sure the official record will be on every congressperson's desk by nine o'clock the following morning. That sounds important. But if you read the *Congressional Record,* you see that there's something strange about the process. The *Record* is not a record of what was said in Congress. Members of Congress wouldn't want to subject themselves to *that.* The *Record* is a record of what the members want the public to think they said.

20/20 examined thousands of pages of the *Record,* and discovered glaring examples of what one has to call wasteful ink. One issue of the *Congressional*

Record said a congressman rose before his colleagues to call soap actress Kelley Menighan "a talented and intelligent woman." The *Record* also said a congressman rose to pay tribute to rock singer Ted Nugent for being "as good with a bow and arrow as he is with a guitar."

A congresswoman praised a grade school band that uses musical instruments made from garbage. There was a tribute to Turkey Lovers' Month, tributes to the birdwatchers of Camp Chiricahua, to beekeepers and their bees, and to a seventy-eight-year-old drum majorette: The *Record* claimed a congressman said, "Mr. Speaker, I ask my colleagues to join me in saluting Dot Hill, who's a legend not only in her own hometown, but throughout the world."

None of those tributes was ever made on the floor of Congress, but they're all in print, enshrined in history along with what really was said. How does this happen? Because the official *Record* is a fake. The law just says it has to be "substantially a verbatim report." Congress took that word *substantially* and ran with it. Why do they add these things?

Well, suppose I'm Congressman Stossel, eager to be reelected. I want to impress my constituents. What's more impressive than public praise in the official *Record* of Congress? It's goodwill in the home district. Ego massage at public expense.

Of course, it would be embarrassing to actually stand in front of my colleagues and talk about Turkey Lovers' Month—no one has time for that—so I'll just use the *Record* to make it seem as if I did. I can even use phrases like, "Mr. Speaker, I rise today," to make it extra convincing that I really did say those things in front of my colleagues. The additions do cost taxpayers millions of dollars, but so what? They don't cost me anything.

We sought out some of the real constituents praised in the *Record*. Young Derek Vaught of Mississippi thought his congressman, Mike Espy, really did rise on the floor to give a tribute to his karate skills. "I thought it was pretty awesome," he said. Derek's father knew better—but he was pleased too: "If they're going to waste money," he told us, "I'd just as soon they wasted it on my son."

The waste calculates out to almost $675 a page. Congressman Collin Peterson of Minnesota noted, "It's as if Congress can't stop wasting money on anything."

It can't.

Not only do members of Congress tell the government printers to add their "extensions" to the *Record*, they even sometimes have them change their words if they don't like what they really did say. In one memorable exchange,

Representative Gerald Solomon got mad and starting screaming at Representative Louise Slaughter.

> **REP. GERALD SOLOMON (R), NEW YORK** What did you say? You're trying to shut me off? You better not do that, ma'am. . . . Who do you think you are?

But you didn't read that in the *Congressional Record*. Solomon or his staff had the *Record* print his comments this way, instead:

> **REP. GERALD SOLOMON (R), NEW YORK** I will say to the gentle lady for whom I have the greatest respect . . .

That is how history will record what happened that day on the floor of the United States House of Representatives. It is only one of several lies printed every day of every congressional session.

When we examined the *Record*'s pages, we found the person who abused the *Record* most was Florida congresswoman Ileana Ros-Lehtinen. She had put in tributes to a local restaurant, to Girl Scout cookies, and to a local car dealer, and she was the author of that tribute to the children who play garbage instruments. Ms. Ros-Lehtinen refused to talk to us about it, so we interviewed the second biggest abuser of the *Record*, Jim Traficant of Ohio.

Representative Traficant had filled the *Record* with tributes to a soap box derby, the anniversary of his grade school, a friend who collected antique cars, the local tennis pro, and more.

Confronting Jim Traficant was an adventure.

> **REP. JAMES TRAFICANT (D), OHIO** John, what are you doing here in the Capitol? I mean, what the hell are you doing with me? Roll that tape. I want to know what you're doing here . . .
>
> **STOSSEL** I'm here—
>
> **REP. TRAFICANT** Jacking me around with these other politicians who are so dumb they can throw themselves to the ground and miss, who blow hundreds of thousands of dollars on free mail, which I don't abuse, and you're here, talking to me about giving some tributes for achievements made?
>
> **STOSSEL** You're wasting money. These tributes are wasting my money.
>
> **REP. TRAFICANT** I didn't ask you that. I asked who sent you here and who told you that my tributes are wasting money—
>
> **STOSSEL** "Sent" me here?

REP. TRAFICANT —because they are [sic] a liar. I do cite some specific achievements in the *Congressional Record*. I don't apologize for it, and I'm glad to be able to cite their achievements. What they should do— these pussies—is sponsor a bill to stop it. Jim Traficant is going to cite the achievements of his constituents as long as other members can.

STOSSEL So it's okay for you to waste some money since your colleagues are wasting much more?

REP. TRAFICANT No, I'm not saying it's wasting money. *You* see it as a waste of money.

STOSSEL But why should I have to pay for that?

REP. TRAFICANT Because that is a practice that is existing here in the Congress, and everybody pays tribute.

Everybody pays tribute and congressmen do almost anything they want. Almost anything. After that interview, Traficant was caught taking bribes and using government employees to do work on his farm. He was convicted of bribery, racketeering, and fraud, expelled from the House, and jailed.

He made no mention of that in the *Congressional Record*.

MYTH: "I pledge to serve no more than (fill in the number) terms in office."

TRUTH: "I feel important now, so I'll cling to power as long as I can."

Occasionally, a politician says he's coming to Washington with a built-in expiration date. He'll be different—not a career officeholder, but a citizen legislator who, like Abraham Lincoln, will serve a few years and then return to private life. Before he was president, Lincoln served just one term in Congress, saying the biggest threat to America would come from "the voracious desire for office, this wriggle to live without toil."

It's not something you hear today's politicians admitting. Take George Nethercutt, of Washington State. In 1994, he ran against the Speaker of the House, Tom Foley, promising he'd serve only six years. Foley had been there for thirty. Nethercutt ran ads in which he proclaimed, "Thirty years is too long."

The ads helped Nethercutt win an upset victory. But then he came to Washington, DC, where members of Congress and senators are royalty. You get an elegant office and a staff to serve you. You get your own private subway. Businesses invite you to exotic places. It can make you feel so special, you regret promising to leave.

Nethercutt announced, "I have changed my mind." The motivation had nothing to do with the royal treatment, he said: "I've thought and prayed a lot about what's right for our state."

Some people we talked to in Washington State weren't thrilled at his change of heart.

> **FIRST MAN** I think he must think that we're pretty stupid.
>
> **SECOND MAN** Once he got in, he just immediately was seduced by the system.

Nevertheless, Nethercutt was reelected. Congress has so rigged the system that even breaking promises doesn't get them booted out. In 2004, the House reelection rate was better than 99 percent.

Once politicians are in power, they tend to stay until they die—or are convicted.

Colorado Congressman Scott McInnis promised he'd serve just three terms. But then he got close to power, and—to hear him tell it—knowledge. He decided he'd been "ignorant" when he promised to be a citizen legislator. "My statement was a statement based on ignorance," he told his constituents. "I discovered how important seniority is."

Get the shovel. McInnis had spent years in his state legislature. He knew what seniority was. They all did. But once they taste glory, they don't want to let go.

Tom Tancredo (R-CO) won in a crowded field thanks to publicity about his pledge. An e-mail he sent to supporters of term limits illustrates how duplicitous politicians can be. Tancredo wrote, "I made a pledge and I intend to stick to it. . . . A citizen legislator is far preferable to a lifetime politician . . . we have always been straight with one another and I never want it to be any other way. I believe your help . . . was crucial in getting me elected." Just sixteen months later, the *Rocky Mountain News* reported that Tancredo told his constituents that "he'd been talking with the Lord, who had absolved him of his pledge."

Zach Wamp (R-TN) pledged to serve twelve years. Asked why he would not limit himself to six years by the *Wall Street Journal,* Wamp replied that he had "crawled across broken glass to get here."

That's why the idea of a citizen legislator is appealing. It implies the office holder wants to serve his country, not crawl over broken glass to feed off it for life.

The good news is that not a single pledge-breaker has won higher office. However, pledge-*keepers* Tom Coburn (OK), Jim DeMint (SC), and John Thune (SD) are now U.S. Senators, and Mark Sanford (SC), John Baldacci (ME), and Bob Riley (AL) are now governors.

MYTH: Public officials are role models for other citizens.

TRUTH: Public officials are often hypocrites.

In 1992, when Presidential candidate Bill Clinton was asked about his drug use, he said, "I have never broken the laws of my country." It turned out to be one of those lawyerly language tricks. That was revealed when a reporter later asked him about laws in other countries.

"The answer to that question is I have never broken a state law," he said. "When I was in England, I experimented with marijuana a time or two, and I didn't like it and didn't inhale."

There was a smirk on his face; it was clear drug use was no big deal to him. Remember the time he played the sax on TV? What got him the biggest audience response that night was talking about smoking dope: "That's how I learned to inhale, by playing my saxophone," he said, with another sly smile. "You blow out and then you have to inhale." Everyone laughed and applauded.

What fun. His vice president did drugs too, and so did other officials.

AL GORE As a student a few times in the army.

BILL BRADLEY, FORMER SENATOR I have used marijuana several times in my life, but never cocaine.

BRUCE BABBITT, FORMER SECRETARY OF THE INTERIOR Didn't seem like a big deal at the time.

President George W. Bush admitted to "mistakes" in his youth. His father, when asked if he had ever smoked grass, said, "No, but I'd hate to speak for my kids." No one seems to take this too seriously. It's something to chuckle about. After all, more than thirty million Americans have tried cocaine, according to the latest National Survey on Drug Use. Ninety million have used marijuana at least once. "It is not a big deal," said Bill Clinton.

But if it's no big deal, why did he and his vice president push for tougher drug laws with longer jail time, and why are we arresting more people than ever, more than 1.5 million Americans a year, on drug charges? The biggest category of arrest? Possession of marijuana. We arrest more people for marijuana than for rape, robbery, murder, and aggravated assault combined. Eight out of ten drug arrests are just for possession—for exactly what the politicians admitted to doing. Ha ha. We'll smoke grass and joke about it, but you, we'll lock up. Hypocrites.

The hypocrisy also comes out when their friends and family get caught.

The son of Duke "Death Penalty for Drug Kingpins" Cunningham (R-CA) was convicted for possession of four hundred pounds of marijuana. *Mother Jones* reports that in court, the congressman cried and pleaded for mercy, explaining that his son "has a good heart. He works hard." The congressman— who denounced "soft-on-crime liberal judges" and railed against "reduced mandatory-minimum sentences for drug trafficking"—won for his son the mercy denied so many others. Cunningham's son got thirty months—half the federal "mandatory" minimum sentence.

In an ironic twist, Congressman Cunningham himself later admitted taking 2.4 million dollars in bribes, including a Rolls-Royce and a yacht. He resigned from Congress and when you read this, he will presumably be in jail.

Likely 2008 Presidential candidate John McCain (R-AZ) has advocated tougher drug laws, but when his wife, Cindy, admitted stealing Percocet and Vicodin from a charity, she was not prosecuted. Percocet and Vicodin are Schedule II drugs, in the same legal category as opium. Each pill theft carries a penalty of one year in prison and a monetary fine. But Mrs. McCain entered a pretrial diversion program and escaped without a criminal record.

Politicians are hypocritical about many parts of their personal lives. Bill and Hillary Clinton talk about the importance of public schooling, and oppose vouchers that would let poor people escape government-run schools. But when the Clintons moved to Washington, they enrolled Chelsea in a fancy private school, Sidwell Friends. Tuition today is around $24,000.

The Heritage Foundation found that almost half the members of Congress with kids sent them to private schools at some point. Only Congressman Jesse Jackson Jr. was willing to talk to me about it. His father, the Reverend Jesse, sent him to the best schools he could find, public or private, depending where they lived. For high school, he went to the exclusive St. Albans School, the same place former Vice President Al Gore sent his son. Tuition is now over $24,000. But even though Jackson enjoyed the benefits of a private education, he votes against giving parents vouchers that would let those with less money have what he had.

> **REP. JESSE JACKSON** When I went to high school, my parents did not have access to a voucher.
>
> **STOSSEL** But your parents could afford [private school]. Lots of people can't.
>
> **REP. JACKSON** Of course, lots of Americans can't afford it.
>
> **STOSSEL** So let them have what you had!
>
> **REP. JACKSON** No one is keeping them locked in now. They can make decisions for themselves.
>
> **STOSSEL** The parent without money is stuck, stuck in the prison of the—
>
> **REP. JACKSON** Well, I wouldn't call it necessarily a prison. It's not the best possible education system that's available.
>
> **STOSSEL** You have kids. Where will you send them?
>
> **REP. JACKSON** They will probably do a combination of public, private, parochial, secular. I want them to have the best possible education that I can provide for them.

Of course he does. And after that interview, we learned that he had enrolled his daughter in private school.

Wouldn't it be nice if everyone had that choice? They don't, because hypocritical politicians suck up to teachers' unions. No vouchers for you, St. Albans for them.

MYTH: "I'm from the government, and I am here to protect you."

TRUTH: Help!

Sometimes the regulators' contempt for market choices leads them to pass edicts so absurd they practically *beg* me to say "Give me a break." For a perfect example, take the Equal Employment Opportunity Commission's attempt to "equalize" the opportunities of men and women at Hooters restaurants.

The EEOC is the agency Congress created to enforce the 1964 Civil Rights Act, the law passed to prohibit discrimination in public accommodation. Hooters is a successful restaurant chain known for attracting male customers by hiring women servers who are well endowed and dressed to show it.

The firm has grown so much that it now employs more than 30,000 people. Many would consider this a success story, but our government didn't. Not because Hooters is using sex to sell—but because all the women servers are, well . . . women. Horrors! Hooters girls are women! "Discrimination!" cried the EEOC.

Racism was what Congress was thinking about when it created the EEOC. But over the years, the agency has found an ever-expanding list of places to regulate. Now the EEOC was saying Hooters violated antibias laws because they don't hire enough men.

The business of Hooters is food, says the government, and "no physical trait unique to women is required to serve food and drink to customers in a restaurant." EEOC lawyers demanded Hooters produce all its hiring data, and then grilled Hooters for *four years*. It cost the company hundreds of thousands of dollars in legal fees alone. Mike McNeil, Hooters' vice president of marketing, told us the EEOC bureaucrats demanded to look at reams of paperwork. "Employee manuals, training manuals, marketing manuals—virtually everything that's involved in how we run our business . . ."

The EEOC then issued a set of demands. First, it invented and "defined" a class of disappointed males who had not been hired by the company. (Of course, those males hadn't *applied* either—but defining the non-existent has never been a problem for government.) The EEOC said, according to McNeil: "We want you to establish a twenty-two-million-dollar fund for this mythical 'class' of dissuaded male applicants. We want you to conduct sensitivity training studies to teach all of your employees to be more sensitive to the needs of men."

What a hoot! Hooters decided to fight back, cleverly, not just in court, but in the court of public opinion.

Hooters waitresses marched on Washington, chanting "Save our jobs." A burly Hooters' manager dressed as a Hooters waitress and posed for cameras, beard and all, demonstrating what a "Hooters Guy" might look like. It was fun to watch, and it worked. The lawyers representing those "dissuaded male applicants" accepted an out-of-court settlement of 3.75 million dollars. This was a lot of money, but just a fraction of the twenty-two million dollars that had been demanded. The EEOC also dropped their demands for sensitivity training; instead, Hooters just agreed to create more jobs like busboys and managers, which didn't have to be performed by women.

Did the Hooters overreach and other EEOC excesses (see Chapter 2, He and She) embarrass the government into shrinking the EEOC? Of course not. It now has 2,400 employees, and spent 326.8 million dollars in 2005—millions more than the year before.

MYTH: Environmental regulators are dispassionate scientists.

TRUTH: Many are radical activists.

I want endangered species protected. I assume you want endangered species protected too. Who doesn't? But years ago, ranchers and farmers told me that government's environmental regulatory agencies had been taken over by religious fundamentalists (environmental fanatics) so hostile to the idea of private property that they'd use the endangered species law to drive just about every landowner off his land.

I thought they were overwrought. But then I learned about what happened with the Canada lynx.

The lynx are furry, adorable animals that look like big housecats. Tens of thousands of them live in North America, but environmental officials weren't sure there were any in the Gifford Pinchot and Wenatchee National Forests in southern Washington State, so they commissioned a million-dollar study to find out.

This can be scary for the people who live and work in those areas because finding threatened species often leads to increased regulation that keeps humans out. The Endangered Species Act has been used to shut down logging, take away water rights, and stop multitudes of construction and development projects. "Area closed" can be the result when endangered species are found. The discovery of threatened or endangered species is especially terrifying news to ranchers and farmers who depend upon use of the land for their livelihoods.

Property rights advocate Mike Paulson told us: "We basically say if you have an endangered species in your area, we're going to take your livelihood away, we're going to destroy your communities, and we're going to make it very difficult for your families to survive." In Colton, California, the discovery of the endangered Dehli Sands flower-loving fly forced San

Bernardino County to move the location of a new medical center—at a cost of three million dollars—to avoid disturbing the "fly habitat." There are dozens more examples of endangered species insanity, but to get to them all I'd have to write another book.

For their study in Washington State, government biologists nailed pieces of carpet soaked with a catnip mixture onto trees, hoping a lynx would rub up against them and leave some fur—evidence of the lynx's existence in this particular forest area. Sure enough, when biologists sent the samples to a lab, they came back positive for hairs from a Canada lynx.

Was this evidence that the threatened Canada lynx had moved into this part of Washington? Actually, no. It turns out that the biologists faked the test. They went to a nearby zoo that has several Canada lynxes, got hair samples, and sent *those* hairs to the lab to be tested. The biologists only admitted that when they were caught by a Department of Fish and Wildlife official. He was retiring, so he didn't fear the wrath of his colleagues. He reported them.

The cheating didn't surprise Jim Beers, a biologist for the Department of Fish and Wildlife for thirty years. He told me he'd seen his agency change from promoting science to pushing fanatical back-to-the-earth environmentalism. He said that biologists at Fish and Wildlife were on a campaign to keep people out of wooded areas.

> **JIM BEERS** The agencies today are—are staffed with environmental radical activists.
>
> **STOSSEL** Extremists have captured a government agency?
>
> **JIM BEERS** That's correct.
>
> **STOSSEL** They don't want people [living in wooded areas]?
>
> **JIM BEERS** No. That's correct.
>
> **STOSSEL** And one way to keep the forests free of people is to find endangered species.
>
> **JIM BEERS** Once you establish that there are any lynx in the area and you say there were some lynx over in this area, or there, the areas in between suddenly become very urgent to not allow the road to be built, not allow the ski slope to come in, not allow grazing. Ultimately not to let you or I drive our wives and kids in for a picnic.

Once caught with their hands in the cage, the biologists announced that they were not trying to cheat, they were just "testing" the lab to make sure it could detect lynx hair by sending a "control" sample; they said they were going to notify everyone of their little "test" as soon as the results were in. Beers said: "That's the same as you telling me that you caught them walking out of the bank with money and they said, 'Oh, we were just seeing if the system works here. We were going to return it tomorrow.'"

If the biologists really were innocently "testing the lab," they would have had a heck of a time correcting the record after the fact. A report from the Government Accountability Office (GAO) said, "There was no procedure whereby the biologists who submitted samples would receive preliminary results, so that they could subsequently notify the laboratory of their unauthorized submissions."

No biologists were fired for this fiasco. They were just "disciplined." The fanatics protect their own. How would environmental fanatics capture a government agency? Well, think about it. Who is more likely to volunteer to take a low-paying job with a bureaucratic agency that has little to recommend it except that it gives you the power of force over ranchers and farmers? A dispassionate scientist or a zealot? It's why in government, the zealots eventually take over.

> **MYTH:** Political leaders promote the general welfare.
>
> **TRUTH:** Political leaders are often busybodies who want to force their preferences on us.

Sometimes I'm convinced that the people who run for office are the most dangerous people. Most of us want to run our own lives, or help people by offering them charity, or selling them things. The people who want to run other people's lives are . . . different. In pursuit of their vision of the perfect world, they justify even absurd restrictions on our freedom. For example:

In Belton, Missouri, it is illegal to throw a snowball.

In New Jersey and Oregon, it is illegal to pump your own gas.

In Kern County, California, it is illegal to play bingo while drunk.

In Illinois, it is against the law to hunt bullfrogs with a firearm.

In Massachusetts, it's illegal to deface a milk carton.

In Fairfax, Virginia, the use of pogo sticks is outlawed on city buses.

In Palm Harbor, Florida, it is illegal to have an artificial lawn.

Some of these silly laws are old, but dumb as they are, they are still on the books. The bureaucrats' bad ideas never go away. They don't repeal old laws; they just pass new ones.

Plan on painting your porch on your day off? Don't do it in Spring Hill, Tennessee. The city council banned any "alteration or repair of any building" in a residential neighborhood on Sundays, even do-it-yourself work.

The mayor of the tiny community of Friendship Heights, Maryland, said he had to protect his citizens from cigarette smoke. He got his town to pass the most stringent antismoking law in America. It banned cigarette smoke not just in restaurants, bars, and offices, but *outdoors* too.

The mayor is a doctor who should have known that only the flimsiest of data suggests secondhand smoke hurts people. The suggestion of slight risk came from studies of people who *lived* with smokers, and were exposed to lots of secondhand smoke at home and in cars. The idea that outdoor cigarette smoke is a meaningful health risk is silly. Granted, secondhand smoke is a nuisance. But so are many things.

But the mayor was a zealot, and Friendship Heights banned smoking anywhere on city property, which meant no smoking on the sidewalks, the streets, the parks.

> **STOSSEL**   You're another of these busybody politicians who want to tell other people how to live their lives.
>
> **ALFRED MULLER**   Well, we're elected to promote the general welfare, and this is part of the general welfare.

The mayor seemed very sincere, and the citizens of Friendship Heights felt protected by his concern. However, shortly after I interviewed him, he was caught touching a fourteen-year-old boy's genitals in a restroom at Washington National Cathedral. The mayor got probation, and the village council repealed his law. Now we finally know what it takes to get a law repealed.

The people who have the biggest passion for restricting others' behavior . . . are the people we should worry about most. Unfortunately, they keep running for office. The good news is that they don't get to run most of our lives.

> **MYTH:** The President and Congress run America.
>
> **TRUTH:** The people run America.

Politicians and the media always talk about who "will run the country." What arrogance!

SEN. JOHN BREAUX [*on CNN*] "We've got to remember we've got to run this country for the next four years . . ." **(11/26/00)**

FLAVIA COLGAN [*on MSNBC*] "As incompetent as Bush is as the president, at running the country right now . . ." **(10/28/05)**

RALPH NADER [*Charlie Rose Show*] "They know who's running the country." **(8/13/05)**

CHRIS MATTHEWS [*Hardball*] "The current crowd running the country now . . ." **(11/2/2005)**

STEVE KROFT [*60 Minutes*] "President Bush, do you think he'll come on?"
JON STEWART: "He's busy running the country . . ." **(10/24/04)**

Get the shovel!

Do these pundits and politicians think that government is so important that if politicians don't call the shots, America stops? Nonsense. Politicians don't run the country. America isn't a car that will crash without a president at the helm. America is run by millions of free people, entertaining themselves, building spectacular buildings, distributing thousands of wonderful, new inventions.

Yes, good government creates conditions that allow good things to happen, and bad government can make life worse, but fortunately, the complex, thriving giant that is the United States mostly runs itself. As Thomas Paine deftly pointed out in *The Rights of Man*: "Society performs for itself almost everything which is ascribed to government."

Government doesn't create new musicals or the old Latin Quarter, or produce today's miracle drugs, or think up new cures for jet lag. Government doesn't build our cars, or supply America with its amazing variety of food, shelter, and clothing. Thankfully, most of life, and the best of it, happens independently of whichever politician is in charge.

CHAPTER FIVE

STUPID SCHOOLS

A re American kids stupid? Comedian Jay Leno's routines with young people make you wonder:

JAY LENO What state holds the Kentucky Derby every year? [a young woman just stands there] Think about it. . . . What state . . . holds the . . . Kentucky . . . Derby every year?

YOUNG WOMAN Kansas?

JAY LENO Name this famous American author: Ernest . . .

YOUNG WOMAN Chump?

JAY LENO Ernest Chump? No, Ernest Hem . . . Heming . . .

YOUNG WOMAN Hemington?

JAY LENO Finish the name of this book: *War and* . . .

YOUNG MAN *Sex?*

It isn't a Hollywood spoof. These are their real answers.

Still, "Stupid" is a nasty word to use in the title of a chapter on American K–12 education. But it was the title of an ABC News special I did, and I'm proud of that show. I had planned to call it "Education" or "The System Is a Mess," but my boss said, "Are you crazy? 'Education' sounds tedious, and 'System' is a boring word. Competition for viewers is more intense than ever; we have to call this show something that will pique people's curiosity. We'll call it 'Stupid.' "

I argued with him, but he was right. "Stupid" is a perfect word because

America's decision to have its public schools run by a government monopoly is stunningly stupid. Having a *union-dominated* monopoly run them is even stupider. Unionized monopolies create ossified, bloated bureaucracies that don't serve people well. Little improves in monopolies.

By contrast, competition is remarkably good at making services better. It changes my behavior at *20/20* all the time. If I weren't threatened by my competitors, I would do story after story on libertarian economics with boring public-policy wonks I find fascinating. The stories would be long and impressive—I'd be impressed, anyway; you might be bored.

It's because I know viewers have choices and a remote control that I'm forced to try harder—to find interesting pictures to accompany the reporting, track down the most interesting experts, walk over hot coals, jump into the Hudson River, and do the other silly things I do to make reports fun.

Competition has given us better TVs, homes, cars, food, phones, and well, everything. The U.S. Postal Service couldn't get it there overnight. None of the brilliant managers of that government monopoly could make it happen. But once others were allowed to compete, Federal Express, United Parcel Service, Airborne Express, etc., suddenly were able to get it there overnight. Now even the post office does it (sometimes). Competition inspires people to do what we didn't think we could do.

So why don't we harness it to teach our kids?

> **MYTH:** Educating children is too important to be left to the uncertainty of market competition.
>
> **TRUTH:** Educating children is too important to be left to a government monopoly.

Think about how many choices you have when it's time to get a new cell phone. The companies offer different plans based on how many minutes you want, how big your family is, if you travel a lot, and a million other things. The cell phone companies don't offer you all of these plans because they care about *you,* just because they care about your *business.*

Why can't education be the same way? If people got to choose their kids' school, education options would be endless. There could soon be technology schools, cheap Wal-Mart–like schools, virtual schools where you learn at home on your computer, sports schools, music schools, schools that go all year, schools with uniforms, schools that open early and keep kids later, and, who knows? If there were competition, all kinds of new ideas would bloom.

This already happens overseas and the results are good.

We gave identical tests to high school students in New Jersey and in Belgium. We asked the Belgian kids, "What did you think of the test?"

> **FIRST BOY**   Well, I thought it was pretty easy considering the tests we usually get here. This was kinda a piece of cake.
>
> **SECOND BOY**   The test was so easy, I think that if the kids in America couldn't do this, they're really stupid.

"Stupid" was harsh, but the Belgian kids cleaned the American kids' clocks, getting 76 percent correct vs. 47 percent for the Americans. We didn't pick smart kids to test in Europe and dumb kids in the United States. The American students attend an above-average school in New Jersey and New Jersey kids have test scores that are above average for America.

The American boy who got the highest score told me: "I'm shocked, 'cause it just shows how advanced they are compared to us."

I asked the New Jersey kids:

> **STOSSEL**   So, are American students stupid?
>
> **FIRST STUDENT**   No, we're not stupid.
>
> **SECOND STUDENT**   I think it has to be something with, with the school, 'cause I don't think we're stupider.

I agree. It's the schools. At the age of ten, students from twenty-five countries take the same test and American kids place eighth, well above the international average. But by age fifteen, when students from forty countries are tested, the Americans place twenty-fifth, well *below* the international average (see chart, page 109). In other words, the longer American kids stay in American schools, the worse they do in international competition. They do worse than kids from much poorer, less-developed countries, like Korea and Poland, which spend much less on education than the United States.

This should come as no surprise once you remember that public education in the U.S. is a *government monopoly*. Families send their kids to schools the government chooses. If you don't like your public school? Tough. If the school is terrible? Tough. Your taxes fund that school regardless of whether it's good or bad.

Government monopolies routinely fail their customers.

AGE 10			**AGE 15**	
RANK	COUNTRY		RANK	COUNTRY
1	Singapore		1	Finland
2	Hong Kong, SAR		2	Korea
2	Japan		3	Hong Kong—China
2	Chinese Taipei		4	Lichtenstein
5	Latvia		5	Japan
6	England		6	Australia
7	Netherlands		7	Canada
8	Belgium (Flemish)		8	New Zealand
8	Russian Federation		9	Netherlands
8	**United States**		10	Macao—China
11	Hungary		11	Belgium
12	Lithuania		12	Switzerland
13	Australia		13	Sweden
14	Italy		14	France
14	New Zealand		15	Czech Republic
16	Moldova, Rep. of		16	Ireland
17	Cyprus		17	Iceland
18	Scotland		18	Germany
19	Slovenia		19	Denmark
20	Armenia		20	Austria
20	Norway		21	Poland
22	Iran, Islamic Rep. of		22	Norway
23	Philippines		23	Hungary
24	Morocco		24	Slovak Republic
24	Tunisia		**25**	**United States**
			26	Latvia
			27	Luxembourg
			28	Spain
			29	Russian Federation
			30	Italy
			31	Portugal
			32	Greece
			33	Turkey
			34	Serbia
			35	Uruguay
			36	Thailand
			37	Mexico
			38	Brazil
			39	Indonesia
			40	Tunisia

Government-run airlines had filthy planes that rarely arrived on time. The best car made by government-run car manufacturers (The "Trabant," the pride of East Germany) couldn't compete with average cars made by private companies.

In America, the phone company was once a government-supported monopoly. All the phones were black, and all the calls expensive. It was illegal to plug in an answering machine—installing a "foreign device," the monopoly called it. Only when the monopoly was broken up did we get lower prices and the variety of phone choices we have now.

So why do we entrust American education to a government monopoly?

Most countries that beat us on international tests also have government-funded schools, but they give students more choice. In Belgium, the government spends less than American schools do on each student, but the money *is attached to the kids,* and they can take it to any school—religious, secular, or government run.

Kaat Vandensavel runs a Belgian government school, but she has to compete. She told us she works hard to impress the parents. "If we don't offer them what they want for their child, they won't come to our school." That pressure makes a world of difference, she says. It forces Belgian schools to innovate in order to appeal to parents and students. Kaat's school offers extra sports programs and classes in hairdressing, car mechanics, cooking, and furniture building. She told us, "We have to work hard day after day. Otherwise you just run out of business. You can't afford ten teachers out of 160 that don't do their work, because the clients will know, and won't come to you again."

"That's normal in Western Europe," Harvard economist Caroline Hoxby told me. "If schools don't perform well, a parent would never be trapped in that school in the same way you could be trapped in the U.S." Vandensavel adds, "America seems like a medieval country . . . a Communist country on the educational level, because there's no freedom of choice—not for parents, not for pupils."

Andreas Schleicher, who administers the international tests given to the fifteen-year-olds (the PISA test), says freedom to choose schools, and freedom for schools to govern themselves, matters more than who runs the schools. Jan de Groof, coauthor of one of the biggest international studies on education, agrees. He says the key is freedom for parents to choose, and second, freedom for schools to create the kind of school they want: "Our research is quite obvious. The more centralized and the more uniform . . . the more . . . the monopoly of the state system, the less the quality of education."

Even within Belgium we saw differences. Since 1989 the Flemish and French sides of the country have had separate school systems. The government pays for schools on both sides, but it gives schools on the Flemish side considerably more autonomy than on the French side. The kids on the Flemish side of Belgium do much better on the international tests.

Surveys show most American parents think *their* kids' public school is pretty good, but that's only because *they don't know what their kids are missing!* Without real competition, they don't know what their kids might have had. One Belgian mother told us that she and her son once lived in America, and she was dumbfounded when he was assigned to a school and she wasn't given a choice. "In America I sort of had to beg, please, please, give me good school for my child. Here in Belgium they're all over the place."

> **MYTH:** American public schools level the playing field.
>
> **TRUTH:** Public schools do not level the playing field, and are more segregated than private schools.

Public school officials say that public schools "are great equalizers" and, unlike private schools, give minorities and the poor the opportunity to succeed. It's nonsense. Public high schools are more segregated than private schools. Jay Greene, author of *Education Myths*, did research that showed "54.5 percent of public-school students were in classrooms that were more than 90 percent white or more than 90 percent minority. Fewer private-school students, 41.1 percent, were in similarly segregated classrooms."

It's not because racists steer kids to different schools. It's because wealthier parents move to where schools are better. Poor people are usually stuck.

Ballou High School is one of the worst in Washington, DC. When we visited, student Lajuan Brown told us that at her school teachers often don't show up. "So basically you have nowhere to go but the hallways; it's like no one cares; there's nothing to do." She knows she's stuck, locked into the school she's assigned to. "I don't have no choice but to go here."

No choice if she follows the rules. She could try to pretend to live in another district. But then she might be caught by the school-zone Gestapo. In San Jose, California, we taped one of these detectives, John Lozana, going door to door to make sure kids attending schools in the Fremont Union

School District weren't lying about where they live. Many do lie, because Fremont schools are better than the dismal schools in the surrounding area.

Lozana takes pride in his work, and we followed him as he entered homes and even inspected kids' rooms for computers, personal photographs, and clothes on the floor that would prove the student *really* lived there. He caught a grandmother who had helped her grandson get a better education by claiming he lived at an address in the good district. "Caught! She's definitely caught," said Lozana with satisfaction. "This boy will not be able to attend our school because he doesn't live in our attendance area."

Two days later I talked to the grandmother about it:

ESTHER TAPANG   I was actually crying, and all I'm wanting to do is just to have my grandchild have a better education.

STOSSEL   It's kind of creepy that they force you to go to the black market to get your kid a better education.

ESTHER TAPANG   Why can't they just let parents to get in the school of their choice?

Because the government monopoly thinks it knows best.

> **MYTH:** Kids learn to read in public elementary schools.
>
> **TRUTH:** Many can't even read in high school.

I can hear you saying, "The schools leave kids stupid? If that's true, it's not the teachers' fault, it's the fault of indifferent parents!"

It's true that parents matter most. Those who read to their kids, ask about schoolwork, and take an interest in their education have kids who do better. When parents fail to do that, a teacher's job is a thousand times harder.

But many parents who do the right things still have no option but to send their children to bad schools. Watching many try to get their kids a better education through the government school monopoly is like waiting for the sun to rise in a windowless room. The parents have a hard time getting anywhere.

Dorian Cain is a senior at Lee Central High School in South Carolina, a school that gets the lowest rating given out by the state of South Carolina. That says a lot, since South Carolina has just about the lowest SAT scores in all of America. When I asked Dorian to read to me from his school's history text, he could not.

> **STOSSEL** You know there is a whole world that can open up to you, if you are able to read.
>
> **DORIAN** Yeah, I know that. I know if I could read better, I wouldn't be such a problem.
>
> **STOSSEL** Did they try to teach you to read?
>
> **DORIAN** From time to time.
>
> **STOSSEL** Well, what did they do?
>
> **DORIAN** They just tell you to read by yourself. Go home and read, which, uh, I wouldn't.
>
> **STOSSEL** But they kept moving you ahead in class?
>
> **DORIAN** Yes, sir.

That's not unusual. The U.S. Department of Education says that a quarter of American high school seniors can't read at a basic level. Dorian's mom has been asking for help from Dorian's schools for years.

> **GENA CAIN** You have to beg. You know whatever you ask for, you, you're begging. I mean you literally have to beg for it, because they have the power.
>
> **STOSSEL** They've had meetings with you to talk about your son.
>
> **GENA** Yes.

We taped one such meeting. It was unbelievable. Lots of educational "experts" were assembled: the director of "programs for exceptional children," Dorian's "resource teacher," his PE teacher, the school counselor, and the district's special ed coordinator. Dorian's mom stared, dumbfounded, as they tossed around official-sounding jargon, like "functional behavior assessment" and "less restrictive environment." The principal said, "I've seen great progress in him. I don't have any concerns." The meeting went on for forty-five minutes. There was lots of paperwork to sign.

Later I asked the chairperson of his district's school board, Deloris Wright, and the district's superintendent, Dr. Lloyd Hunter, about their schools' failures. I was surprised that they seemed so calm about it:

DELORIS WRIGHT Our children are doing fairly well.

STOSSEL You have kids, like Dorian, who can't read! Isn't it your job to teach them how to read?

DR. LLOYD HUNTER It is the school's job to teach children how to read.

STOSSEL You keep advancing some of these kids, even though they can't read.

DR. LLOYD HUNTER That may very well be.

STOSSEL Can't every kid learn how to read?

DR. LLOYD HUNTER We believe that every child can. But the outcome you will get from a school is going to be dependent upon the capacity of the school.

STOSSEL You've had twelve years; you've spent $100,000 on these kids. You can't teach a kid to read?

DR. LLOYD HUNTER I'm not sure that we have students that we've had for twelve years that are, that are not reading. I do not accept that.

He may not accept it, but Dorian couldn't read. We decided to send him to Sylvan Learning Center. Could a private company succeed where the public school system failed? *Yes.* In just seventy-two hours of instruction, Dorian's reading comprehension jumped two grade levels.

In that short time Gena noticed a change in Dorian. The family had always received *Sports Illustrated* in the mail, but suddenly Dorian was reading it. Also, with no prompting from her, Dorian started using flash cards to teach himself vocabulary at home. "I'm more confident," he said.

How can Sylvan teach in weeks what the government school failed to teach in twelve years? "We're accountable to our parents. We're accountable to our students. We do what we say we're gonna do," says Stephanie Hollander, a manager at the Sylvan Center Dorian attended. "If we don't have students in the center, then we don't have a business. We need to have happy parents."

The Sylvan program cost about $3,000. South Carolina's government schools spent nearly $100,000 on Dorian's "education."

MYTH: Public schools are underfunded.

TRUTH: Public schools have lots of money.

The U.S. spends "so much for war," said a protest sign at a teachers' union rally, "so little for schools." Parents and educrats both list "lack of money" first when asked about the problems with schools. *Everyone* knows there isn't enough money.

In South Carolina, those school officials who failed to teach Dorian to read told me they needed more money:

STOSSEL How much money would be right?

DELORIS WRIGHT How much? Oooh. Millions. And it would really make it right.

STOSSEL They're spending ten thou per kid now. Fifteen thou, twenty thou?

DELORIS WRIGHT Twenty thou, twenty-five, thirty. The more, the better.

The more, the better, sure. But do the math: She said $10,000 per kid was not enough, but $10,000 per student is $250,000 per classroom of twenty-five kids. And it's all operating money—not capital expense—the land and building are already paid for. With $250,000, couldn't you hire several good teachers, and have plenty left over for supplies and lavish field trips?

The truth is, public schools are rolling in money. Even the teachers' slogan about schools vs. war was wrong: In 2004, America spent 454 billion dollars on the military (including the war in Iraq) but 536 billion dollars on public schools. What we all "know" is not so.

America spends more on schooling than the vast majority of countries that outscore us on the international tests.

But the bureaucrats still blame school failure on lack of funds, and demand more money. In 1985, Kansas City judge Russell Clark said the city's predominantly black schools were not "halfway decent" and he ordered the government to spend billions more. So they did.

They renovated school buildings, adding enormous gyms, an Olympic-size swimming pool, a robotics lab, TV studios, a zoo, a planetarium, and a wildlife sanctuary. They added intense instruction in foreign languages. They spent so much money that when they decided to bring more white kids to the city's schools, they didn't use buses—they paid for 120 taxis.

Reporters gushed at the improvements.

KANSAS CITY TV REPORTER Any student who wants to learn French, for example, today can enroll in a total immersion program where every course taught is in French.

STUDENT Goodness!

What did spending billions more accomplish? Nothing. In fact, the schools got worse. In 1999, two billion dollars later, the Kansas City school district failed eleven performance standards and lost its accreditation for the first time in the district's history.

Jay Greene points out that many school districts have increased spending without results. "We've doubled per-pupil spending, adjusting for inflation, over the last thirty years, and yet schools aren't better."

Here is a graph of the increased spending (yes, it's adjusted for inflation):

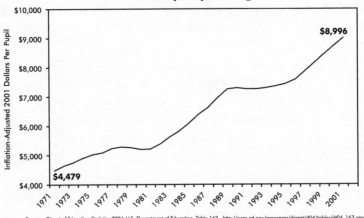

Per-Pupil Spending

$8,996

$4,479

Source: *Digest of Education Statistics 2004*, U.S. Department of Education, Table 163. http://nces.ed.gov/programs/digest/d04/tables/dt04_163.asp

Here are student achievement and graduation rates:

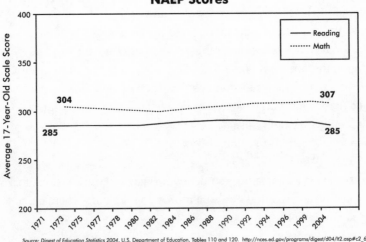

NAEP Scores

304   307

285   285

Source: *Digest of Education Statistics 2004*, U.S. Department of Education, Tables 110 and 120. http://nces.ed.gov/programs/digest/d04/lt2.asp#c2_6

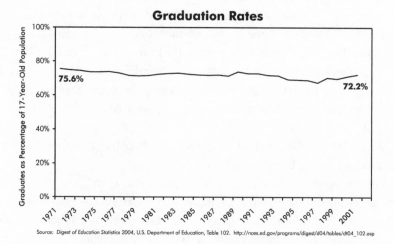

Graduation Rates

75.6%

72.2%

Source: *Digest of Education Statistics 2004*, U.S. Department of Education, Table 102. http://nces.ed.gov/programs/digest/d04/tables/dt04_102.asp

The spending line goes up, but achievement and graduation rates are flat. Doubling spending failed to make schools better.

"Everyone has been conned—you can give public schools *all* the money in America and it will not be enough," says Dr. Ben Chavis, a former public school principal who now runs the American Indian Public Charter School in Oakland. His school spends thousands less per student than Oakland's government-run schools spend.

Chavis saves money by having students help clean the grounds and set up for lunch. "We don't have a full-time janitor," he told me. "We don't have security guards. We don't have computers. We don't have a cafeteria staff."

Students who can't afford lunch get boxed lunches from a local restaurant in return for weekend work. There's no gym; for PE his students move the tables and use the cafeteria, or just run laps around the block. Competition forces Chavis to innovate.

CHAVIS I see my school as a business. And my students are the shareholders. And the families are the shareholders. I have to provide them with something.

STOSSEL You've boosted the scores from where they were. Spending less money.

CHAVIS It's not about the money.

STOSSEL But what about kids who have come from broken families, poor families?

CHAVIS Poor kids are the easiest ones to motivate. Give me the poor kids, and they will outperform the wealthy kids who live in the hills.

STOSSEL What if a kid just doesn't do the work?

CHAVIS I'm going to embarrass them. [In front of the] other kids I say, do you want to grow up pushing a cart like these homeless guys on the street? I take them down to the corner, where the guys are pushing the carts. I say, do you want to grow up to be like this?

Since Chavis took over four years ago, his school has gone from being the worst in Oakland to being among the best.

All over America there are dynamic schools that spend little, but outperform government schools. In Russellville, South Carolina, we taped students at Teresa Middleton's school leaping out of their chairs to answer questions in her "math game"—screaming the answers in excitement.

Middleton makes learning fun. When she walks into the classroom her students are already asking, "Can we play this today? Can we do relay math? Can we play bingo? Can we play phonics around the world?"

Middleton built her school in 1996, after watching students fail in public schools. She was fed up with the inefficiency she saw. Now, when her students transfer from her school to a public school, their parents say that they are *way* ahead of their peers.

Middleton charges parents about 3,000 dollars per child, less than half of the 8,000 dollars the government gives to the surrounding public schools. But even with less money, her students do better. Middleton told us, "I've had three-year-olds sounding out words. I have one [student] who's already been diagnosed autistic, but we have him counting by fives." Her customers (parents) are willing to pay her 3,000 dollars, even though they already pay for their public schools through property taxes, to get that kind of superior performance. One parent told us, "It's worth the extra effort, the extra money, because of, I call it, return on your money."

One of the bureaucrats' favorite arguments is that "we need more money so we can have smaller classes." But the public school student-teacher ratio has already fallen from an average of 24.7 students per teacher in 1965 to 15.9 students in 2002. It's logical to believe that more teachers would improve results, but in government schools, it has made no difference in student performance.

> **MYTH:** Teachers need teaching certificates to teach well.
>
> **TRUTH:** They don't.

All over America, thousands of Catholic schools outperform government schools, while spending less than half as much money. I confronted a New York City school principal about that.

> **STOSSEL** Your average teachers make more than the top they pay at Catholic schools. But they are getting it done.
>
> **THELMA BAXTER** They get the job done because they want to be where they are teaching. But please understand that many of those teachers are not as well-qualified. Some of them are teaching without a four-year degree. Many of them are teaching without a master's degree.

Oh, what a shame. But look at the results! The Catholic schools do better! Maybe teachers don't need master's degrees or a four-year course from an education college.

Above all, note what Baxter said: "They get the job done because they want to be where they are teaching." What a telling indictment of her public schools! Baxter's teachers, like her students, have little choice, and apparently don't "want to be where they are teaching." The lower paid, less "qualified" teachers in Catholic schools want to be there.

> **MYTH:** Catholic schools succeed because they expel the problem kids.
>
> **TRUTH:** Catholic schools educate problem kids.

Government school officials often argue that the Catholic schools do better for less money only because they have the power to select their students. The public schools must take everyone.

> **THELMA BAXTER** The Catholic schools can select the students who attend.
>
> **STOSSEL** They can throw out the troublemakers?
>
> **THELMA BAXTER** That's the truth.

STOSSEL Do they throw a lot out?

THELMA BAXTER Yes.

Actually, they *can,* but they rarely do. I interviewed Monsignor Wallace Harris, who ran a school in a New York City slum not far from Thelma Baxter's public school. His school looked very different. It was orderly. Although class sizes were large (thirty-six kids), the kids paid attention:

STOSSEL With thirty-six in a class, how can you teach? It's too many.

MONSIGNOR WALLACE HARRIS We manage.

STOSSEL [They say] you can throw out the troublemakers.

MONSIGNOR WALLACE HARRIS No, can't do that. Won't do that. . . . If one or two out of the entire population of five hundred were asked to leave for disciplinary reasons, it would be unusual.

STOSSEL So what do you do when you have a kid who's making trouble?

MONSIGNOR WALLACE HARRIS You start talking to the parents right away.

That's the difference. Few kids are expelled, but parents and kids know it could happen, and that changes behavior. Catholic schools educate plenty of "problem" kids.

New York City's public schools have eight thousand administrators. It's where much of your tax money is wasted. At Catholic school headquarters, there are only thirty administrators. At Harris's school, he's in charge. It's up to him to convince the parents that his school is the best.

STOSSEL You get to just make the decisions?

MONSIGNOR WALLACE HARRIS Yes.

STOSSEL You don't have to call the head of the school board, get permission?

MONSIGNOR WALLACE HARRIS No. I'm expected to fix it right away.

STOSSEL What if you don't?

MONSIGNOR WALLACE HARRIS It will be my head that rolls.

That freedom to fail is a reason that, in city after city, the Catholic schools do better although they spend less than half as much. In New York City, the Catholic high schools serve the same "disadvantaged" population as the government schools, but the Catholic school four-year graduation rate is 99 percent, vs. 54 percent for the government schools.

> **MYTH:** Public school officials will experiment to help kids.
>
> **TRUTH:** Public schools officials resist any change.

The government schools' professional educators say they are open to all kinds of experimentation. They oppose competition from private schools, but say they are open to government-approved charter schools. That's what they say. But just try to open a charter.

Educators told us that getting one started is like beating your head against a wall.

"It was a horror story," South Carolina charter school principal Nancy Gregory told us. "The gobbledygook they put you through. It wasn't, what can we do to help you? It's, here's what you can't do . . . [the education bureaucrats] are very—very threatened by school choice, charter schools. They're very threatened [by] turning loose the reins of power."

Nancy persevered and succeeded in creating a thriving charter school, but she says she took the risk only because she knew her next career step was to retire. "You know that you're dead—you're dead in your profession when you do this kind of thing."

In Lee County, South Carolina, where lousy schools failed to teach Dorian to read, a group of parents spent years trying to start a new charter school, only to have the school board fight them every step of the way. The bureaucrats filed objections all the way to the state Supreme Court.

> **STOSSEL** You haven't made this easy for them.
>
> **DELORIS WRIGHT** It's not that we've made it hard.
>
> **STOSSEL** You haven't delayed it? Come on! You took it all the way to the state Supreme Court.
>
> **DELORIS WRIGHT** The application was not filed in a timely manner.
>
> **DR. LLOYD HUNTER** Change is always difficult.
>
> **STOSSEL** Why did you take it all the way to the state Supreme Court?
>
> **DR. LLOYD HUNTER** The school district was protecting its interest.

South Carolina parent Jenny Sanford told me, "They see it as money leaving their school or leaving their little area. And so it's all about money. So they do everything they can to make it difficult to start a charter school."

Jenny Sanford isn't just *any* parent, she happens to be the wife of South

Carolina's governor. After Mark Sanford was elected, the Sanfords and their four boys moved to the state capital in Columbia. Their first big challenge was: Where will we send our kids to school?

They wanted to send them to public schools, but the middle school near the governor's mansion was rated "below average." The Sanfords quickly learned that *they* wouldn't have to send their kids to that school—they could get access to the *best* schools because of the governor's position. Mrs. Sanford told me that school superintendents called and wrote her, inviting her to "choose their best schools and send my children there. And I said, 'But it's not fair because if I lived down the street here, [I] wouldn't be allowed to do that.' They said, 'You're married to the governor! So forget the rules.'"

That's how it works; the privileged get special breaks. The Sanfords didn't think it was fair for them to take advantage of that, so they dug into their own pockets and sent their kids to private school. Then the governor proposed a plan that would make it easier for all kids in South Carolina to have the same choice they had. He called his plan "put parents in charge." It would allow parents to pick any school they wanted, and if they chose to leave the government schools for a private school, they'd get a tax credit to help pay the tuition.

Letting parents choose, he said, would start competition between schools.

> **GOVERNOR SANFORD** People expect and demand choice in every other area of their life. Nobody would accept the notion of, I only get one kind of toothbrush. We're all made better by competition.
>
> **STOSSEL** People say the kids are too important to leave them up to the market, to competition. They might fall through the cracks.
>
> **GOVERNOR SANFORD** The kids are in fact falling through the cracks right now!

He's right about that. In South Carolina about half of the kids don't graduate from high school within four years. But how did the education establishment react to the governor's plan? School boards objected. Teachers' unions objected. PTAs sent *kids* home with letters saying, "Contact your legislator. How can we spend state money on something that hasn't been proven?"

The state legislature rejected the school-choice proposal sixty to fifty-three. It was a "great victory" for education, said state school superintendent Inez Tenenbaum.

INEZ TENENBAUM   It was an unproven, unaffordable, and unaccountable plan.

STOSSEL   Well, it's unproven because politicians, unions, won't let anyone try it. But why not let a thousand flowers bloom?

INEZ TENENBAUM   Because you're acting like these flowers are going to bloom. You have no idea what the private sector is going to produce.

STOSSEL   That's the beauty of it! The private sector constantly produces more than you or I as individuals could imagine, because a million minds create.

INEZ TENENBAUM   I don't buy that.

Tenenbaum said there was no need for an "unproven" scheme because her schools were getting better all the time.

INEZ TENENBAUM   We need to stay the course. If you look at every indicator for South Carolina schools, South Carolina is not last. We have been ranked as having some of the highest standards of learning in the entire country.

STOSSEL   But the kids don't achieve them. You're *last* in SAT scores.

INEZ TENENBAUM   SAT is an indicator that really shouldn't be used to judge any state.

STOSSEL   Aren't the parents better judges than your tests, if the parent says, "I hate this school, I wanna put my kid in [another] school"?

INEZ TENENBAUM   Parents can get out, parents have public school choices.

STOSSEL   [A] lousy public school versus another lousy public school! Why not give them more choice, why not let them take half the money you spend, and try these private alternatives?

INEZ TENENBAUM   Because you do not have the same kind of accountability in private schools that you have in public schools.

Accountability? The head of a government monopoly has the nerve to talk about accountability? Accountability is why *private* schools perform better. Every day they are held accountable by parents, and if they fail the kids, the school administrators lose their jobs.

Government schools are accountable only to politicians. It's why almost no school is ever closed, no matter how bad it is. No one loses his job when the kids fail.

It's not news that government monopolies perform poorly. The fall of the

Soviet Union is not a secret. Why would we think a monopoly would work for schools?

> **MYTH:** Teacher excellence is rewarded.
>
> **TRUTH:** Mediocrity is rewarded.

The only thing worse than a government monopoly is a *rigidly unionized* government monopoly. In American cities, most schoolchildren are stuck with exactly that.

At a high school in New York, students told us some of their teachers don't try very hard. "I'm standing, today sixth period, outside my room, 'cause I don't know where my teacher is," said one, adding, "One of my teachers tells me he does this for the health benefits."

This seems odd because teachers I know *want* to help kids learn. Some are passionate about education. They take extra courses to learn how to be better teachers. Some pay out of their own pocket to learn the latest techniques.

Yet again and again, kids told us, "You got teachers that say, 'I don't care, I get paid for it anyway.'"

I shouldn't be surprised. If you pay everyone the same, and pretty much guarantee their jobs, there's little incentive to try harder.

I talked to a group of NYC high school students.

STOSSEL Are there teachers that students dread?

GROUP OF STUDENTS (In unison) Yes!

PATRICIA STUART They talk like—like they're dead, and—and it makes you want to go to sleep. And when you do go to sleep, they get mad. But you—but you can't help but go to sleep, 'cause they—they talk like they—like somebody is forcing them to be here. When they don't have no enthusiasm, we don't have no enthusiasm.

Some teachers are bored, and others aren't very smart.

In 1999 I tried to create an informal national teachers test. Which teachers would prove the smartest? ABC affiliates approached teachers in dozens of cities. But in city after city, teachers refused to take the test. I interviewed a group of New York City teachers who declined to take our test. They were suing New York because the state had the nerve to use a test called the National Teacher Examination or NTE, to partly determine benefits and pay. Some of these teachers had failed the NTE test repeatedly.

> **FIRST WOMAN** I've taken the NTE probably twenty times, maybe more.
> **FIRST MAN** I've taken it numerous times. I lost count.
> **STOSSEL** Usually, if you take something and you fail, you study so you can pass.
> **SECOND MAN** There's nothing to study from.
> **SECOND WOMAN** I don't need to be tested.
> **STOSSEL** You test the kids. Why shouldn't we test you?
> **THIRD WOMAN** If I'm tested by outsiders, that's unfair. Every day that we go into the classroom, that's a test.

Their lawsuit claimed the test was racist, because many who flunked the test were members of minority groups.

> **MARC PESSIN, SOCIAL STUDIES TEACHER** Now, I will give you an example of a common question. Let's see if you get it. What is the hue of that wall?
> **STOSSEL** Hue? That means color of the wall?
> **MARC PESSIN** I'm asking you the question.
> **STOSSEL** Beige.
> **MARC PESSIN** All right. You are lucky because, based on your understanding, the word hue is understood to mean color. People who come from poor neighborhoods, those people may not have the enriched vocabulary that the people who make the test have.

The word *hue* is too tough a word for a *teacher*? Joel Klein, chancellor of New York City's public schools, complained to me, "We tolerate mediocrity [because] people get paid the same, whether they're outstanding or average or way below average."

The schools Klein manages are one of the biggest government monopolies outside of China. Klein made headlines when he led President Clinton's Justice Department's attack on Microsoft, for what he called "monopolizing computer software." But Microsoft was a hotbed of competition compared to Klein's new organization, a monopoly so heavily regulated that even dangerous teachers sometimes don't get fired.

STOSSEL You can't fire them?

JOEL KLEIN It's almost impossible.

It's almost impossible because of the byzantine steps a principal must take to fire a bad teacher. See pages 128–131 for a chart of the steps.

The rules were well intended—to make sure that teachers get due process. The union worried that principals would play favorites, hiring friends and family members, while firing good teachers. If public education were subjected to the competition of the free market, the bureaucratic rules would be unnecessary, because enough parents would hold bad principals accountable by sending their kids to a different school the next year. The bad schools would close. But government schools never close, so the school monopoly must operate according to paralyzing rules.

The rules are so onerous that principals rarely even try to fire a teacher. Most just put bad teachers in pretend-work jobs, or sucker another school into taking them. They even have a name for it: the "dance of the lemons."

JOEL KLEIN We have a system in which we don't distinguish among people. And as a result of that, we don't reward excellence.

STOSSEL Why don't you reward excellence?

JOEL KLEIN Because it's barred by the contract.

The contract: 205 pages of work rules. Union monopolies create documents like that. The rules forbid paying excellent teachers more, and made it almost impossible to fire even the teacher who sent sexual e-mails to his sixteen-year-old student.

JOEL KLEIN This is the most unbelievable case to me because the e-mail was there, he admitted to it. It was so thoroughly offensive.

STOSSEL And he confessed.

JOEL KLEIN Well, we had the e-mail.

STOSSEL So, I would think, they would just—fire him.

JOEL KLEIN You can't fire him. . . . We've paid him. He hasn't taught, but we've had to pay him, because that's what's required under the contract.

They paid him more than $350,000. Only after six years of expensive litigation were they finally able to fire him, and Klein is still paying hundreds of teachers who are said to be incompetent, violent, or guilty of sexual misconduct.

Afraid to let these teachers teach, they put them in "rubber rooms." They're not made of rubber—it's just what they call the places where they house teachers they're afraid to let near the kids. Teachers in rubber rooms read magazines, play cards, and talk to each other. While they waste time, they collect their salaries, at a cost to New York City taxpayers of twenty million dollars a year.

Insane as it is to have rules that make it practically impossible to fire even the worst teacher, the teachers' unions defend the rules. And teachers' unions have extraordinary power. Labor-friendly legislation usually *requires* teachers to pay dues—even if they disagree with the union. This creates a political weapon that politicians ignore at their peril.

In New York, teachers' union president Randi Weingarten demonstrated that political power when, in 2005, she got more than 20,000 teachers to show up for a rally at Madison Square Garden. I had to wear earplugs to stand the noise, as teachers chanted and screamed insults at anyone who opposed their agenda. Twenty thousand people willing to show up and *scream*. It's no wonder politicians tremble.

After the rally, Weingarten defended work rules I asked her about. Even the one that said no teacher was allowed to help a disabled kid exit a bus.

STOSSEL No cafeteria duty, study hall duty for teachers?

RANDI WEINGARTEN Teachers have professional duties!

STOSSEL Permit members to retire without penalty, at age 55.

RANDI WEINGARTEN Yes.

STOSSEL Teachers work "uniform six-hours-and-forty-minute days."

RANDI WEINGARTEN Which is what normally happens in the private sector.

In the private sector people work uniform six-hour-forty-minute days? Only in unionized monopolies can people get so arrogantly out of touch. After my interview with Weingarten, she and Chancellor Klein agreed to a new contract that gives her teachers a 15 percent raise. She agreed to change some of the stupider rules, like "no study hall duty," but other rules still stand, and that complex chart (pp. 128–131) that shows what it takes to fire a teacher was done *after* the contract "simplified" the process.

The teachers did make a big concession, though. They agreed to work ten minutes a day more.

Of course many teachers—the better ones—work much longer than six hours and fifty minutes at home, grading papers and preparing for the next day's classes. But some teachers told me they were "afraid to work past three

HOW DO I FIRE AN INEPT TEACHER?

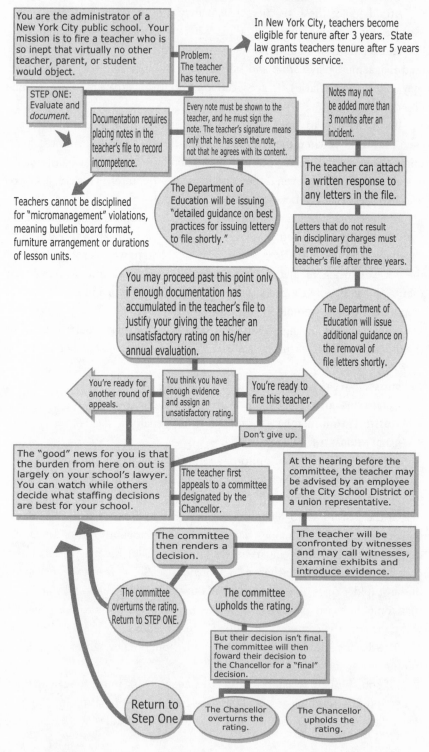

You are the administrator of a New York City public school. Your mission is to fire a teacher who is so inept that virtually no other teacher, parent, or student would object.

Problem: The teacher has tenure.

In New York City, teachers become eligible for tenure after 3 years. State law grants teachers tenure after 5 years of continuous service.

STEP ONE: Evaluate and *document*.

Documentation requires placing notes in the teacher's file to record incompetence.

Every note must be shown to the teacher, and he must sign the note. The teacher's signature means only that he has seen the note, not that he agrees with its content.

Notes may not be added more than 3 months after an incident.

Teachers cannot be disciplined for "micromanagement" violations, meaning bulletin board format, furniture arrangement or durations of lesson units.

The Department of Education will be issuing "detailed guidance on best practices for issuing letters to file shortly."

The teacher can attach a written response to any letters in the file.

Letters that do not result in disciplinary charges must be removed from the teacher's file after three years.

You may proceed past this point only if enough documentation has accumulated in the teacher's file to justify your giving the teacher an unsatisfactory rating on his/her annual evaluation.

The Department of Education will issue additional guidance on the removal of file letters shortly.

You're ready for another round of appeals.

You think you have enough evidence and assign an unsatisfactory rating.

You're ready to fire this teacher.

Don't give up.

The "good" news for you is that the burden from here on out is largely on your school's lawyer. You can watch while others decide what staffing decisions are best for your school.

The teacher first appeals to a committee designated by the Chancellor.

At the hearing before the committee, the teacher may be advised by an employee of the City School District or a union representative.

The committee then renders a decision.

The teacher will be confronted by witnesses and may call witnesses, examine exhibits and introduce evidence.

The committee overturns the rating. Return to STEP ONE.

The committee upholds the rating.

But their decision isn't final. The committee will then foward their decision to the Chancellor for a "final" decision.

Return to Step One

The Chancellor overturns the rating.

The Chancellor upholds the rating.

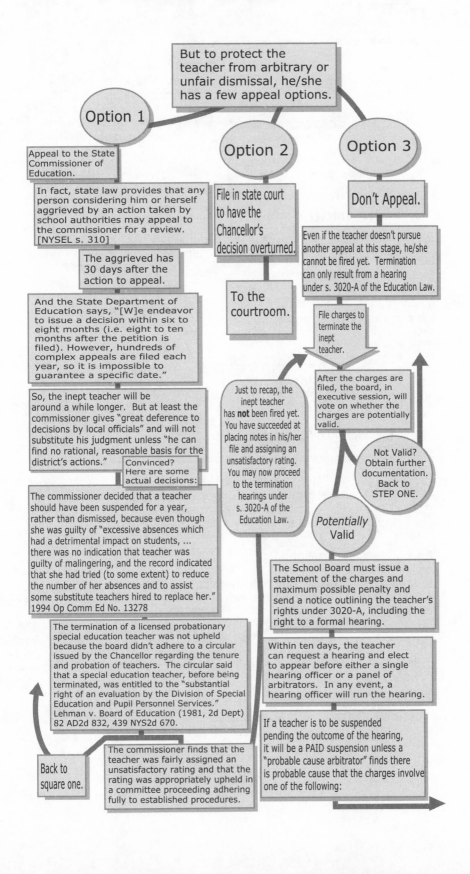

But to protect the teacher from arbitrary or unfair dismissal, he/she has a few appeal options.

Option 1

Appeal to the State Commissioner of Education.

In fact, state law provides that any person considering him or herself aggrieved by an action taken by school authorities may appeal to the commissioner for a review. [NYSEL s. 310]

The aggrieved has 30 days after the action to appeal.

And the State Department of Education says, "[W]e endeavor to issue a decision within six to eight months (i.e. eight to ten months after the petition is filed). However, hundreds of complex appeals are filed each year, so it is impossible to guarantee a specific date."

So, the inept teacher will be around a while longer. But at least the commissioner gives "great deference to decisions by local officials" and will not substitute his judgment unless "he can find no rational, reasonable basis for the district's actions."

Convinced? Here are some actual decisions:

The commissioner decided that a teacher should have been suspended for a year, rather than dismissed, because even though she was guilty of "excessive absences which had a detrimental impact on students, ... there was no indication that teacher was guilty of malingering, and the record indicated that she had tried (to some extent) to reduce the number of her absences and to assist some substitute teachers hired to replace her." 1994 Op Comm Ed No. 13278

The termination of a licensed probationary special education teacher was not upheld because the board didn't adhere to a circular issued by the Chancellor regarding the tenure and probation of teachers. The circular said that a special education teacher, before being terminated, was entitled to the "substantial right of an evaluation by the Division of Special Education and Pupil Personnel Services." Lehman v. Board of Education (1981, 2d Dept) 82 AD2d 832, 439 NYS2d 670.

Back to square one.

The commissioner finds that the teacher was fairly assigned an unsatisfactory rating and that the rating was appropriately upheld in a committee proceeding adhering fully to established procedures.

Option 2

File in state court to have the Chancellor's decision overturned.

To the courtroom.

Just to recap, the inept teacher has **not** been fired yet. You have succeeded at placing notes in his/her file and assigning an unsatisfactory rating. You may now proceed to the termination hearings under s. 3020-A of the Education Law.

Option 3

Don't Appeal.

Even if the teacher doesn't pursue another appeal at this stage, he/she cannot be fired yet. Termination can only result from a hearing under s. 3020-A of the Education Law.

File charges to terminate the inept teacher.

After the charges are filed, the board, in executive session, will vote on whether the charges are potentially valid.

Not Valid? Obtain further documentation. Back to STEP ONE.

Potentially Valid

The School Board must issue a statement of the charges and maximum possible penalty and send a notice outlining the teacher's rights under 3020-A, including the right to a formal hearing.

Within ten days, the teacher can request a hearing and elect to appear before either a single hearing officer or a panel of arbitrators. In any event, a hearing officer will run the hearing.

If a teacher is to be suspended pending the outcome of the hearing, it will be a PAID suspension unless a "probable cause arbitrator" finds there is probable cause that the charges involve one of the following:

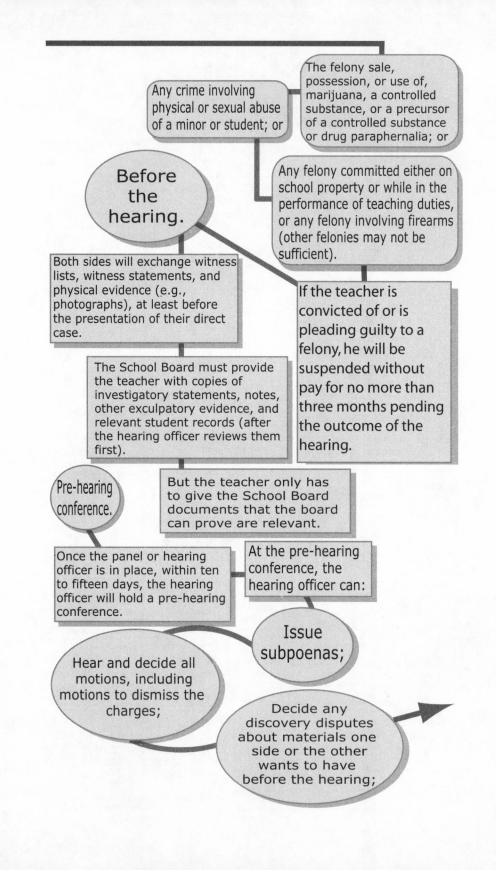

Any crime involving physical or sexual abuse of a minor or student; or

The felony sale, possession, or use of, marijuana, a controlled substance, or a precursor of a controlled substance or drug paraphernalia; or

Any felony committed either on school property or while in the performance of teaching duties, or any felony involving firearms (other felonies may not be sufficient).

Before the hearing.

Both sides will exchange witness lists, witness statements, and physical evidence (e.g., photographs), at least before the presentation of their direct case.

The School Board must provide the teacher with copies of investigatory statements, notes, other exculpatory evidence, and relevant student records (after the hearing officer reviews them first).

If the teacher is convicted of or is pleading guilty to a felony, he will be suspended without pay for no more than three months pending the outcome of the hearing.

Pre-hearing conference.

But the teacher only has to give the School Board documents that the board can prove are relevant.

Once the panel or hearing officer is in place, within ten to fifteen days, the hearing officer will hold a pre-hearing conference.

At the pre-hearing conference, the hearing officer can:

Issue subpoenas;

Hear and decide all motions, including motions to dismiss the charges;

Decide any discovery disputes about materials one side or the other wants to have before the hearing;

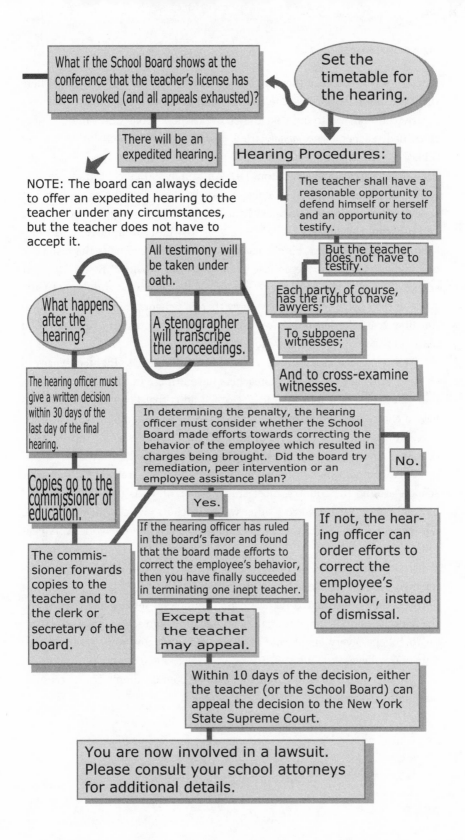

What if the School Board shows at the conference that the teacher's license has been revoked (and all appeals exhausted)?

Set the timetable for the hearing.

There will be an expedited hearing.

Hearing Procedures:

NOTE: The board can always decide to offer an expedited hearing to the teacher under any circumstances, but the teacher does not have to accept it.

The teacher shall have a reasonable opportunity to defend himself or herself and an opportunity to testify.

All testimony will be taken under oath.

But the teacher does not have to testify.

What happens after the hearing?

Each party, of course, has the right to have lawyers;

A stenographer will transcribe the proceedings.

To subpoena witnesses;

The hearing officer must give a written decision within 30 days of the last day of the final hearing.

And to cross-examine witnesses.

In determining the penalty, the hearing officer must consider whether the School Board made efforts towards correcting the behavior of the employee which resulted in charges being brought. Did the board try remediation, peer intervention or an employee assistance plan?

No.

Copies go to the commissioner of education.

Yes.

The commissioner forwards copies to the teacher and to the clerk or secretary of the board.

If the hearing officer has ruled in the board's favor and found that the board made efforts to correct the employee's behavior, then you have finally succeeded in terminating one inept teacher.

If not, the hearing officer can order efforts to correct the employee's behavior, instead of dismissal.

Except that the teacher may appeal.

Within 10 days of the decision, either the teacher (or the School Board) can appeal the decision to the New York State Supreme Court.

You are now involved in a lawsuit. Please consult your school attorneys for additional details.

p.m." in school because they might "get in trouble with the union." Where there are union work rules, the laziest members drag everyone else down.

By contrast, we found that the charter schools that were free of union rules had teachers who *happily* tried new things. At Friendship, a charter school in Washington, DC, the students come from the most crime- and drug-ridden areas of Washington, DC. Amazingly, 90 percent graduate, and nearly all graduates go on to college, usually becoming the first people in their families to do so. Principal Michael Cordell says it happens because he and his team can run his school as he sees fit. "Education moves at a thousand miles an hour and there's new ways to teach kids. That's the beauty of our school—we can move as fast as our kids are moving." Being a charter school gave him the freedom to get rid of teachers who didn't make the grade. If they don't perform, they know there's a chance they'll be fired. After the first year, Cordell didn't re-hire one-third of them. He rewards good teachers with promotions and more money.

The students at Friendship notice the difference. Eighteen-year-old Gbeye Nyahn says, "I think the teachers have it more in them to want to actually put their best foot forward." Cordell adds that knowing his students have a choice forces him and his teachers to try harder. "We have that pressure, we have someone always picking up the phone, [saying] this isn't acceptable, we can't settle for just being good enough."

Such competition stimulates innovation. At the successful KIPP charter schools around the country, most students stay in class until five p.m. and have school on Saturday every other week. Teachers give out their cell phone numbers and are available to answer questions about homework every evening.

In Boston's tough Dorchester neighborhood, the Cadman Academy charter high school—whose students are almost exclusively from poor and minority families—graduated its first class of nineteen seniors last year. While the national norm is for about half of low-income high school graduates to go on to college, every single one of Codman's graduates were accepted into four-year colleges.

Too bad *more* kids and parents across the country aren't given access to *those* kinds of schools.

> **MYTH:** Teachers are underpaid.
>
> **TRUTH:** Under-*what*?

At that rally in New York City, angry teachers told me they were "horribly underpaid."

I see why they might feel that way. Teachers *are* charged with the incredibly important task of educating our kids—one of the most important jobs in the world.

FIRST TEACHER We work hard.
STOSSEL What do you make now?
SECOND TEACHER Seventy thousand.
STOSSEL How much do you make?
THIRD TEACHER Sixty thousand dollars.
STOSSEL What should you make?
THIRD TEACHER Eighty-five thousand.

Is $60,000 to $70,000 for a nine-month job "underpaid"? These salary statistics don't even include the perks that are part of teacher compensation. New York City teachers have a pension plan with a government guaranteed 8.25 percent return, their pensions are not taxed by the city or state, and they get ten days per year sick leave.

Nationally, most teachers make less. K–12 teachers average $45,081 a year. But most teachers only work nine months a year. If you look at the average *hourly* K–12 teacher wage ($30.91), it's more than chemists ($30.64), computer programmers ($28.98), registered nurses ($26.87), and psychologists ($28.49) make.

Whatever teachers earn today, if there were a free market in education—*good* teachers would make *much* more. Don't believe it? Remember, many schools spend $250,000 per classroom. If parents had choices, they would insist on the best teacher for their kids. Demand for the good teachers would bid up their value. The best would make $200,000 a year.

I don't even know what the word *underpaid* means in a free society. No one is forced to become a teacher or to keep teaching if other opportunities arise. If teachers were paid too little, we'd have teacher shortages. We don't. In Missouri, for example, there are 25 applicants for every teaching job in elementary schools. There are sometimes shortages in certain subjects, like math and science, but that's because of the insane pay-everyone-the-same rules, not a general underpayment problem. At KIPP charter schools, teachers are mostly nonunion, but they make about 15–20 percent more than their public school counterparts.

There are costs and benefits to every job and the free market is better able to figure those costs and benefits into a salary. One-size-fits-all contracts at unionized government schools just punish good teachers and reward bad ones.

MYTH: Homeschoolers are religious wackos whose children don't learn to socialize.

TRUTH: Homeschooling is a good option for some parents fed up with lousy government schools. Homeschooled kids do well.

More than one million kids are being homeschooled in America today. That's 2 percent of the school-aged kids, and that number has been growing by 10 percent every year. Some parents choose to homeschool for religious reasons, but a growing number are just fed up with the public schools.

Critics say that kids who learn at home don't learn how to get along with their peers. Homeschoolers answer: Why assume that school is the best place for kids to get "socialized"? Isn't school where you're supposed to pay attention to the teacher, not your peers? Homeschooled kids socialize all the time—at places like Boy Scouts, ballet lessons, soccer teams, and church choirs. Many get together for classes with other homeschoolers.

South Carolina teacher Tristen Sharpe was named the "teacher of the year" by her school. Her two boys attended the same school, and she noticed one of them was falling behind. His teacher said, "I just don't know what to do." Sharpe decided *she* knew what to do. She quit her teaching job to homeschool both her sons. Soon other parents asked her if she would homeschool *their* kids as well. Tristen says, "As many as I can take, I take." She has a long waiting list. "Parents who have called say, 'Is there anything that you can do? Is there anything? What part of the day is available? I'll do anything.' "

When we visited Tristen at her home school, we were struck by how excited the kids seemed about learning. Caymen Young, who hated her math class in public school, told us, "I love math, I'm a math freak." Science class was held at a pond behind Tristen's house; the kids caught tadpoles and ran over to show us how they go through life stages. A rope swing attached to a tree became a physics lesson. For geometry, they built a fort.

Brian Ray taught in both public and private schools before becoming President of the National Home Education Research Institute. He says home-schooled students blow past their public school counterparts in terms of achievement. "In study after study, children who learn at home consistently score 15–30 percentile points above the national averages," he says. Home-schooled kids also score almost 10 percent higher than the average American high school student on the ACT.

I don't know how these homeschooling parents do it. I couldn't do it. I'd get impatient, and I'd fight with my kids too much. Yet more than a million kids learn at home, and they outperform the kids from the public schools.

> **MYTH:** Vouchers will hurt the public schools.
>
> **TRUTH:** Vouchers make all schools better.

One way to improve schools is to give parents education "vouchers." A voucher might be worth the $10,000 government schools spend per child, or much less. A $5,000 voucher would cover tuition at most Catholic schools. The important point is that the voucher attaches the money to the student. Since parents can take the voucher to any school, that will force the schools to compete.

Critics of school vouchers say vouchers will "destroy public education." They say the most active and informed parents will pull their kids out, leaving the public schools with a concentration of "problem" kids whose parents are less involved. As the involved parents withdraw, that will "pull money from the public schools." It sounds plausible. Since the American education establishment has prevented any large-scale voucher programs from starting, those myths are tough to test.

However, in 1990, the city of Milwaukee did create a voucher program for some kids. When the program started, the Milwaukee school superintendent, Robert Peterkin, scoffed, "The idea that competition is just going to spark improvement for all schools is something that has no basis in fact."

Peterkin was wrong. In 2001, Harvard economist Caroline Hoxby did research to see what vouchers had done to nearby public schools. Hoxby found that kids who used vouchers to go to private schools raised their scores, *and* the kids in the competing nearby public school did too. The private school vouchers made the *public* schools change. "[Public] school principals were allowed to have a lot more autonomy," she said. "They counseled teachers out of teaching altogether who really weren't performing or showing up on the job—they put in new 'back to basics' curricula in some primary schools that really needed it so that reading skills and math skills would go up." Test results at those public schools went up by 8.1 percent in math, 13.8 percent in science, and 8.0 percent in language.

It shouldn't surprise anyone. Competition makes us better. The public schools didn't want to lose their students to voucher schools, so they tried harder. They did a better job.

They don't lose money either. The voucher is worth $3,878 less than what the government spends per child ($11,178) at the public schools, so every child that uses a voucher to go to a private school leaves the public schools with extra money. Per-pupil spending at the public schools in Milwaukee has gone *up* since vouchers began.

> **MYTH:** Vouchers will saddle the public schools with the "problem kids."
>
> **TRUTH:** Vouchers help "problem kids" too.

Defenders of government schools claim private schools do better only because they don't take the "problem" kids, the special-needs kids, who are more difficult to teach. The private schools "don't want the kids who are more expensive and time-consuming," they say, so if all parents are given vouchers, the smarter kids will go to private schools, and "special-needs kids will be left behind."

But it's not true. In Florida, students with disabilities are eligible for a voucher ranging in value from $3,885 to $22,248, depending on the severity of their condition.

"The students who participate in this program are not having great difficulty finding private schools eager to take them on, even when they have very severe disabilities," says author Jay Greene. "[The schools are] quite happy to take on those students, because they bring a lot of resources that help those schools teach those students."

Twelve-year-old Joseph and fifteen-year-old Alan Bauer left their public school to attend a private school that caters to students with learning disabilities. Alan has gone from having behavior problems and nearly failing grades to being on the honor roll. Their mother was in tears as she recounted the improvements.

Government-run school educrats claim that they must fight vouchers to "protect" the special-needs kids, but it's the government schools that leave these kids behind.

Kids like Kyle Hammond. He has ADD. When he was in public school, he told his grandmother, Dale, that he didn't have to study because he already had a copy of the test with the answers highlighted.

STOSSEL They were giving him the answers?

DALE He said, "Nana, they've done it lots and lots of times—they're teaching me to cheat!" and that's exactly what they were doing so they could pass him on to the next grade. The No Child Left Behind thing, you know? Send him up to the next class! Get him outta here! They really don't care.

Kyle now attends a private school, and he's doing much better. His grandmother says. "He is not the same child." It's "problem" students like Kyle who have the most to gain from choice.

MYTH: Vouchers violate the separation of church and state.

TRUTH: Not if parents choose the schools.

Most parents given school vouchers use them to send their kids to religious school. In 1999, the Ohio Education Association and other groups (like People for the American Way) filed a lawsuit saying that Cleveland's voucher program violates the separation of church and state guaranteed by the First Amendment ("Congress shall make no law respecting an establishment of religion . . .").

The lawsuit was a big threat to voucher programs. Allowing kids to choose religious schools is probably the only way a voucher program can work—at least at first—because today most nongovernment schools have some religious sponsor—usually the Catholic Church.

The public-interest law firm, the Institute for Justice, defended Cleveland's voucher program, arguing that so long as parents and kids *chose* to go to the religious school, rather than being *forced* by the state, the program did not constitute the establishment of religion.

The U.S. Supreme Court agreed. Cleveland parents eligible for the vouchers were elated. Roberta Kitchen said, "Now I have the same opportunity to choose a good school for my child that wealthier parents have had for years. School choice means that my children will no longer be ignored or taken for granted. If my children aren't getting the education they need, we have the power to choose something better. We can now vote with our feet."

Allowing people to take education money to the school of their choice is not a new idea. After World War II, the GI Bill sent 2,230,000 veterans to college, including religious schools like Notre Dame (Catholic), Brigham Young (Mormon), and Baylor (Baptist). The military allowed the soldiers to choose any accredited school. GI Bill "vouchers" helped create vibrant competition between American colleges, and they became the world leaders.

Wouldn't it be great if kids in our K–12 system could have access to that excellence too?

> **MYTH:** K–12 public education is one of the best parts of America.
>
> **TRUTH:** K–12 public education is a disgrace.

The United States didn't *always* have state-run schools. Parents homeschooled kids and communities set up their own schools. Teachers made little, but people always volunteered to teach, to help kids. Only in the 1830s was there a campaign to have state governments centralize education.

People then had a healthy suspicion of state-run education. After the Massachusetts State Board of Education was formed, it was promptly abolished on the grounds that, "The establishment of the Board of Education seems to be the commencement of a system of centralization and monopoly of power in a few hands, contrary, in every respect, to the true spirit of our democratical institutions; and which, unless speedily checked, may lead to unlooked-for and dangerous results."

How right they were.

But Horace Mann, often called the father of public education, touted public schooling as a tool to cure all sorts of social ills. He said that once there was public education, "nine-tenths of the crimes in the penal code would become obsolete." As usual, the reality produced by the collectivists didn't match their promises.

The collectivists' dreams of the perfect became the enemy of the good. Left alone, competing private schools would have expanded and used charity money to serve the poor—serving them far better than the government monopoly does now.

How sad that we "protect" our children from the benefits of competition by forcing them into a monopoly. What if we forced you to get your food that way? You'd pay taxes to support the "food system" and then you'd be assigned to one restaurant, where you'd eat every meal. What kind of service would you get?

Monopolies don't innovate. Why does the school year run from September to June? Because the public schools still use the *farm* calendar as a model of when kids should be in school. In 1830, kids needed the summer off to plant and weed the crops. Andrew Coulson, author of *Market Education,* points out, "Of course, we're no longer an agrarian society and so demands for schooling have changed, but public schools are not an organization that is responsive to consumer demand." No kidding. Some parents would prefer year-round schools. Today less than 2 percent of families get their incomes from farming. Has the education system responded? No.

Why can't kids learn math from video games? Why can't teens attend school at night, when their body clocks are more ready? Why can't there be *choice?*

Public education is sacrosanct, untouchable. But government education has become mediocre. People say America has the best education system in the world, but that's only because they don't know any better.

Hard-core libertarians say that the only solution is to abolish government involvement in education—to separate not just church from state, but *school* from state. Parents would pay for their kids' schooling, and charities would pay for the poor.

But I suspect that Americans are so used to the "education entitlement" that government-funded education is here to stay.

Still, government-*funded* is different from government-run.

We ought to give our kids access to schools that are as good as the other products and services we have in life. The way to do that is to unlock the chains of the government monopoly and give parents a choice.

The customers should get to decide where they want to learn.

CHAPTER SIX

CONSUMER CONS

'm a consumer reporter. My new enemies like to call me a "former" consumer reporter who "sold out and became a corporate shill," but I'm still a consumer reporter. I just realized there were bigger fish to fry. I saw that big government hurts consumers much more than business.

However . . . That doesn't mean that businesses aren't ripping us off. They are, and they'll do it every chance they get. Competition, media coverage, and (occasionally) legal prosecution limit their opportunities to scam consumers, but there's still plenty of deceit to shovel out.

I had great help uncovering the deceit. When you call and say, "I'm from ABC News," scientists, economists, and all kinds of researchers are eager to lend their expertise. Or test products. Then we'd call the companies. They were not as willing to talk, but once we had the research, we could go back and forth between the sellers and the skeptics until we were satisfied that we'd found the truth.

The lessons I've learned from ABC's research have saved me money, and trouble, and I'm eager to share them with you.

> **MYTH:** Brand names are better.
>
> **TRUTH:** Brand names cost more.

You've seen the plainly packaged "generic" or "no-brand" products. You may have tried them and liked them. They *are* cheaper; they can be 30 to

50 percent cheaper than brand names. Why, then, do so few of us regularly buy the no-brands?

Because we're afraid of them.

The plain-looking labels do suggest "inferior." People wonder: Are they dirty? Older? Lower quality?

Actually, many come from the same place as the brand names.

Take peas, for example. Their "grade" is determined largely by *when* they are picked. A pea is at its peak—young, sweet, tender—for only half a day. Peas picked then are likely to be government grade A.

Those picked eight hours later may be graded B or C, because they are older, and therefore a little starchier. Peas may also lose their A grade if they do not "have a good appearance."

Grade A peas usually get name-brand labels slapped on them, while no-brand labels go on grade B or C cans. Usually, I say, because when we bought peas from stores around the country, hid the labels, and had a government grader re-grade them, he found that two no-name brands were a higher grade than what he found in a can of Del Monte, which cost about twenty cents more.

In general, the no-brand foods tended to be lower grade. But as was the case with the peas, lower grade doesn't necessarily mean "bad." If you know how insignificant the difference between higher and lower grade is for some foods, you may not care about the grade.

Lower grade rice is just rice with colored or broken kernels left in. No-brand spaghetti is made the same way, in the same factory, as Prince spaghetti. The flour they use for no-brand spaghetti is simply less finely ground.

The only difference between brand-name and no-brand peanut butter is in the size of the peanuts used. Larger, smoother ones go into the brand; the smaller, wrinkled peanuts into the no-brand. A twenty-eight-ounce jar of Skippy's brand name often sells for $1.80 a jar more than the no-brand. Nutritionally, there is no difference. In fact, every nutritionist we talked to said when it comes to food, no-brand is just as nutritious as brand names.

Taste, of course, is the main reason that we buy one food over another. So we ran a taste test: no-frills spaghetti against Prince's; no-brand peas and peaches against Del Monte's; plain-wrapped peanut butter vs. Skippy. We paid a scientific testing laboratory to bring in a random sample of fifty adults to taste the peas, spaghetti, and peaches, and kids to taste peanut butter. No taster knew the purpose of the test. They didn't know they were comparing brands to generics; all they knew was that they were there to taste two foods and tell us which they liked best.

The result: Most testers did prefer the brand name peas and spaghetti, but the no-brand peaches and peanut butter tested equal to the brands. When we told them what they'd picked, testers were surprised. One said she was "educated" by the test: "I never buy the no-name brands; I just thought they were inferior quality, not that I had any basis to go on."

My favorite interview was with a smart shopper who said: "When my kids see a generic label, they all say 'it's junk,' or 'it's cheap.' [So] sometimes I buy jelly in a generic brand and put it in a Welch's jar, and they eat it and they don't know."

Other tests have also shown that, when they don't see the label, many people prefer the taste of the generic. You might as well try it. It's cheaper, and you may like it *more*. Give your family a blind taste test.

Ironically, consumers are less suspicious of non-food generics, like household cleaners, napkins, and garbage bags, but with those products, there *is* more reason to be wary.

We tested liquid dish detergents. The soap industry actually has a standard test for comparing them called the "dish-count test." It is just what it sounds like: The researchers wash dishes by hand and record what works. America's best seller, Ivory, cleaned thirteen dishes while the best-performing generic, Pathmark's no-frills, only washed eleven.

Likewise, Glad garbage bags held more garbage than generic bags. The generics tore (that was good TV!).

Brand name soaps, bags, paper towels, etc., *are* usually better, stronger, thicker, whatever. They are probably worth the extra money.

But the brand name food? Probably not.

MYTH: Bottled water is better than tap.

TRUTH: Most of you are being conned.

It started when a French company called Perrier put a few ounces of water in an elegant bottle, and convinced Americans it was cool to pay a lot of money for it. We've been getting soaked ever since.

Today, Evian has surpassed Perrier in sales; it's now the chic French water of choice. It costs more than gasoline—about five dollars a gallon—and if you'd rather wear it than drink it, you can pay ten dollars for a five-ounce aerosol can (ingredients: "aqua" and nitrogen).

Then there are Aquafina, Dasani, and the dozens of new brands of bottled water that have jumped into this billion-dollar business, including bizarre ones like Venus, "the Water for Women," and Trump Ice, with the Donald scowling on the label. I'd have to be pretty thirsty to buy that.

Water comes out of public fountains for free. It comes out of your tap for pennies. Why buy it in bottles?

"Because it tastes better," people told us. So ABC News ran a taste test. We put two imported waters, Evian and Iceland Spring, up against Aquafina (America's best seller), American Fare (Kmart's discount brand), Poland Spring (which is bottled in America, not Poland), and some water from a public drinking fountain in the middle of New York City.

We asked people to rate the waters. Only one water got "bad" ratings. Which one? Why, monsieur, that would be Evian, the most expensive; it came in last in our test. The water our testers liked most came from Kmart, which costs a third of what Evian costs. (Maybe that's why "Evian," spelled backward, is "naive.") Aquafina ranked second. Poland Spring came in fifth.

Tied for third were the fancy import from Iceland and . . . drum roll . . . *New York City tap water.* In other words, reservoir water—squeezed through the antique pipes of New York City before emerging from a water fountain in Harlem—tastes as good as expensive imports. Even people who told us that they didn't like tap water did like it, when they didn't know it was tap water.

Satirists Penn and Teller got a trendy California restaurant to let them fool customers with a "water steward." Like a wine steward, he had lots of fancy bottles, and most diners said they loved their elegant waters. "Oh, yeah, definitely better than tap water!" said one. But tap water is just what it was—the "water steward" filled the fancy bottles using the hose on the restaurant's patio.

If taste doesn't justify the price of bottled water, maybe "purity" does. Many people believe that bottled water is cleaner. So we sent bottled and tap water samples to microbiologist Aaron Margolin, of the University of New Hampshire, to test for the bacteria, like E. coli, that can make you sick. "No difference," he said.

Some people worry more about traces of chemicals in water, like chlorine, lead, chromium, copper, and iron. It's possible that you will ingest more of these from some tap waters than bottled, but trace amounts of chemicals are not only harmless, they may even be helpful; that's why iron, copper, and chromium are in vitamin pills.

More scientific tests than ours have also found that tap water is as good for you as bottled waters that cost 500 times more. Even the Bottled Water

Association doesn't deny it. I asked the man they recommended we interview, Dr. Stephen Edberg, of Yale University's School of Medicine, "Is bottled water healthier than tap?" He gave me this sparkling gem: "I wouldn't say, uh, it's healthier than tap water. I mean, uh, it's both, they both provide, uh, water."

That's right: All those companies that charge you an arm and a leg are selling you, uh, water. I can't argue with that. They certainly are selling you water.

In a few parts of the country, your local tap water may not be as safe or tasty, but in most of America, if someone tells you to buy bottled water, get out your shovel.

> **MYTH:** Expensive coffee tastes better than cheap coffee.
>
> **TRUTH:** Probably not.

Do you pay big bucks for "better quality" coffee? Maybe you spring for Dean & DeLuca's beans, which cost twelve dollars per pound. Well, wake up—after you have someone give you a bottled water taste test, have them give you a blind taste test for coffee, because chances are you're wasting your money.

Fancy coffee companies do take great pains to create "better" coffee beans. "Specialty beans are roasted and ground for this important test, the cupping," intones a video the Specialty Coffee Association of America sent me. In the cupping, experts "sip small portions of the brewed coffee and judge its taste, body, and aroma."

The best of what they approve is later sold by companies like Dean & DeLuca, Starbucks, and Oren's Daily Roast, which cost plenty. Compare their prices: twelve and ten dollars a pound—to the five dollars for Folgers, America's best-seller, and four dollars for Marques de Paiva, sold by Sam's Club and Wal-Mart.

When coffee is available for less than four dollars a pound, why spend three times that? We invited people to sample some Nescafé instant coffee and the five brands of coffee I mentioned above, but didn't tell them which was which. Then I sat down with some of the tasters, most of whom had clear preferences. One compared coffee to "fine wine."

Some tasters, like Mr. "Fine Wine," could indeed identify their favorite.

His was Starbucks, which did well on our test. In fact, even a woman who told us she hated Starbucks liked it when it wasn't labeled Starbucks. "Maybe I'm picking the wrong coffee," she said.

Remarkable things happen when you take off the label. Taryn Cooper discovered that her preference was instant coffee. "That's interesting, because like, I feel like instant coffee is kind of sacrilegious," she said.

We invited the six coffee companies to send representatives to watch and/or take our test. Only the Oren's rep, Genevieve Kappler, had the guts to go in front of our television camera and announce to the world which coffee she preferred—when that coffee was identified only by number. Would it be the brand she's paid to hawk? A competitor's? She waited nervously as I told her the result:

"The one you liked best was—Oren's. You picked yours."

"Yes!" she said, adding smugly, "The best coffee will certainly not be the cheapest."

That statement would have been more convincing had other tasters liked her coffee. But most didn't. Half listed it as "bad." Kappler had a quick answer to that: "None of these coffees were brewed the way we do," she said. "So the result is not going to be as good as it could be."

Really? Our brewing was supervised by Kevin Sinnott, author of *Great Coffee: The Coffee Lover's Guide*. If a guy who writes books about coffee isn't brewing it correctly, who is?

Still, at least Kappler took the test. Rich Bertagna, the Folgers representative, backed out. He said he would not take a taste because other testers "smelled of perfume." (This must explain why there is never any odor in coffee shops.)

On our test, Starbucks came in first. A close second went to, surprise, the cheap Sam's Club brand, Marques de Paiva. Oren's came in a distant third, closely followed by Nescafé, the instant coffee. The most expensive brand, the twelve dollars a pound Dean & DeLuca's, ranked second to last, and dead last was Folgers, America's best seller.

When I asked Bertagna about that, he said, "Well, every morning millions of Americans enjoy waking up with Folgers for the great taste and value."

At least Folgers is cheap.

> **MYTH:** Premium dog food is better.
>
> **TRUTH:** Not to your dog.

Pet foods now take up huge amounts of supermarket shelf space—which is surprising because fifty years ago, almost no one bought pet food. We fed our animals table scraps. No more. Now pet food is a fourteen-billion-dollar business—that's more than the gross domestic product of ninety-four countries. With so much money at stake, pet food companies work hard at pleasing the customer. But just who is the customer: the one with the cold, wet nose or the one with the money?

Visit a pet food company, as I did, to look into this, and you see that they go out of their way to try to please the one who never eats the food. Friday mornings at the Alpo factory, the executives meet to critique the product. They smell it. They check the way the food slips from the can—this is known (you can't make this stuff up) as the "plop factor."

Dogs are color-blind. But the executives used terms like "good color." This is because we pet owners believe that our pets like what we like. So the companies make pet food that mimics human food.

What dogs like most would disgust their owners. Read the label on many dog foods and you'll see: "water and meat by-products." "By-products" doesn't mean steak. It means things like lungs, intestines, and gullets. Gullets are the throats of cattle. They are black, totally covered with charcoal, when they are dumped into the dog food "slurry." The blackening is required by law to make sure no one sells gullets as people food.

When I talked with Alpo president Frank Krum, he told me the slurry changes from day to day. "The mix may change . . . Instead of putting 30 percent lungs in, we may put in 25 percent lungs and put in 5 percent udders. But you've got to keep udders in—dogs love udders."

It may disgust you that your animal eats udders, but organ meats like udders, livers, and lungs are good sources of protein and actually better for your pet than steak. They are also what your dog likes most. If you don't believe that, next time you're on the plains of Africa, watching wild dogs chase down their dinner, check out what they eat first: the stomach and other very smelly organs.

But the dog food companies have to appeal to the owners; that's why the marketers do all that smelling. Frank Krum told me they had to change one Alpo product that dogs loved because the owners thought it stank.

"Surprisingly, we found that some of the poorer smelling products are preferred in the kennel."

All the big companies keep hundreds of cats and dogs in research kennels, but the marketers packed into skyscraper kennels on Madison Avenue matter more. They worry about humans, and so on supermarket shelves, you'll see what they call "premium" pet food, brands like Lick Your Chops, Science Diet, and Sheba. "Premium" means it costs more.

Does that mean it's any better? I put that question to the dean of Tufts Veterinary School. "I find it difficult to find any scientific evidence that there are differences that matter," said Dr. Franklin Loew. "There's no reason to pay more unless you, for some reason, *feel good* paying more. If it says, 'complete dog food,' or 'complete cat food,' it will meet all the same requirements that any of the more expensive brands will meet."

"Complete," or "complete and balanced." You don't see that on people food. What it means is that government bureaucrats set standards that say, "If your pet eats this food and nothing else all its life, that's okay, because this is all it needs." You can find this guarantee in even the cheapest supermarket brands, so shovel away all the Madison Avenue hype: There's no need to pay more.

> **MYTH:** Buying in bulk saves a lot of money.
>
> **TRUTH:** Only if you do it right.

More people are buying in bulk at places called warehouse clubs. You have to pay to join. Is it worth it? Sometimes.

Chains like Costco, the leader in sales, and Sam's Club, which has the most stores, are enormously popular. These stores are huge bare-bones warehouses—packed from floor to ceiling with practically everything.

The sheer volume of goods for sale, says Phil Lempert, editor of Supermarketguru.com, drives sales. "You look at the pallets and you go, wow, it must be cheap. I want to buy it."

That's certainly true. When I first went to Costco, the vast aisles of merchandise were intoxicating. I felt compelled to shove things into my cart whenever the crew wasn't taping me. It's a reason warehouse clubs make lots of money.

Price Club was the first major club, selling office supplies at a discount to small businesses back in the 1970s. It merged with Costco, and today, seventy million people are members of Costco, Sam's Club, BJ's, and other clubs.

The prices are good: You can save 20 percent to 30 percent compared to supermarkets or department stores. But there's a catch—you have to become a member, and that costs about forty dollars a year—or a hundred dollars if you get a club's "premium card," which gives you 2 percent cash back on your purchases.

You need to buy a lot to justify paying a hundred-dollar membership fee.

Teresa Arca makes it work by partnering with her friends. They call it the "buddy system." They use Arca's membership card, and then divide up the items later; all of them share in the savings. Arca says Costco has saved her "from two to four thousand dollars a year."

But some people lose money shopping at warehouse clubs, because they spend more than they normally would. One woman at Costco told us: "You can come in here and think you're going to spend twenty-five to fifty dollars and you go out spending two hundred dollars, easy. You know what they should call it? 'Costco Surprise,' because when you get to the register, everybody's face is like, *What?!*" Researchers also told us that having all that food around the house makes people overeat. Cornell University marketing professor Brian Wansink tracked the eating habits of 240 club shoppers for two weeks. He found most of them ate more because they had more food in the house. "Some people even open the stuff on the way home!" Wansink said.

Club shoppers told Wansink they were buying food for a month, but most ate half the food within ten days of buying it.

So here's the advice from the experts:

- Use a shopping list to avoid "impulse buys."

- Don't buy in bulk if the product might spoil.

- Don't buy it if you're just going to get fat eating it.

- Use a buddy system to justify the membership money.

If you do that, you can save big bucks.

> **MYTH:** Buying on the Internet risks identity theft.
>
> **TRUTH:** The risks are small.

Columbia University professor Sree Sreenivasan had a knowing smile on his face when he told us: "I get a lot of people telling me 'I don't want to shop online,' but these are people very comfortable giving their credit cards to a complete stranger at a restaurant who will then go in the back, swipe the information, and bring them the bill." Sreenivasan, a specialist in computer commerce, says buying over the Internet is not a big risk. "It's in the companies' interests, these big corporations, to make sure that your information is safe," he told us, "because their reputations are riding on it."

One study tallied up the known causes of identity theft, and found that Internet purchases were related to less than 12 percent of them. Even that number, experts say, can be reduced by two simple safeguards on the consumer's end of the transaction: Make sure you are dealing with a "secure" site that encrypts information (the Internet address line in your browser should begin *https://* and not just http://), and check your computer for "spyware," sneaky software intruders that can compromise confidential information.

You can also protect yourself simply by reading your credit card statements. If you find a fraudulent charge and report it to the credit card company promptly, your liability will be no more than fifty dollars.

> **MYTH:** Diamonds mean love.
>
> **TRUTH:** Diamonds mean money to a South African cartel.

When Americans think about diamonds, they think about love. Seventy percent of American men who propose give their bride a diamond engagement ring. Diamond jewelry has come to symbolize love.

We also think of diamonds as valuable investments, valuable because they are so rare.

But we think both those things—because we've been conned.

Diamonds only mean love, and cost more than gold, because one brilliant company convinced people that diamonds were special.

The marketing strategy was born a hundred years ago in the mines of South Africa, when huge deposits of diamonds were found, deposits so rich that miners could practically just scoop the diamonds out of open pits. Before that, the discovery of a diamond was so rare that diamonds had become status symbols among royalty. But with the South African discovery, diamonds were suddenly ordinary. Prices plunged.

Then a smart Englishman, Cecil Rhodes, bought lots of the suddenly cheap diamond mines, and established a monopoly on the diamond supply.

Here's how it worked: Rhodes's company, De Beers, talked most every diamond-producing country into selling its diamonds only through his company; in exchange, De Beers guaranteed it would buy all of their diamonds, and promised to use its monopoly power to keep the price of diamonds high. The deal brought De Beers an astonishing amount of control over the world's diamonds—as much as 80 percent of the market.

New diamond discoveries and changing political alliances—the disintegration of the Soviet Union, for example—have reduced De Beers's world share to about 65 percent, but that still leaves them with enough clout to manipulate the market. To keep prices high, De Beers hoards diamonds. That makes diamonds seem more rare than they actually are.

But that's only half of their strategy. Since people were becoming aware that diamonds were really as common as cheaper gems, DeBeers might have been stuck with a huge stockpile of diamonds that no one wanted. De Beers played the market brilliantly. It launched an advertising and public relations campaign to manipulate the world into believing that diamonds were the proper way to express love. "And they succeeded—they created the marriage market," says author Edward Jay Epstein.

Epstein wrote a book about the diamond monopoly, and how De Beers conquered America's men: "Here was a country of a hundred different cultures that had just really come together at the end of the nineteenth century. There were no common traditions, no one knew how they were supposed to behave, and they [De Beers] said this in a very simple way: 'You relate to women, you give them a little glittering pebble; they put it on their finger.'"

Movie studios took up the cause. Leading men went to their knees, proffering diamonds glittering in Technicolor, as glamorous movie stars swooned at their scripted proposals. "Diamonds Are a Girl's Best Friend" became a Hollywood anthem. Diamond sales boomed.

The diamond message changes depending on the type of diamonds De Beers has in its warehouse. When it had lots of large diamonds, De Beers ran ads that said, in essence: "The bigger the diamond, the more you love her."

Then Russia increased the mining of small diamonds. Since De Beers had to fulfill a purchase contract with Russia, it suddenly had more small diamonds than it could sell. So De Beers started promoting the idea that, after years of marriage, if a man really loved his wife, he would show his devotion by giving her an "eternity ring"—a ring with lots of small diamonds on it. It worked. Today thousands of American women wear eternity rings because of a South African company's need to accommodate Russia.

Just as amazing, De Beers convinced women to covet diamonds, even though other rocks are just as pretty.

I ran a test. I borrowed a big diamond—worth $65,000—and a piece of cubic zirconium worth less than a hundred dollars. Could people tell the difference? No. At jewelry stores where couples were shopping for diamond rings, people had no idea which one was the real diamond. One bride told me, "It's sickening, that's what it is, sickening."

Could *jewelers* tell the difference? No. You cannot tell just by looking. One jeweler was convinced both were fakes. At the Gemological Institute of America, the director of grading showed me how *they* have to use machines to test for fakes. I told him: I should go on TV and tell people to buy a fake, since even jewelers cannot tell the difference! He said, "Down deep inside, you know you don't have the real thing, and that's the most important point."

Get the shovel. If people can't see a difference, the diamond cartel has pulled off a scam. Using clever advertising, they got people to spend thousands of dollars for rocks that look exactly like ten-dollar rocks. If that isn't a scam, I don't know what is.

I wish I could convince my wife.

At least diamonds are a good investment. If they don't actually convey love, they do at least hold their value. If you need money, you can sell them and recover what you paid for them, or much *more*.

That's what people think. But that is also a myth. I ran another test; I borrowed my assistant's diamond ring—which three appraisers said was worth $2,400.

Then we took it to twenty jewelers, saying we wanted to sell it. Some offered $500, some $800, one $1,200. No one offered anything close to $2,400. I went back to some of those same stores with a camera crew to see if they would offer more when they were on TV. Most did, but even with the camera there, no one offered more than $1,500. One jeweler admitted you're likely to lose money if you sell a diamond because the retail mark-up is at least 100 percent.

STOSSEL If I brought this ring to you and said I want to sell it, what'll you
give me in cash?

JEWELER Probably in the area of eleven to twelve hundred dollars.

STOSSEL So half what I might have bought it for retail.

JEWELER It could be even less than that.

STOSSEL I shouldn't buy something like this for investment. It's foolish.

JEWELER I'm not saying you should.

STOSSEL People do all the time.

JEWELER We are all ignorant, only about different things.

The diamond industry makes money off our ignorance.

Diamonds may be a girl's best friend, but they're a dubious investment,
and they are only a girl's best friend because the girl has been conned. Eventually, cheap diamonds may overwhelm the De Beers monopoly; then prices will
plunge. As Edward Jay Epstein told me: "Only a fool or a lunatic would invest
in diamonds."

> **MYTH:** Premium gas is better for your car.
>
> **TRUTH:** Only if you have an odd car.

High-octane premium gas costs about twenty cents more than regular.

Because premium costs more, it's logical to think it's better for your car.
It's called "premium," after all. At a NASCAR race, fans told us that they buy
high octane because it gives them better gas mileage, more power, and a
cleaner engine. Regular gas, one woman told us, "leaves a lot of gunk in your
engine, you know. That's what my daddy taught me."

But her daddy and many of you are wasting your money. Had she asked
the NASCAR drivers, she would have learned the truth.

"Believe me, I've pumped gas in from about every gas station there's
been in," NASCAR driver Joe Nemechek told us, "you put the regular in
there, it keeps on running."

For 90 percent of the cars sold today, high-octane is no better. It
won't give you better mileage, more power, or a cleaner engine. Some older
cars need higher octane because without it, they may knock or ping. And
cars with high compression, high-revving engines like Ferraris, Bentleys,

Jaguars, Acuras, Mercedes, and Corvettes need higher octane gas to run smoothly.

But that's about it. Check your owner's manual. Most cars have low-compression engines. They don't need high-octane gas, and you're wasting your money if you buy it. Even the gas companies admit that most of you don't need it (though they don't go out of their way to tell you that).

> **MYTH:** Brand name gas is better.
>
> **TRUTH:** Brand name gas costs more.

The big brands like Mobil, Chevron, BP, Shell, and Sunoco spend a lot on ads to persuade you to buy their gasoline, and the ads have worked. At gas stations, people tell us:

FIRST MOTORIST I get better gas mileage with brand-name gas, Sunoco, Mobil.

SECOND MOTORIST I would not go to a Wal-Mart gas station.

That's good news for Big Oil, and good news for those of us on TV who want companies to know their advertising works, so they'll buy more ads. But it's not a smart move for consumers.

All gasoline, brand-name and no-name, comes from the same refineries. Brand names do use some different additives, but there's no evidence that makes them superior. Save your money.

> **MYTH:** Hair-growth potions grow hair.
>
> **TRUTH:** The few that work don't work very well.

Millions have been spent on antibaldness potions. Every year there are new promises: *"This* chemical really *does* work!"

The snake-oil sellers get away with it because hair growth is so slow, and improvement so subjective, that even the promoters get fooled.

I remember fondly an interview I did over twenty years ago with a man

named Bob Murphy. He was the president of a company called New Generation Products, and Entrepreneur magazine had just named him "Entrepreneur of the Month" because his baldness treatment was going to make him
rich. What was odd, however, was that Murphy himself had little hair.

ROBERT MURPHY We get letters saying, "Great. It's changed my life."

STOSSEL If this product works so well, how come you're still a little bit
bald?

ROBERT MURPHY It works for everybody on a different degree, John. I've
gotten approximately 50 percent of my hair loss back.

STOSSEL This is a picture of you three years ago.

ROBERT MURPHY Right.

STOSSEL And you now have much more hair?

ROBERT MURPHY Oh, yeah.

STOSSEL Can you show us?

ROBERT MURPHY Sure, sure. I mean, all this is new in here *[pointing to head]*.
All this is new.

It certainly looked as if he had more hair than in the old picture, but I
thought it might have had something to do with the way the light from a
flashbulb bounces off a bald head. So I borrowed Murphy's Polaroid camera,
and he let me take a similar snapshot of his head. Sure enough, in the photo-
graph he looked as bald that day as he had in the "before" picture.

STOSSEL There's no difference.

ROBERT MURPHY *[looking shocked]* Yeah, there's no difference at all.

STOSSEL The flashbulb just makes the hair go away.

ROBERT MURPHY Okay, okay, it's—you're correct. I don't know what to tell
you.

Murphy had been showing off a newspaper column in which people said
New Generation had worked for them. He didn't know that we would make
the effort to track those people down.

STOSSEL All these people are happy with the product?

ROBERT MURPHY Certainly.

STOSSEL Well, we called them up today, and they don't use it anymore,
and they say it didn't work.

ROBERT MURPHY Some of them . . .

STOSSEL   Everyone in this article. You're passing this article out. "No flim-flam." Sounds like it is a flimflam. It makes me think you are a crook.

ROBERT MURPHY   Well, the way you're putting this is—it's true. It does appear to be so.

Finally! After years of confronting scam artists, calling them crooks, someone admitted that they did appear to be a crook! Murphy was the only one who ever did, then or since. It didn't seem to hurt him much: He's still selling his potions on the Internet.

Today, there actually are products that have been shown to grow hair: Propecia and Rogaine. They are the only baldness drugs the government says do work. Rogaine passed the double-blind tests because the researchers actually counted the hairs on the test subjects' heads and found a slight difference. But that doesn't mean ordinary people can *see* a difference. 20/20 called thirty dermatologists who prescribe Rogaine and found that fewer than one in ten of their patients had hair growth that was noticeable.

Propecia has shown more promise. It works by inhibiting the body's formation of the hormone responsible for the thinning of hair follicles. The American Hair Loss Organization says: "Propecia is the first drug in history to effectively treat male pattern baldness in the vast majority of men who use it."

But if Propecia works, why are there still so many bald people walking around? Because while it may work for many, it doesn't necessarily work very well. Just like Rogaine, results were measured by counting hairs on test subjects' heads and even then, one-third of those who take it never see any results. Also, you have to take it every day, forever, because if you stop, whatever benefits you've seen will gradually go away.

Disappointment over hair-loss treatments has brought increasing business to wig makers. Toupees for men (custom "hair replacements," as the suppliers like to call them) can be expensive. Men pay an average of three thousand dollars for two "units"—two, so they can switch off while one is being serviced. Women can pay up to two thousand dollars for a high-quality wig, which may need to be replaced, but it is a cost many are eager to pay, especially those losing their hair during cancer treatment.

One hairdresser I interviewed, Madeleine White, told me, "They tell us that it's more devastating for them to lose their hair than it is to lose a breast, because it's more visible. They would rather take the chance of dealing with the cancer than losing their hair. I have known women who have refused the treatment." That was hard to believe, but we called cancer hospitals and they said, yes, some women refuse chemotherapy when a side effect is hair loss.

More men and women are going to hair transplant surgeons. The surgeons transplant hairs the way you might repot plants. They dig holes in your bald spot and then take a "plug" of flesh and hair from the back and sides of your head (where even balding people usually have plenty) and replant it in those holes. Patients may have to return for six or seven separate operations. I interviewed Beverly Krofchick after her fourth session. She'd had 264 holes dug in her head, and was ready for more. "As you look into the mirror, you think, Gee, you know, I really like what I see. I really like all the hair I'm getting, and you become greedy and you want more!"

The transplants can cost as much as ten thousand dollars per visit, but people told me they have no doubt that they were worth it. The transplants made some look like they had tree farms on their heads, but to each his own.

The best solution to hair loss is to do what the men of the Bald-Headed Men of America Association do. They celebrate baldness, holding an annual "sexiest head" contest, and a parade, where they chant: "Bald is beautiful!"

Excess testosterone causes hair loss, they told me, so that means "we real men don't waste our hormones on silly things like growing hair."

A good attitude solves so many problems.

MYTH: Roaches check in; they don't check out.

TRUTH: Most roaches won't check in.

Cockroaches have lived on Earth some 350 million years, and now they want to live with us. In the South, people call the big American cockroaches "water bugs" or "Palmetto bugs." We Northerners are more likely to be tormented by the smaller German roaches. What is it about these bugs that gets people so worked up?

They're ugly, but so are ants. Ants don't freak us out. Roaches freak us out. I think it's because they *dart*.

Roaches clearly bring out hatred in people. Insecticide manufacturers conduct focus groups in which consumers tell the researchers that when they see the bugs, they want them dead, *fast*.

FIRST FOCUS GROUP MEMBER If you see that they're dead, at least you know
that you got some of them.

SECOND FOCUS GROUP MEMBER My son will kill them with his bare hands and
say, "Here, Mama!"

Our hatred of roaches has been good to the insecticide companies. The
biggest is the maker of Raid, the SC Johnson corporation. SC Johnson scientists have spent thirty years searching for better ways to kill roaches. Along
the way, Raid researcher Dr. M. Keith Kennedy told us that he's developed an
affection for them.

"We pay a great deal of attention and detail to rearing our bugs," he told
me. "We have top quality, grade-A cockroaches here."

Yes, he did say "rearing our bugs." After all, if you're going to try to find
the best way to kill roaches, you have to raise lots of them. They do that in
the "insectory," a big room filled with jars of cockroaches. This is not a place
you want to visit.

With so many people saying that they want to "see them dead," Raid's
advertising features sprays and traps that visibly execute the pests, like the
Roach Motel. But products like those rarely solve a roach problem.

Spraying Raid or anything else on the roaches you see isn't going to accomplish much, because for every roach you see, there are hundreds hiding behind the walls. Since just one pair of roaches can produce 20,000 babies, it
doesn't accomplish much to spray the ones you happen to see. Equally point-
less are the traps, the Roach Motels, where "roaches check in—but don't check
out." The boxes do trap the few roaches that walk in, by gluing their feet to the
floor. But so what? Most of the roaches won't ever visit the roach motel.

Foggers, which fog up the house with poison gas, are better killers because they carry the pesticide into more hiding places. But you have to leave
the house for hours, because the chemicals go *everywhere*.

Experts told us there is a better and easier solution: bait, like Raid's
Combat. The roach goes into the Combat disk and eats poisoned food. The
poison kills the roaches slowly, which is good because it gives the roaches
time to crawl back into their nest and poison their thousands of brothers and
sisters. The roaches do all the work. Every expert we spoke to said, if you
want to kill roaches, bait works best.

But bait is boring. It kills invisibly, behind the walls. Raid knows that
won't satisfy its customers' wish to murder roaches. So the day I visited
Raid's cockroach-filled traveling van, Raid was pushing the expensive spray. I
gave Raid entomologist John Randall grief about that.

STOSSEL This spray costs five dollars a can.

DR. RANDALL Yes.

STOSSEL So what I don't get is that you're out promoting the most expensive product, which doesn't work as well.

DR. RANDALL We're promoting the premium product that we think, used in concert—the fogger, the aerosol, and the bait—works the best.

STOSSEL But you don't promote the bait. You don't even have it out here.

DR. RANDALL Well, we have the bait here. We do.

STOSSEL In the truck somewhere?

DR. RANDALL Yes, somewhere.

STOSSEL If you were going to use one product, what would you use?

DR. RANDALL It's an interesting question. [pause] The bait, if you had to pick one.

Shovel away the spray and the Roach Motel. Buy the bait.

Bait works best on ants too.

MYTH: Funeral directors will help you select an inexpensive funeral.

TRUTH: Some will prey on you in your time of need.

"The abuse of the consumer in the funeral industry is absolutely vast," said Jessica Mitford. Forty years ago, Mitford wrote a scathing best seller charging that American funeral homes bullied grieving families into paying too much. She was right then, and I've discovered that since then, not much has changed.

The average cost of a funeral and burial in this country is about $6,500. You may want to pay that, because an elaborate ceremony helps you get over the death of a loved one. But often people pay because they don't know that they could pay $2,000 or less. When a loved one dies, you don't have the heart to shop around. That gives a funeral director a perfect opportunity to manipulate you. For a report on *20/20*, we visited twenty-six funeral homes in four states. Some people gave us fair and compassionate service. But half the time, salespeople lied to us, broke laws, or misled us in some way.

A Connecticut funeral director said he would help our producer select an inexpensive funeral. "We'll keep [the price] down," he said as our hidden camera rolled. "Keep it simple, and then you'll know everything that's going on by the time you leave here. Will you trust me with this?" The "trust" resulted in a big bill: $2,300 for a casket, another $800 for a container to put the casket in, $1,600 for professional services, and so on. This "inexpensive" funeral would have cost more than $7,000.

A well-informed consumer might ask for the funeral home's price list, which would make it easier to make price comparisons. The law says funeral directors must offer the list to customers, but it's yet another consumer law that's widely ignored. Here are some sales tactics our hidden cameras caught when producer Mark Golden asked about buying a less-expensive casket.

> **FUNERAL HOME SALESMAN 1** To be perfectly frank and honest with you, the metal casket is about one step above a Maxwell House coffee can.
> **FUNERAL HOME SALESMAN 2** It's called a morgue box. You go to a lumberyard, get lumber, and slap it together with some nails. It's very, very plain.

It's like listening to car salesmen; they want to sell you options and fancier models. One wanted us to shell out two thousand dollars for a protective vault: "This is to protect the casket," he said, "because the weight of the earth, thousands of pounds, will push down the casket and crush it." Another extolled the virtues of a more expensive, specially sealed casket: "Water can't get in, air can't get in, bugs can't get in, little critters can't get in."

"They are constantly selling protective things, protective caskets, protective vaults, to protect your loved one," said researcher Karen Leonard, who worked with Jessica Mitford. "This is outrageous, really. When you put a body in a protective casket, instead of the natural process of decomposition, drying out and becoming a skeleton, instead you get a slimy, moldy, much slower process and it's much more gruesome. But they're not telling you that."

Cremation is cheaper, and some funeral directors were contemptuous of it. One said, "That's like saying my father's death is an inconvenience, make it go away." When we asked about prices for cremation, we were quoted up to $3,300 for "the cremation package." Cremation doesn't need to cost anywhere near that much. Nonprofit groups often make cremation arrangements for as little as four hundred dollars; you can find them at the Funeral Consumer's Alliance website at www.funerals.org.

A still cheaper alternative is donating your body to science, another choice not very popular with the funeral industry. When our producer asked a Connecticut funeral director about that option, he was told: "We just went through this very recently with Yale–New Haven Hospital. A woman wanted to leave her body to science. She donated it to Yale. Yale refused. They have so many bodies, they don't know what to do with them." But it was a lie; Yale told us they rarely reject bodies, and the nearby University of Connecticut said they have an active body donation program. For those who donate their body through the program, the school assumes all costs associated with procuring the body upon death, cremation of the remains, and returning the ashes to the family. All free.

Of course, funeral homes in America couldn't get away with charging so much more if people just knew that there were cheaper alternatives. Now that you know you can buy a burial for two thousand dollars, a cremation for four hundred dollars, or donate to science for free, it will be harder for them to rip you off.

MYTH: Businesses rip us off.

TRUTH: Most don't.

For years, I did a consumer report every day. As a TV reporter for stations in Portland, Oregon, and then in New York City, I had no trouble finding companies doing nasty things. When I went to work at *20/20*, I continued to report on the phony diet remedies, baldness cures, breast enlargers, mail-order frauds, etc. that kept fooling consumers, no matter how many times we said that they were bunk.

But I eventually noticed that most crooks behind these frauds were small-time con artists. My bosses would say, "That's a clever scam, but is it worth putting on *20/20*? Is it a rip-off big enough for a *national* newsmagazine?" Often it wasn't. Consider the examples in this chapter: Maybe you're paying too much for brand-name peas, roach spray, or for a phony baldness cure. It's annoying, but not that huge a deal. Cheaters can't cheat that much or that long, because word gets out. Honest companies take away their customers.

This might not happen in the funeral or diamond business. Overpaying for funerals persists because a funeral is a one-time purchase, we don't like to talk about death, and some newspapers won't even accept funeral price advertising because they think it's in bad taste. So word doesn't get out. The diamond scam persists because consumers are so smitten by the advertising that they *want* to believe. But these are the exceptions. Usually, the companies that give consumers the most value at the best price are the ones that grow. The cheaters and rip-off artists remain fringe operators. There are a few big Enron-like scams, but they are the exception. There are more than twenty-one million businesses in America, and the vast majority survive by serving their customers well.

Even Halliburton. Halliburton is the whipping boy for the left. But assume everything its critics say is true: The Bush administration overpays Halliburton, Halliburton is hugely inefficient, steals from the government, subcontracts to cronies at outrageous prices, and funnels millions to Dick Cheney and his friends. Halliburton is still able to get meals to troops, deliver mail, wash millions of bundles of laundry, and transport fuel for half the money that the government needs to do it. In fact, the Congressional Budget Office says that if contractors like Halliburton were replaced in Iraq, it would take three soldiers to do the work of one private sector employee.

Because the private sector is subject to competition, it will always serve consumers better than government does, even when it's flawed.

It took me too long to see that the biggest villains were not businesses. The real villains are the people who say they're "going to help us": government—and "public interest" lawyers.

CHAPTER SEVEN

THE LAWSUIT RACKET

A s a believer in free markets, I should like lawsuits, since they promise a free-market solution to problems. Instead of clumsy, one-size-fits-all government regulation, lawsuits can offer individual justice. As Walter Olson, author of *The Rule of Lawyers*, put it, plaintiffs' lawyers could be called a supplement to Adam Smith's invisible hand, acting like an invisible fist. If you hurt someone or break the law, the fist will hit you back. In theory, solving problems through litigation should be a good thing.

But in practice, litigation hurts many more people than it helps.

It took me years to realize that. When I started doing consumer reporting, personal-injury lawyers were my best source. They were eager to help me because they recognized a common interest: They could advance their cases in the realm of public opinion by helping me do stories. As we'll see, this partnership between reporters and lawyers has evil effects, but it's hard for reporters to resist because trial lawyers are such good sources. They do expensive fact-finding that is easily recycled into print and broadcast pieces.

I felt so self-righteous doing those stories. The lawyers and I were the good guys fighting the bullies. Get the shovel. Now I realize that it's the *lawyers* who are the bullies, and I was just part of their hustle.

MYTH: Lawsuits help the little guy.

TRUTH: For every one helped, hundreds are hurt.

"Lawsuit wins $1 million for injured child" is the headline after a child is allegedly injured by a medical device. The headline implies that justice is served.

The lawsuit is clearly good news for the family taking care of the child.

But the headline leaves out a great deal. First, the suit cost everyone involved—and that includes you—much more than a million dollars. In addition to the million-dollar settlement, there were the court costs and the legal fees charged by the defense lawyers—*many* defense lawyers, considering the plaintiff probably sued not just the maker of the medical equipment, but the surgeon, an internist, some nurses, the hospital, and God knows how many others. Lawsuits routinely name as many as a dozen people, because to not include someone who is later revealed to be at fault may expose the lawyer to a charge of legal malpractice.

For the lawyers and people like me, a lawsuit is just another part of our work, but for most people it's a life-wrecking experience. Nurses are terrified. Doctors lose their concentration and can't sleep. Their hard-earned reputations are trashed by newspapers quoting plaintiffs' lawyers, who paint deceitful pictures of the doctors' incompetence and negligence. The doctors are forced to hire defense lawyers who eat up their time, energy, and entire life savings. Patients suffer while their physicians spend several hours a week with attorneys, preparing for and giving depositions. The suit drags on for years.

Soon doctors begin practicing hyper-defensive medicine, ordering expensive and largely unnecessary tests to avoid lawsuits. Some of the tests are painful for the patients. Today 51 percent of doctors recommend invasive procedures like biopsies more often than they believe are medically necessary.

Doctors become more secretive, talk less openly with patients, and become averse to acknowledging any mistake. Insurance premiums rise, and both doctors and hospitals pass the cost on to patients. Newly fearful, the medical device manufacturer decides to stick to proven technologies, dropping its plan to pursue a new line of tools that would make surgery less painful and less risky. I could go on, but you get the idea.

Many people suffered pain, fear, and financial loss to arrive at that million-dollar settlement. More bad news: The family of the child did not get a million dollars. They got only $600,000 after the lawyer deducted his expenses and fee.

Were the "incompetent" or "negligent" people at least punished? Probably not. The device manufacturer/doctor/hospital/nurse may have been innocent. A Harvard study concluded that most people who win malpractice settlements are not victims of malpractice.

In order to cover what the lawyers take, the price tags of all consumer goods are a little higher. Lifesaving products are especially penalized by the "lawyer tax." A manufacturer who produces pacemakers says lawsuits add thousands of dollars to the cost of every pacemaker. Lawsuits punish hundreds, if not thousands, of innocent people.

Critics of lawsuit abuse tend to focus only on the *cost* of litigation. The cost *is* nasty. But the higher cost is just the start of the nasty side effects. What's worse is that fear of lawsuits now deprives us of things that make our lives better.

> **MYTH:** "Defective-product" lawsuits make products safer.
>
> **TRUTH:** Product lawsuits deprive us of safer products.

Sure, fear of the "invisible fist" makes manufacturers more careful. Some lives have been saved because the litigation threat got companies to make their products safer. That's the "seen" benefit.

But that benefit comes with a bigger unseen cost: The fear that stops the bad things, stops good things too. Fear suffocates the innovation that, over the past century, has helped extend our life spans by almost thirty years. Every day, we lose good things.

In 1987, Monsanto developed a substitute for asbestos—a new fire-resistant form of insulation that might save thousands of lives. But Monsanto decided not to sell it for fear of lawsuit liability. Richard F. Mahoney, the CEO at the time, said, "There may well have been a safe, effective asbestos replacement on the market, and now there isn't."

Why do we have to worry about shortages of flu vaccine? Because only four companies still make it. And why is that? Because when you vaccinate millions of people, some get sick and sue. Between 1980 and 1986, personal-injury lawyers demanded billions of dollars from vaccine manufacturers. Most didn't win, but it was enough to scare many American drug companies out of the business.

In 1986, Congress stepped in. To help curb the lawsuits that discouraged vaccine production, the government established a fund called the National Childhood Vaccine Injury Compensation Program. The fund would pay victims' families directly, so they wouldn't have to hire lawyers and suffer the delays of litigation. This reform was supposed to entice vaccine makers back into production, but drug companies were still leery, fearing that plaintiffs' lawyers would sue them anyway.

They were right to worry. Forty years ago, Eli Lilly developed a mercury-based preservative called Thimerosal that was used in many children's vaccines. Plaintiffs' lawyers jumped on scaremongers' claims that mercury causes autism in children. Although a government-issued review found no such link, more than 100 autism lawsuits have been filed against vaccine makers since the National Childhood Vaccine Injury Compensation Act passed. No wonder most drug manufacturers still steer clear of vaccine research.

Even when new vaccines are discovered, drug companies are sometimes afraid to sell them. The FDA has approved a vaccine against Lyme disease. Want some? Forget about it. No company wants to take the risk.

Fear of being sued reduced the number of American companies researching contraceptives from thirteen to two.

After scientifically groundless lawsuits against breast implant makers bankrupted Dow Corning, Japanese silicone makers stopped producing a pain-reducing silicone coating for hypodermic needles. A company director said, "We're sure our product is safe, but we don't want to risk a lawsuit."

Union Carbide has invented a small, portable kidney dialysis machine. It would make life much easier for people with kidney disease, but Union Carbide decided not to sell it. With legal parasites constantly circling, the risk of expensive lawsuits outweighs the possible profit.

Are you pregnant? Miserable with nausea because of morning sickness? Bendectin would probably cure it. For twenty-seven years, doctors prescribed the drug to over thirty-three million women because it was so good at stopping nausea and vomiting. But you can't buy Bendectin today. You can't buy it because lawyers kept suing Merrell Dow, which made it, claiming the drug caused birth defects.

Studies did not show that Bendectin caused birth defects, and Merrell Dow won most of the lawsuits. But after spending a hundred million dollars in legal fees and awards, the company gave up selling the drug. Bendectin has never been effectively replaced, and morning sickness is now a major contributor to dehydration during pregnancy.

Dr. Paul Offit, Professor of Pediatrics at the University of Pennsylvania School of Medicine, says, "Within two years of discontinuing Bendectin, the incidence of hospitalization for dehydration during early pregnancy doubled; the incidence of birth defects was unchanged."

Those are just a few examples of what we've lost. We can't even begin to imagine the life-saving products that might have existed—if innovators didn't live in a climate of fear.

MYTH: Malpractice lawsuits protect patients.

TRUTH: Malpractice lawsuits hurt many patients.

In hospitals, lawyers have bred so much fear that patients are *less* safe. "Everybody walks in mortal fear of being sued," New York surgeon Edgar Mandeville told me. He's a professor of obstetrics who appears on lists of "New York's Best Doctors," yet he has been sued more than a dozen times. His medical specialty, obstetrics, is a high-risk legal target: 76 percent of American obstetricians have been sued. I understand that there are bad doctors, but are three-fourths of our obstetricians bad?

I sat down to talk about this with one of America's most successful trial lawyers, Dickie Scruggs.

> **DICKIE SCRUGGS** There are only a few of the physicians who are causing all of the problems.
> **STOSSEL** But then how is it fair that three-fourths of the obstetricians get sued?
> **DICKIE SCRUGGS** Well, that's why they have insurance.

People often give answers like that, as if they believe insurance makes everything free . . . maybe money grows on insurance trees.

But *you* pay for that insurance, through higher prices. You also pay for Dickie Scruggs's two airplanes, his yacht, and his platinum lifestyle. He's the king of the "class action" suit, banking millions from asbestos litigation and a billion dollars—that's right, a *billion* dollars—from the monster settlement against the tobacco companies. Big Tobacco settled that case for *$206 billion*— most of which is being paid for by Little Smokers in higher cigarette prices.

Scruggs is an admirer of another master litigator, former senator and vice-presidential candidate John Edwards. "It is an art form," Scruggs told me, "and John Edwards practiced it very successfully." Edwards sure did. And he had a major impact on Dr. Mandeville's field, obstetrics.

Edwards made between forty and eighty million dollars (he won't say how much), mainly by suing doctors and hospitals. He earned some of his biggest fees suing on behalf of children born with cerebral palsy. Edwards said that the CP was caused by a lack of oxygen getting to the baby's brain during delivery. Edwards argued passionately that if the doctor had only done a cesarean section, the child's cerebral palsy would have been prevented.

Edwards has some clever courtroom tactics. He once won a record verdict after impersonating the injured infant in the womb. "Right now, I feel her," he told the jury. "I feel her presence. She's inside me, and she's talking to you, [and she's saying] 'I'm having problems, I need out!'" The jury responded by awarding 6.5 million dollars.

One thing doctors learned from the antics of Edwards and other lawyers was to do more cesareans. The incidence of C-sections has more than quadrupled—from 6 percent of all births in 1970, to 28 percent in 2003. C-sections are more common today for many reasons, but fear of a cerebral palsy lawsuit has had a big impact. You would think, if Edwards's argument were correct, that this would have eliminated nearly every case of cerebral palsy. But that's not the case. Dr. Mandeville, who usually wields a scalpel, helped me with the shovel this time:

> **DR. EDGAR MANDEVILLE**   There has not been one small decrease in the cerebral palsy rate across the board!
>
> **STOSSEL**   You would think it would've gone down after doing all these . . .
>
> **DR. EDGAR MANDEVILLE**   It would seem, wouldn't it, sir? It would seem.

Wary of John Edwards and his colleagues, doctors still are quick to do C-sections. "Better safe . . . than sorry," one told me.

> **STOSSEL**   And that means more pain for the woman?
>
> **DR. EDGAR MANDEVILLE**   The pain is clearly worse, significantly worse.
>
> **STOSSEL**   But natural childbirth is painful.
>
> **DR. EDGAR MANDEVILLE**   But nowhere near as painful as a scar this long on your belly. And a cesarean section has a three- to five-fold risk of death, from things like hemorrhage, infections, pulmonary embolism, any number of other things.

I don't mean to be a scaremonger—C-sections are relatively safe, but they are major surgery. Many more women today endure unnecessary pain and an increased risk of death during childbirth because lawyers like John Edwards have frightened doctors into doing C-sections.

The irony is that scientists now say cerebral palsy is seldom caused by anything a doctor does in the delivery room. Is Edwards giving his millions back? No.

We are just beginning to learn about the more subtle unhappy side effects of malpractice lawsuits. Secrecy is another. Remember Charles Cullen, aka the "killer nurse"? He was fired from one hospital after another, but the hospitals didn't tell the next hospital: "Don't hire him! We think he might have killed patients." Fear of a lawsuit silenced them. The chief medical officer at Somerset Medical Center in Somerville, New Jersey, where Mr. Cullen last worked (and may have killed twelve to fifteen patients) said, "If anything good comes from this, it would be to reform the system where we're prevented from telling one another what we know out of fear, quite frankly, of being sued."

Fear of lawsuits also means doctors are more likely to conceal mistakes. A Department of Health and Human Services study concluded that "Hospitals, doctors, and nurses are reluctant to report problems and participate in joint efforts to improve care because they fear being dragged into lawsuits, even if they did nothing wrong." As a result, "As many as 95 percent of adverse events are believed to go unreported."

It's a lose-lose situation: We patients lose because doctors cover up mistakes. And lawyers walk away with our wallets.

MYTH: The threat of lawsuits makes the world a safer place.

TRUTH: Lawsuits take away our choices.

Lawsuits don't just decrease our safety, they also take the fun out of life.

Get this: Atlanta Braves outfielders have been told, "Don't toss balls to fans anymore. It's just too lawsuit-risky."

Camps cut back on horseback riding. Schools drop gymnastics programs. They may be fun activities, but God forbid someone gets hurt.

Do your children want to learn diving? Good luck finding a pool with a diving board. Pool managers have removed them because they're scared of lawsuits.

Remember the days of swimming in *nature's* water holes? Forget about those days. Increasingly, people who head over to the old swimming hole are met with signs that say Keep Out.

Those signs went up in High Falls, New York, at a swimming hole on Robert Every's property. His property had been enjoyed by generations of townspeople, and that was fine with Every. But then his lawyers told him that if someone got hurt, he might be sued. Up went the fence and the Keep Out signs. "The reason I'm afraid of being sued," Every said, "is because they can take everything I own."

He's right. Litigation in America is so expensive that one lawsuit can take everything you own—even if you win.

Do the Keep Out signs make us safer? Actually, not necessarily—because they encourage people to take even bigger risks. Several summers ago, a twenty-one-year-old man who was unable to get to Robert Every's swimming hole by the main entrance because of the locked gate and Keep Out sign, went to a more dangerous part of the swimming hole to gain access. He drowned.

And what does closing off swimming holes mean for kids? Fewer learning experiences. Children learn by testing their limits. Some kids fall and get hurt swimming or climbing trees. But are we a happier or safer society now that kids aren't even given the chance to try?

> **MYTH:** Lawsuits protect children.
>
> **TRUTH:** Lawsuits make the world a colder place.

There's a profound change taking place in schools that you may not be aware of, but the impact on your child could be dramatic. Teaching used to be a hands-on profession, where a hug or a pat on the back is given as encouragement. But today, most teachers keep their distance, with good reason.

Albert Thompson, a substitute teacher in Chicago, was told to teach a fourth-grade class. He told me, "I spent one day with this particular class—six hours that changed my whole life."

Thompson had volunteered to work in troubled neighborhoods, where he thought he could help kids who most needed it. To maintain order in those classrooms, he insisted on rigid discipline. Some kids resented that. Thompson wasn't concerned about their resistance until he woke up one day and was horrified to find himself being talked about on television.

"Nine girls and one boy allege a substitute teacher fondled them here on Friday," said the newscaster. "Counselors are talking with any students traumatized by the incident."

One girl said Thompson touched her breasts. A boy said Thompson felt his penis while standing in front of the class. Ten children said he'd molested them. Thompson told me, "That's a conspiracy," but who would take the word of a substitute teacher over so many children's accusations?

Fortunately for Thompson, good police work revealed that it was all a lie. One girl, angry about being disciplined, had paid ten classmates a dollar each to make up a story about Thompson molesting them. Charges were dropped.

Thompson quit teaching and went to work at a health food store. He's too nervous, he says, to go back into the classroom. Some teachers told us that Thompson was lucky, because the charges were dropped fairly quickly. Other innocent teachers have had their lives destroyed.

I interviewed a group of teachers who, between them, had more than a hundred years of teaching experience. Sandy Linkimer said she hears even fourth and fifth graders using phrases like "child molestation" and "lawsuit" to get even with teachers they don't like. "They know that word. They know it's a weapon, you know."

It's changed the way teachers teach. When they were trained, they were told, "Kids need physical affection." But now, if a child starts to touch them, they pull away.

SHARON CLEGHORN You cringe and grin and bear it and hope, "Please get away from me."

STOSSEL Isn't it a terrible thing for the child?

SHARON CLEGHORN Oh, the child probably feels she's rejected.

RICHARD CLEGHORN It's robbing the child.

CHRIS WICHSER You may be pushing them away from even learning because they shut down and they don't want to be bothered.

STOSSEL When you started teaching, did you think twice about hugging a child?

CHRIS WICHSER Not really. I would encourage them maybe to sit on my lap. You know, "Would you like to sit on my lap today and help me read the story?" Today I would never do that.

STOSSEL So she comes and she wants to sit on your lap. You—

CHRIS WICHSER I would say, "Well, you know what? You can sit right here next to me, and that'll be just fine." Maybe if the parents are looking in the window—"What's my daughter doing, sitting on her lap?"

STOSSEL Would you drive a child home?

JOAN GRAY Never.

The former president of the country's biggest teachers' union, Keith Geiger, told me he instructs his teachers to keep their distance: "We are telling teachers, in the overall, 'Teach, but don't touch.'"

To get the message out, teachers' unions get lawyers to lecture teachers on how to protect themselves. We videotaped lawyer Michael Rothchild telling a group of teachers: "Don't invite them home. Under any circumstances, no matter how much you want, don't invite them home. Suicide. Don't do it!"

The bathroom is a particular problem for kindergarten teachers. Kids sometimes need help cleaning up.

> **CHRIS WICHSER** The toilet paper roll needs to be changed. I would have never thought twice about that. I always have a couple of extra rolls, 'cause it happens—go in, change the toilet paper, come out. Not now. Now, I call the nurse, and she will go in and wipe them, and I stand by the door. And then she will immediately go and call the parents and say, "This is what I just did."
>
> **STOSSEL** Isn't this nuts?
>
> **CHRIS WICHSER** We have been told that this is the way that you need to protect yourself. A child on your lap has been called "institutional abuse." We're losing something—some kind of interaction between the children, and I feel bad for them.

Me too. It's not just teachers who are backing away. Doctors, Scout masters, and camp counselors are turning off their affection because they fear a lawsuit. In the name of protecting kids, lawsuits make the world colder for them.

MYTH: Lawsuits increase safety by getting companies to post warning labels.

TRUTH: Lawsuits decrease safety by creating meaningless warnings.

Lawyers make millions by telling juries, "The accident wouldn't have happened if my client had been properly warned!" Cringing companies respond by putting warnings on *everything*.

A hair dryer comes with the instruction, "Never use while sleeping"; birthday candles warn, "Do not use the wax as earplugs"; a power drill label says, "not intended for use as a dental drill."

My recent favorite is a big fishing lure with a warning label that reads: "Harmful if swallowed."

Karen Eppinger added the warning to her fishing lures. Her family had been using lead to make Dardevle lures for almost a century in Dearborn, Michigan, doing quite well without posting warning labels at all. Then, politicians in California decided to require businesses to provide a "clear and reasonable" warning before exposing anyone to any one of 700 chemicals, including lead. The law is one more potential gold mine for plaintiffs' lawyers, so fear of it had the usual unintended effects.

"We had to very quickly have labels printed up," Karen told us, "because Wal-Mart was being sued. Cabela's and Bass Pro were being threatened with lawsuits because the bass lures going into California did not have a warning label to not eat them."

Actual size

As you can see, I doubt that you could get one of these things down your throat. But even if you could, Karen's lures contain only a tiny trace of lead, so you'd have to swallow lots of them to get enough lead to hurt you. But that didn't matter. Karen's lawyers had her in a panic, and she had to re-label and re-box her lures. "It cost us somewhere between $10,000 and $15,000," she said.

It's a reason products cost more.

> **MYTH:** Fast food makes you fat.
>
> **TRUTH:** You make yourself fat.

I like fast food. It tastes good, it's cheap, and it's . . . fast. That's why McDonald's, Burger King, Wendy's, Kentucky Fried Chicken, and Taco Bell are so popular. They serve nearly 100 million people every day.

Of course, eating fast food too often can make you fat. People know that.

But some lawyers say some people don't know, so they're suing. George Washington University professor John Banzhaf told me, "What we're trying to do is the same thing against the problem of obesity that we did so successfully against the problem of smoking."

He should know.

Banzhaf was in the forefront of lawsuits against cigarette manufacturers. "People used to say that those suits were frivolous," he noted. "Well, today we call those lawyers 'multimillionaires.'"

Unfortunately, we do. He and other busybodies may have bad ideas that most people reject, but because they are lawyers and lawyers get to use force, they almost always win—if not at first, then eventually. They just keep suing until they do; they lost 700 lawsuits before they started winning against the cigarette makers, and then they won big. As part of that settlement Big Tobacco has shelled out thirteen billion dollars in attorney fees alone—enough to buy the lawyers 80,000 Bentleys. The food business is even bigger, Banzhaf told me. "It's the next tobacco!"

> **STOSSEL** Don't *we* make ourselves fat? It isn't McDonald's fault if I go in there and have three milkshakes. It's my fault.
>
> **JOHN BANZHAF** Isn't the industry partially responsible if they misrepresent or fail to warn?
>
> **STOSSEL** You could go after Girl Scout cookies, potato chips, ice cream. There are lots of things that make us fat.
>
> **JOHN BANZHAF** There may be lots of things that make us fat. But a study suggests that the current epidemic of obesity was caused in large part by the fast food companies.

They always find some study. If they're lucky, it'll impress a jury. I think obesity is caused by people eating too much and not exercising enough. Maybe he'll sue sofa makers next: "Sofas encourage sloth!" Or maybe he'll sue *20/20* and me—for encouraging people to watch TV on Friday nights.

McDonald's at least is fighting these lawsuits, and so far it has held off Banzhaf and his ilk. But the legal fees are hidden in your Big Mac.

> **MYTH:** Antidiscrimination laws stop discrimination.
>
> **TRUTH:** Not even close.

I became a consumer reporter because I don't like bullies. I was bullied as a kid, and helpless to do anything about it. But as a reporter with a camera and an audience, I could expose the bullies. At first, as I've said, I thought businesses were the bullies. But then I realized that businesses depend on our voluntary cooperation, but lawyers get to use force. It's lawyers who are the bullies.

Even lawsuits that they call "public service" often look like shakedowns to me.

In 1990, Congress passed the Americans with Disabilities Act, the ADA for short, with the best of intentions: to eliminate barriers—physical or legal—for the disabled. The ADA also created a nasty, extortion-like business for lawyers like Anthony Brady of Camden, New Jersey.

Brady partnered with a disabled person and filed dozens of lawsuits against small businesses, charging them with failure to obey the ADA. He's not a law enforcement officer, but his bar association card is all he needs: An obscure provision of the ADA entitles private lawyers to file suit to enforce the law. Brady turned that legislative gift into a cash cow.

He sued a two-story strip club in Florida, on the grounds that it discriminated against people in wheelchairs because they couldn't get a lap dance upstairs. Discrimination! Emotional distress! screamed Brady's suit. The club must pay damages—and Anthony Brady's legal fees, of course.

The small businesses he sued told us that the lawsuits felt like someone coming after them with a bat. No matter how absurd the charge, they were forced to hire lawyers and their lawyers told them, "Settle for a smaller amount now or you'll have to pay me a fortune, and then feel more pain when you have to go to trial." Business owners didn't need a law dictionary to figure it out. "What a rip-off," one of them said. "What a rip-off!"

Scores of businesses have been sued by law firms like Brady's. One suit, filed by William Tucker and Lawrence McGuinness, complained that the Peter Pan Diner in Fort Lauderdale, Florida, wasn't up to code. Among other things, they said the diner's bathroom had a paper dispenser that was a *half inch* higher than the ADA requires.

The renovations were cheap compared to what the restaurant had to pay to settle with Tucker and McGuinness: $3,500. The lawyers should send some of that money to Washington to thank their shakedown partners in Congress.

> **MYTH:** Class action lawyers get justice for consumers.
>
> **TRUTH:** Class action lawyers get rich at the expense of consumers.

Congress may be kind to lawyers, but there's another branch of government even kinder to them: the judiciary. After all, while "only" 41 percent of congressmen are lawyers, virtually 100 percent of judges are. And in some jurisdictions, politics narrows the gap between black robes and pinstripes to a *very* thin line. One of those places is Madison County, Illinois.

Madison County has about 250 thousand souls spread out over a rural landscape. The tiny county seat of Edwardsville has a population of less than 25,000. Yet the courtrooms in Edwardsville are extraordinarily powerful magnets to law firms from New York to California.

Why? Because they have a history of being hospitable to that most lucrative of legal inventions: the class action suit.

A class action suit is a lawsuit brought on behalf of a class of plaintiffs—consumers, for instance. In theory, this is a good way to protect consumers. If a business rips you off for ten dollars, you can't justify suing; just meeting with a lawyer once would cost more than that. But if the lawyer can bundle thousands of those alleged rip-offs into one case, suddenly those rip-offs are worth pursuing. It's why the class action business boomed. Most of us have been a "plaintiff" in some of those cases.

The news arrives in the mail with an important-looking letter from a law firm you've never even heard of, let alone retained. At first glance, it looks like you've won a sweepstakes: You're entitled to "benefits won" by "your" lawyer. The reality is different.

One letter I got told me I had sued the Aiwa company and won a settlement. I have an Aiwa CD player, but I had no idea I'd sued them. The notice said some of the Aiwa players have an inability to read CDs, leading to "failure of audio output." Mine worked fine, but I was entitled to collect some money anyway because Aiwa had supposedly ripped people off.

When you read the letter from the lawyer, it's hard to figure out what you've won. My Aiwa settlement explained (in tedious and tiny print) that

I would get more or less money depending on whether my stereo broke, was repaired, had to be shipped, etc. Laborious reading told me I was entitled to ten dollars. To get that, I must get the model number of my CD player and then "provide the documents and information described in Part III of the accompanying claim form . . ." It's confusing enough that most "clients" don't bother to apply for their share. But the lawyers aren't confused at all—they took home $1,687,500 from the case. They're the *privileged* class!

Class action lawyers routinely get much more than any class member. In a settlement with General Mills over cereal that allegedly was exposed to a pesticide, lawyers got nearly two million dollars—consumers got coupons for free boxes of cereal. Settlements like that inspired *St. Louis Post Dispatch* columnist Bill McClellan to write an article calling class action lawyers worse than bank robbers. "Bank robbers don't rob the banks and then pretend they're doing it for us, they just rob it," he told me.

St. Louis class action lawyers sued *McClellan* for libel, demanding he pay them three million dollars. McClellan knew about class actions because St. Louis borders Madison County, Illinois.

Why is Madison County a nirvana for class action lawyers? "The parasite circus moves from place to place," law professor John Beisner told me. "They pick out certain counties where they believe they will get traction with their lawsuits."

Campaign contributions help the lawyers get traction. As I drove around Madison County, I was struck by all the signs promoting the election of this judge or that one—posted on law firm property. Ninety percent of judicial campaign donations in this area come from lawyers. It looked as if lawyers were getting their friends elected judge, and the judges then rewarded their supporters in court.

Madison County looks like one of the "magic jurisdictions" described by class action king Dickie Scruggs. In these jurisdictions, says Scruggs, "the trial lawyers have established relationships with the judges. . . . It's almost impossible to get a fair trial if you're a defendant in some of these places. . . . The cases are not won in the courtroom. They're won on the back roads long before the case goes to trial."

I wanted to ask Madison County judges about that, but they didn't want to talk to me. One former judge, though, did agree to defend the reputation of the local bench. He told me campaign contributions don't influence decisions, and said class action lawyers file so many cases in Madison County because judges there are "so efficient."

STOSSEL You're quicker here?

FORMER JUDGE Yes. And we've got some of the best trial lawyers in the country. We have plaintiffs' lawyers and judges in this area that have a lot of experience handling complex litigation. There's some good hardworking guys.

STOSSEL But harder working and smarter than all of America?

FORMER JUDGE Our lawyers are as good as they get.

This former judge had presided over a class action suit filed against a big phone company. Lawyers claimed the company charged a fee for a warranty on phone lines without first making sure people wanted it. The company said it had done nothing wrong, and just settled to avoid expensive litigation. Companies usually settle. Pay the lawyers to go away.

Columnist McClellan told me, "I mean, it's sort of like the mob, you know. They'll break your window unless you give them the money. So you think, hey, it's easier just to give them the money than to have them break the window."

The former judge approved the settlement, but the customers didn't get much out of it. The settlement gave consumers awards like fifteen-dollar phone cards, but gave the lawyers a whopping sixteen million dollars.

I told the judge that these class-action settlements sounded like extortion. He smiled and said, "You could say that about any settlement then, couldn't you?"

I could.

Madison County needs a shovel.

MYTH: Public interest lawyers serve the public interest.

TRUTH: Public interest lawyers force you to pay for their political visions.

In Chicago, "public interest" lawyers filed a class action suit on behalf of panhandlers. It was a case of lawyers asking taxpayers, "Brother, can you spare a few hundred thousand?" I take that back. Lawyers don't ask—they demand.

Chicago's police were arresting people for panhandling. Lawyer Mark Weinberg sued, saying that the law violated beggars' free speech rights, and claimed that he represented Chicago's beggars.

Weinberg had a point about the free speech. Asking for money is a form of free speech. We could respectfully argue about the line between panhandling and aggressive panhandling, or free speech and threatening speech.

In the 1990s in my hometown, some panhandlers asked for money while washing windshields, whether you wanted it washed or not. Mayor Rudy Giuliani had police arrest the beggars. I gave him a hard time about that.

STOSSEL Isn't it benign . . . a needy person asking for help?

RUDY GIULIANI Of course it is. However, when the needy person might . . . put a knife in you, then you got to sort of take a different look at it.

Giuliani's actions were popular in New York. And now I have to say he was right, I was wrong. The city became safer because Giuliani's crackdown set a different tone—it made it clear that a higher level of civility was expected in the public square.

But when Mark Weinberg won his lawsuit, people in Chicago were soon hassled by beggars. We videotaped them following people. One cursed people who didn't give her money. That didn't seem to bother "their" lawyer.

STOSSEL So I can go to Chicago and bother people on the street?

MARK WEINBERG Well, you can exercise your first amendment rights and ask somebody for a quarter, yeah.

STOSSEL Can I ask them again if they say no?

MARK WEINBERG Yeah, you could ask them again.

STOSSEL I can ask repeatedly?

MARK WEINBERG You can ask repeatedly in the same way that a politician can ask you to vote for him repeatedly, when he's trying to shake your hand.

STOSSEL Who asked you to decide for all of Chicago?

MARK WEINBERG Well, I know panhandlers and they agreed with me that something should be done.

So this one lawyer, who "knows" panhandlers, gets to set panhandling policy for the entire city. It's bad enough that the "public interest" lawyers have that power, but what's worse is that they collect your tax money when they exercise it. As part of the settlement, Weinberg's "clients," the beggars, got (if someone could find them) fifty dollars each, or four hundred dollars if they could prove they'd been arrested. Weinberg and his partner got $375,000.

MARK WEINBERG John, this is not a case of greedy lawyers getting paid astronomical sums.

STOSSEL Sounds like one to me! $375,000 for you?

MARK WEINBERG Yeah, I actually think my lawsuit is a really great example of the system working.

"The system working" or *"working the system"*? Get the shovel.

After I did a "Give Me a Break" segment about this on *20/20,* Chicago's city council did pass a law that allows prosecution of "aggressive" panhandling. Chicago pedestrians can relax a little. However, they'll have less to relax *with,* since they are now hundreds of thousands of dollars poorer.

Think about that next time a lawyer tells you he's doing "public interest law."

MYTH: Lawyers sue to right injustice.

TRUTH: Lawyers sue because they can.

Some successful lawyers get so comfortable with their ability to bully that they overreach.

If there were an award for chutzpah—for a lawyer with brass business cards—a clear contender would be Howard Siegel of New York City.

He's the lawyer for a famous person, and so he wrote a letter, on very swanky stationery from his swanky law firm on Park Avenue, to the *Atlanta Journal-Constitution.* The letter said, "Your publication employs the writing services of an individual using the name Bill Wyman; we believe this to be a seriously misleading and, arguably, an intentional unauthorized exploitation of our client's name."

The newspaper was guilty as charged: It employed a reporter named Bill Wyman, whose byline regularly appeared in the paper. The lawyer's client was also Bill Wyman—the comatose-looking bass player for the Rolling Stones. The Bill Wyman I talked to was more amused than angry.

STOSSEL What do they want you to do?

BILL WYMAN They want me to stop using my own name, or they've said that I could use it if I ran a prominent disclaimer.

STOSSEL It's your real name?

BILL WYMAN Absolutely.

STOSSEL But [quoting from the lawyer's letter] "you're not entitled to utilize in a way that's misleading or likely to cause confusion to the public."

BILL WYMAN Do I think that any sane person thinks that Bill Wyman of the Rolling Stones is gonna be writing for the *Atlanta Journal-Constitution*?

Wyman of the *Atlanta Journal-Constitution* has been Bill Wyman longer than the rock star Bill Wyman. The musician was born William Perks; he changed his name to Wyman three years after Atlanta's Bill Wyman was born. The reporter had the name first!

But reasonableness is rarely the standard when lawyers can make money bullying others.

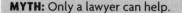

MYTH: Only a lawyer can help.

TRUTH: Only a lawyer is allowed to help.

Lawyers are good at working the system because they generally write the rules. One of their rules says: "No one may compete with us, especially if they work cheap."

Okay, no law puts it that way, but that's a good description of the "unauthorized practice of law" rule. UPL is a self-important rule that says: "Only lawyers can give legal advice." Another way to put it is that lawyer bullies don't like others on their playgrounds, so they use their special powers to keep them out.

Jerome Papania of Lake Charles, Louisiana, had the nerve to challenge them.

JEROME PAPANIA Seven deputies came in, put me under arrest.

STOSSEL Seven deputies?

JEROME PAPANIA Seven of them booked me, fingerprinted me. They handcuffed me as I got to the jail.

Jerome's offense was helping some nursing home residents and some of his neighbors fill out legal forms for wills and bankruptcy. The real offense to the legal profession was the "fees" he charged for his help: fifty dollars for a will, ninety dollars for a bankruptcy. What an insult to such a noble calling (what a threat to its expensive tastes)!

Have you priced a lawyer lately? They're easy to find; they're multiplying much faster than the general population. Still, more lawyers doesn't mean *cheaper* lawyers. In principle, Americans have equal access to the legal system. In reality, most of the time, only the rich do.

Jerome told me there was a big demand for his services: "It wasn't just a matter of liking it—people *needed* it."

Jerome's neighbor Lurline Marcantel wanted to draw up a will, but couldn't afford to do it the Bar Association way: "It costs too much. Why should I pay $250 for a man to help me know where to put that little bit that I'm leaving to my children?"

A long illness and big hospital bills left Sharon Cormier's family hounded by creditors. "They would call and get very ugly and demanding on the phone," Sharon told me. "They were going to garnish my husband's wages, and then we would have been nowhere."

The only way out was to file bankruptcy. But the lawyers wanted five hundred dollars: "If we had five hundred to pay an attorney to handle a bankruptcy," Sharon said, "we would have the money to pay for our bills and our debts that we owe!"

Jerome helped her, and the local prosecutor, Richard P. Ieyoub, didn't like it at all. He charged Jerome with "unlicensed practice of law," an offense that in Louisiana carried a maximum sentence of two years in jail. I was tempted to use a shovel, but instead I took a camera crew to see Ieyoub, who said it was important to prosecute Jerome because he might not give good advice. Of course, some lawyers don't give good advice either.

> **STOSSEL** Why not let the customer choose? His customers knew he wasn't a lawyer.
>
> **RICHARD IEYOUB** But the customers may not know the effect of having bad legal advice.
>
> **STOSSEL** You lawyers are just trying to keep everything under your control.
>
> **RICHARD IEYOUB** That's absolutely false. I think lawyers in general get a bum rap. We are a very fine profession. I'm telling you that there are lawyers in this area that will do things for poor people, first of all, free of charge and certainly at approximately the same price that Mr. Papania was doing.

STOSSEL Sorry, but we called around and we couldn't find that.

RICHARD IEYOUB Well, I can name you a lawyer that does it. I would not like to say his name over the air.

But when the camera was off, he still wouldn't give me names. He said he "couldn't remember, but it would be easy" for us to find those lawyers. So we called more than a dozen, trying to find anyone who would help the poor the way Jerome did. We called and called, but no one would help them at Jerome's prices, let alone for free.

During the interview the prosecutor also said that he would let me see complaints his office had received about Jerome. But after the camera stopped, he wouldn't let us see them. He gave us only one name, Mary Sallier, saying she was a complainant. When we sought Mary out, she told an entirely different story about her experiences with Jerome. "I felt he knew what he was doing," she said. "He drew the papers up for me. It was a simple uncontested divorce."

The prosecutor told us that Jerome was a threat to the public because he was giving advice in a "technical field." But helping people fill out forms for wills, bankruptcy, or mutually consensual divorces is not so "technical" that only the holy mandarins of the legal bar should be allowed to do it.

Normally, when we buy things, we have a lot of choice. You can buy a Lexus, but you can also buy a Chevy, ride a bicycle, or take the bus. When you buy law, however, the lawyers insist you must buy only the Lexus or maybe a Mercedes. You have no choice.

When the Constitution was adopted, there was nothing that said a lawyer had to help you with the paperwork. It wasn't until about a hundred years ago that lawyers got UPL statutes passed—under the guise that they were protecting the public. As Jerome told me, "It's like a basketball game where the lawyers own the court, they own the basketball, they're the referees, and only they get to play."

Jerome was convicted, fined five hundred dollars, and put on probation for six months. The government was never able to collect the fine: Sadly, Jerome had to declare himself indigent because the sheriff's deputies had confiscated his computers and files he needed for his bookkeeping practice. They destroyed his livelihood.

In Arizona two years ago, the nonprofit Institute for Justice beat back an attempt by the state's Bar Association to make it illegal for consumers to hire nonlawyers to "prepare any document in any medium intended to affect or secure legal rights for a specific person or entity."

The proposed rule would have shut down two hundred independent paralegals and document preparers who were offering Arizonans low-cost alternatives to high-priced attorneys. The Bar Association claimed it had received four hundred consumer complaints against non-lawyers practicing law in Arizona, but when the Institute for Justice tracked down the "complaints," most turned out to be bogus. A large number of them were actually either complaints *against* lawyers, or complaints filed *by* lawyers, rather than consumers. The Arizona State Supreme Court took a shovel to the Bar Association's proposal.

But in every state besides Arizona, lawyers still rule the roost.

In fact, in many states, laws require a lawyer to be present whenever a real estate deal is closed. Texas lawyers tried to stop a publisher from selling *books* that help people save money by telling them how to write their own wills.

In Delaware, a woman named Marilyn Arons helped parents argue for their disabled kids' educational rights before the state Board of Education. Since most of these parents couldn't afford a lawyer, Arons, whose own child was handicapped, helped them for free. Lawyers complained to the Delaware Supreme Court, and Marilyn had to stop helping parents out. Too bad. I guess the lawyers needed more protection than the handicapped children.

If we let the lawyers make the rules, they won't stop until they've taken all our time, our freedom, and our money.

CHAPTER EIGHT

EXPERTS FOR EVERYTHING

E
xperts are important to my work. We always seek them out when we prepare reports, and I am gratified by their willingness to give their time and share their knowledge. Ego plays a part because most want "face time" on TV, but it's not just about ego; their field of expertise is important to them, and they want to make sure we "get it right."

But getting the *right expert* can be tough—there are plenty of phonies and pretenders out there. The crackpots are often the ones who make the most noise. In fact, I bet expertise correlates inversely with the amount of advertising an "expert" does, and the time he spends on TV. We've learned we have to look beyond the uniforms, publication credentials, clerical collars, and mahogany desks to figure out if someone knows what he is talking about.

Some of the pseudo-experts are so persuasive, so glib, that they make nonsense plausible.

> **MYTH:** Experts can cure homosexuality.
>
> **TRUTH:** Experts delude themselves.

The slogan "Just say no" usually refers to drugs, but today it might refer to homosexuality, because some "experts" say being gay is a choice, and anyone can just say no. Most of these "experts" are leaders of religious groups that run therapy programs that claim to help homosexuals get in touch with their inner, hetero, selves. The movement has proven powerfully attractive to thousands of men and women who want to be "normal." The therapists gave us videotaped testimonials from people who claim it worked:

> **MAN**   A decade ago I walked away from homosexuality through the power of Jesus Christ.
>
> **FIRST WOMAN**   I was in it for six years.
>
> **SECOND WOMAN**   Four for me. We both walked away from it.

I wanted to meet some of these people who "walked away from it" to ask my own questions. The biggest of these groups is called Exodus International. It named itself after the book in the Bible that details the Israelites' emancipation from slavery. Exodus says: "In the same way, people who have experienced change from homosexuality have shared similar stories of being set free from something that they felt enslaved them." When I asked Exodus for an interview, they said I should talk to successful gay-to-straight graduate Alan Chambers.

> **STOSSEL**   You were gay, but you're not now.
>
> **ALAN CHAMBERS**   I'm not gay anymore.
>
> **STOSSEL**   And this was something new that you learned?
>
> **ALAN CHAMBERS**   Yeah. It was like puberty at age twenty-five.

Chambers says he's been straight for fifteen years now and married for eight years. Today he's president of Exodus.

> **STOSSEL**   The men who used to turn you on no longer do?
>
> **ALAN CHAMBERS**   No, they don't.
>
> **STOSSEL**   And women do turn you on.
>
> **ALAN CHAMBERS**   My wife turns me on.
>
> **STOSSEL**   You can just choose to deny feelings?
>
> **ALAN CHAMBERS**   Yes.

Exodus and most similar programs say that God changes people through prayer—God with the help of group therapy and aversion therapy. One program teaches: "If you have homosexual thoughts, inhale ammonia." Some programs tell gay men, "Take up sports," and lesbian women, "Wear makeup."

I'm skeptical. Saying gay people can choose to be straight implies that they choose to be gay. I don't believe anyone *chooses* to be gay. It's hard to be gay. Kids know parents will be upset, and siblings and schoolmates may make fun of them, if not beat them up. To suggest that gays could become straight, if they just *try,* seems absurd. Many spent years trying very hard not to be gay, before accepting it. Gays might learn to repress homosexual feelings, but to actually become straight? I don't think so.

But Exodus had stunning "success stories" like their poster boy John Paulk, who proclaimed on an Exodus video, "I have been out of homosexuality for fourteen years. I've been married for eight years."

Paulk, who was the chairman of Exodus when he made that video, was often interviewed about his success. He and his former-lesbian wife became a *Newsweek* cover story. His transformation was featured on *Oprah* and *60 Minutes.* But then some gay activists spotted Paulk having a drink in a Washington, D.C., gay bar. When they pulled out a camera, he ran away.

He later said he didn't know it was a gay bar; he just wanted to use the bathroom. Still later, he admitted the use-the-bathroom story was a lie, but he said he didn't go there for sex. He just wanted to see "what the scene was like."

When I pressed Exodus to back up its claim that "thousands have successfully changed," they said they kept no records. "It's impossible to keep track," they told us. That's odd. If I had "changed thousands," I'd want to document that.

We, however, had little trouble finding people who tried to change, but failed. Some made earnest and heartbreaking efforts, without success. "I wanted my family's acceptance, bottom line," one woman told us. She is a member of the largest gay and lesbian church congregation in the country, the Cathedral of Hope in Dallas (average attendance: 1,700). We watched one Sunday morning as its dean, Reverend Michael Piazza, looked out over a packed church and asked, "How many of you tried some way in your life not to be gay?"

Most of the people in that church raised their hands. Later, some told me how they had tried Exodus and other programs in hopes of escaping "what they had become." Homosexuality violated their religious beliefs, and "experts" told them they could not really be gay.

FIRST MAN You know, "God wouldn't create somebody gay," you know? "How horrible," you know?

SECOND MAN "God doesn't make mistakes."

FIRST WOMAN Well, that it was a given, because it—it was a sin. I mean, that—that's the premise.

JOHN STOSSEL Nobody has to be gay?

SECOND WOMAN Right—right.

THIRD MAN You finish the program and you'll be heterosexual and, you know, you'll—you'll live the happy, fulfilled life that, you know, everybody else lives.

STOSSEL And did it help?

FIRST WOMAN No. It just doesn't work.

STOSSEL For all of you, it just failed?

FIRST WOMAN Yes.

THIRD MAN Miserably.

STOSSEL Is it possible you just didn't try hard enough? Pray hard enough? Didn't try hard enough to become straight?

SECOND MAN Well, you can pray for brown eyes. It doesn't mean you're going to wake up in the morning with brown eyes . . .

FOURTH MAN The leader of my particular group at one point changed his mind and tried to seduce me.

For some, trying to change their sexual orientation was so painful that they wanted to end their lives.

STOSSEL This drove many of you to consider suicide?

FIRST MAN Yes.

SECOND MAN Yes.

FIRST WOMAN Yeah.

STOSSEL Almost all of you are nodding your heads.

FIRST WOMAN I couldn't bear to disappoint my family anymore.

THIRD MAN It's like, "What's wrong with me? Why isn't this stopping? Why am I so bad?" And the guilt just keeps building and building.

FOURTH MAN Two or three times a week you're reminded that you're defective, that something's wrong with you, that there's something about you that God hates. And you can't go through ten years of that unscathed.

Reverend Piazza summed it up, with his own, dignified version of *Get Out the Shovel*: "You know, we have thousands of ex-gays," he told us. "They're teaching them repression; psychological and emotional repression. Now whoever thinks that is healthy needs to go back to school."

> ⚑ **MYTH:** The "experts" on TV know which way stocks will move.
>
> ⚒ **TRUTH:** Give that expert a banana.

Putting money into the stock market has, historically, been a good move. Stocks go up and down, but eventually, most go up. So if you invest and hold on, odds are you'll do quite well. Most experts say that, and I have no quarrel with them on that score. As my former Princeton professor, economist Burton Malkiel, told me, "The stock market is like a gambling casino with the odds in your favor. Over the long pull, it beats inflation, and beats it by a great deal."

So if the stock market is a good investment, it's logical to think that an *excellent* investment could be had by following the advice of the "experts." On CNBC and other financial advice shows, they sound so confident:

- "The cyclicals, the autos—forget them. They won't perform and therefore, any rallies, I'd sell them if I still had them."

- "It's over for IBM."

- "I think Pfizer has room to increase 30 percent within six months."

These are men and women who make their living studying stocks, so one might think following these experts' advice would help your investments go up even more. That's where I *do* quarrel.

I'm not alone. "Most of the guys on TV—they're not that good," says Jim Cramer. He should know: He's on TV himself (CNBC) and runs a website, thestreet.com. Cramer is not known for holding his tongue under any circumstances, but he says that at least he has no hidden motives. Many other TV talking heads work for firms that do business with the companies traded on the exchange. They have an incentive to promote those companies. "I think, that if you knew their firms were getting paid from the company," Cramer told me, "it would help you form a better or a wiser judgment."

> **JIM CRAMER** A guy comes on TV. Thought process at home: "There's a person who has looked at the whole industry and is making judgments about what are the best stocks." Wrong! Wrong! The worst are guys who say that they love a stock and they're *selling* the stock. That happens all the time.

STOSSEL I mean, that's just lying to people. That's just suckering them.

JIM CRAMER Look, it—it's part of the process.

Part of the process: An "expert" goes on TV to hype a stock because he wants to dump the stock on you. Most conflicts are less venal. You could call it human nature—people recommend people and companies they know. Or, slightly more venal: companies with whom they're doing business.

One spring, Goldman Sachs created a list of e-commerce companies most likely to survive. Seven of the eight top candidates were—surprise!—clients of Goldman Sachs. You could have learned about those corporate relationships in the research reports, but it's always in the fine print at the end. Who reads that?

Most stock predictors are making honest guesses, not touting their friends or their businesses, but the "experts" don't have to have conflicts to lose you money.

"I ended up losing just over forty thousand dollars," David Talevi told us. That was a year's salary for Talevi, who managed a trailer park in Wells, Maine. He lost it buying stocks they recommended on TV. "You just took their word for granted," he said. "I figured, you know, 'This thing is going to take off.'" This thing crashed instead, and Talevi got burned.

How could the TV experts be so wrong? They are well-educated people who call and visit individual companies, and study the balance sheets, new products, and marketing techniques. You'd think this would give them an advantage. But it doesn't, says Princeton's Professor Malkiel, because what they learn is information all the analysts have. Malkiel wrote a book about the process called *A Random Walk Down Wall Street*. He studied stock movements of the past, and concluded that the advice produced by the in-house experts has little value. "Most of it is just absolute nonsense," he told me, "and most of it is really designed to get people to trade more than they should."

The brokerage firms want you to trade more, because they charge a commission on every trade. But despite floors of skyscrapers filled with people analyzing stocks, year after year the trading advice that comes out of most of the big brokerage firms is no better at selecting winners than throwing darts at the stock table, or having a monkey throw darts. In fact, the advice is usually worse! I know this is hard to believe, but people who chart the brokerage firms' recommendations say it's true.

"Let's look at the numbers," as they say on the financial shows: Over the fifteen years ending October 31, 2005 (the most recent figures at the time of this writing), only 5.72 percent of actively managed mutual funds had beaten the 500 stocks that make up the Standard & Poor's Index. In other words, 94 percent did worse. Over that fifteen-year period, you had a 94 percent better chance of making money if you ignored the advice from those well-paid professional stock-pickers.

STOSSEL So all these experts are fooling themselves?

PROFESSOR MALKIEL It's like giving up a belief in Santa Claus. Even though you know Santa Claus doesn't exist, you kind of cling to that belief. Now, I'm not saying that this is a scam. They genuinely believe they can do it. The evidence is, however, that they can't.

None of the big firms would talk to me about their failure to outperform dart-throwing monkeys, so I interviewed successful money manager Robert Stovall. He used to run research departments at EF Hutton and Dean Witter Reynolds, and he defended the experts . . . sort of.

ROBERT STOVALL One-third of the money managers tend to beat the market every year.

STOSSEL Two-thirds do worse!

ROBERT STOVALL Two-thirds do worse, but it's different ones each time.

STOSSEL Why do these brokerage firms have these big research departments if they don't make money?

ROBERT STOVALL Everybody has a boss. Professionals won't buy Coca-Cola or some other stock unless they have reports in the file produced by well-known analysts so if something goes wrong with the stock they buy, they can show their boss, "Hey, I've got a big file on this stock. All these analysts said it was a good one. Something went wrong." That's known as prudence.

STOSSEL So, even if the research is lousy, it protects them?

ROBERT STOVALL That's right.

It's why I invest in index funds. Lower fees. No foolish trading.

Next time you hear the experts on TV, smugly making predictions, get the shovel. Better yet, get a monkey with a shovel.

MYTH: This chiropractor can cure your child's asthma.

TRUTH: Take your child and run.

Chiropractors claim to know how to treat back pain. It's hard to know if they really can, since back pain often comes and goes on its own. Some medical doctors say chiropractors don't know what they're doing, but some MDs don't know what they're doing, so who can judge?

What's unsettling is that many chiropractors claim that they can help patients with problems that seem to have nothing to do with the back. And some have expanded their practices to address children's illnesses, like colds, ear infections, asthma, bed-wetting, and more.

Companies offer to teach chiropractors how to "build their practice." One company told chiropractors to offer free steak dinners to parents who would listen to their pitch. The children got coloring books showing the joys of chiropractic adjustment.

Chiropractors claim their treatments are better because they are "natural." This appeals to many parents—unthreatening treatments—no pills, no shots, no medication, no surgery.

Chiropractors say spinal adjustment gets rid of what they call "subluxations"—bones out of alignment that press on nerves. They claim that allows "messages to flow freely from the brain," and lets the body heal itself.

"It's all nonsense and scare tactics," Dr. Murray Katz of Quebec told me. He was the director of one of North America's biggest pediatric medical centers, and he'd become concerned about what chiropractic "experts" were promising. Katz is just one of many skeptical medical doctors, but Katz is unusual in that he's taken the time to really study what chiropractors do. He put in the time to visit chiropractic colleges, and sit in on courses. He joined the International Chiropractic Pediatric Association. He came away a nonbeliever.

"Patients don't get better," he told me. "People *believe* they're getting better. We know that ear infections can go away in two days. We know an asthma attack can stop acutely. We know that bed-wetting—eventually people outgrow it."

If the child outgrows it after seeing the chiropractor, the parents credit the chiropractor. Since chiropractors usually have kids come in for repeat treatments, there's a good chance that chiropractic will get credit for curing a self-limiting illness. I interviewed parents—some in the office of Dr. Larry Webster of Atlanta—who were convinced that their chiropractor was an expert in "natural" healing. He and other chiropractors we watched had a wonderful bedside manner. Dr. Webster played with the kids and took lots of time to explain things. Parents loved that, and for many, the chiropractor was the only doctor they saw.

STOSSEL Do you go to a pediatrician too?

MOTHER I don't go to a pediatrician.

STOSSEL Your son then gets no vaccinations?

MOTHER Not at all.

That's a scary thought. If more parents give their kids "natural," vaccine-free treatments, we are more likely to suffer outbreaks of whooping cough, measles, and other diseases vaccines have suppressed.

Dr. Webster claimed he had cured deafness in kids.

DR. WEBSTER Probably my most dramatic has been the kid from São Paulo, Brazil. And now the child's hearing normally.

STOSSEL Can I talk to these families?

DR. WEBSTER Well, if you got the—São Paulo, Brazil, I don't know.

STOSSEL We can call Brazil.

DR. WEBSTER Sure, okay, and that's no problem.

When the camera was off, he said he couldn't find the number.

Many pediatric chiropractors were inspired by a couple who call themselves the "Baby Adjusters," Palmer and Jennifer Peet. They showed others how to promote their practice with things like free T-shirts, and how to make "adjustments" to a child's spine in a way that let their bodies "heal themselves," ultimately banishing ear infections, colds, and asthma.

They told me they were simply passing along what they had learned by helping thousands of children, but as you'll see, the conversation got uncomfortable when I tried to get specific.

DR. PALMER PEET They come in with a fever. We adjust them. The child goes to bed and they get up the next morning and it's as if there was never anything wrong with them. We've had case after case.

STOSSEL You say, "Chiropractic works and medical procedures usually fail."

DR. JENNIFER PEET In some cases that's true, and I don't think that you will get people to argue with that too much.

STOSSEL "Usually fail"?

DR. PALMER PEET From the histories of literally thousands of children that we've taken when we've checked them in our office, many of them have come to us as medical failures.

STOSSEL And you can help these children more than the conventional doctor could?

DR. JENNIFER PEET If they have a vertebral subluxation, I'm the only kind of doctor that can help them.

STOSSEL And how many people have subluxations?

DR. JENNIFER PEET About 95 percent of children have vertebral subluxations.

The Peets passed out literature that said: "Subluxations, if left undetected and uncorrected, are life threatening."

STOSSEL Someone might just drop dead if they're not treated?

DR. JENNIFER PEET That's correct.

DR. PALMER PEET That's correct.

STOSSEL [reading from their literature] "Now is the time to tell your patients that subluxations are slowly killing their children."

DR. JENNIFER PEET That's true.

DR. PALMER PEET That's true.

STOSSEL You're scaring people for money.

DR. JENNIFER PEET Oh, no.

"This is not a fight between doctors and chiropractors," Dr. Katz told me. "It's a fight between science and superstition. There are hundreds of millions of dollars being spent to treat fifteen or twenty million children a year for 'subluxations' which *none of them have*."

Which none of them have? The "experts" imagine them? Many medical doctors say subluxations don't even exist—that if you show different chiropractors the same X-rays, the chiropractors won't even agree on where the subluxations are. I thought that would make for a revealing test.

STOSSEL You can pick up subluxations on X-rays?

DR. PALMER PEET Absolutely.

STOSSEL Really?

DR. JENNIFER PEET And it's 97 percent. That's very high.

STOSSEL Well, let me ask you to do one, then, or do a few.

DR. JENNIFER PEET I can't. I don't have a view box.

DR. PALMER PEET Yeah, we don't have the equipment.

DR. JENNIFER PEET Sorry, we're not set up yet.

DR. PALMER PEET Also, we don't have the time, 'cause we have to—

STOSSEL Well, if we leave them with you or—

DR. JENNIFER PEET Well, it would depend on what kind of X-rays they were. Let me have a look at them. *[I gave her some X-rays.]*

DR. JENNIFER PEET This isn't a very good X-ray. Who took these? And that one, you can't analyze that.

STOSSEL If you can't read these X-rays, can we take some of your X-rays and take them to other chiropractors and see if they see the same thing?

DR. JENNIFER PEET Yes.

I was looking forward to doing that, but when the camera was off, the Peets said they wouldn't give them to us.

So we did a different experiment. A boy named Blake had recurring ear infections. A *20/20* cameraman with a hidden camera accompanied Blake's mother as she took her son to nine chiropractors. If pediatric chiropractic were a science, you'd think that the chiropractors would agree on what's wrong with Blake. But they didn't:

FIRST CHIROPRACTOR Blake has a misalignment between the second and the third bones in his neck.

SECOND CHIROPRACTOR It's on the right side of his neck between the first and second bones.

THIRD CHIROPRACTOR There is a weakness in the adrenal glands.

FOURTH CHIROPRACTOR There is a jamming of his occiput. That's the top bone in his—

CAMERAMAN His what?

FOURTH CHIROPRACTOR The occiput, which is the back bone of his skull.

And so on. Although the chiropractors found different problems, they agreed on one thing: They could help. The treatment would be expensive because it would last anywhere from several weeks to a *lifetime*.

We tried again with a different child. Kodi also had chronic ear infections, and ABC paid to have him examined by eight chiropractors.

Again, all eight found a problem, but not the same problem. One chiropractor said Kodi had a pinched nerve in his neck. Another said Kodi's left leg was shorter than his right. Bizarrely, another said his right leg was shorter than his left. Two said the problem was nutritional. One said Kodi was deficient in zinc, while another said food sensitivities were the problem. "Stay away from corn, cow's milk, and white flour," the chiropractor told Kodi's mom.

He never even examined Kodi's ears.

It's sad that people waste their money on "natural" healing; it's worse when they waste your money. Unfortunately, insurance covers many of these treatments, so we all have to pay for this weirdness. Politicians, lobbied by chiropractic associations, sometimes force insurance companies to pay for it. Medicare and Medicaid often pay for it. Your higher taxes and higher insurance premiums subsidize dubious treatments.

Even chiropractors are critical of some of the practices we uncovered. The American Chiropractic Association says there's no evidence that subluxations are life-threatening, and that comments like those made by the Peets are irresponsible.

Charles DuVall, of the National Association for Chiropractic Medicine, a smaller chiropractic group, was more critical, saying pediatric chiropractors make all chiropractors "look like absolute quacks."

STOSSEL Is there a lot of money in this?

CHARLES DUVALL Oh, there is so much money being ripped off. They want the patient to start from the day they're born and be treated *forever*.

Think about that before taking your child to a pediatric chiropractor.

MYTH: Violent video games create violent kids.

TRUTH: Experts get TV coverage by claiming games cause violence.

Self-appointed experts are sometimes so successful in propagating their arguments that the original source gets lost in the confusion. That's often how "conventional wisdom" gets born.

Psychologist and author Dave Grossman gained notoriety with a book provocatively titled *Stop Teaching Our Kids to Kill*. He argued that violent video games are a terrible influence on our kids. Grossman was interviewed by the Associated Press, newspapers, and TV stations all around the country. He made national appearances as an expert on Fox's *O'Reilly Factor,* and Court TV. He made plausible-sounding psychological arguments, like: "We are teaching children to associate pleasure with human death and suffering. We are rewarding them for killing people."

Grossman had credentials. He was a former army psychologist who specialized in training solders to kill without hesitation. "It is very difficult to get a human being to kill," he told me. "We have to rehearse the act." He said he used video games in his army work. "These things are murder simulators."

After the spate of awful shootings in high schools, Grossman volunteered to be an expert witness in a lawsuit filed by families of victims demanding money from video game makers. He says the game makers are responsible for the violent actions of the children they "influence" because the video games are "programming many of our children to kill."

Grossman cited a Paducah, Kentucky, shooting, where fourteen-year-old Michael Carneal shot eight of his classmates, inspired, said Grossman, by the video games Doom and Quake.

DAVID GROSSMAN This boy fires eight shots. He gets eight hits on eight different kids. Five of them are head shots. The other three are upper torso. Where did he get that from? The video games.

STOSSEL They should pay?

DAVID GROSSMAN They were an accessory to the crime. We are teaching children to associate pleasure with human death and suffering. We are rewarding them for killing people. And we are teaching them to like it.

STOSSEL Where do you draw the line? What about wrestling on TV?

DAVID GROSSMAN Wrestling is something that adults can have. But kids shouldn't.

STOSSEL It's mostly kids who watch wrestling.

DAVID GROSSMAN Kids are killing each other. As they imitate what happened on wrestling.

STOSSEL It shouldn't be on television?

DAVID GROSSMAN Should pornography be on television?

Hmm. Frankly, I'd be happy if fake pro wrestling were off TV, but that's not the point. The point is that autocrats claim all kinds of entertainment have bad effects, but there's little evidence of that.

When I asked kids about Grossman's claims, they laughed about the idea that games or films or TV shows would make kids do violent things. "Who are you going to believe?" Grossman asked me. "The kid? Or the surgeon general?"

Grossman was a very compelling speaker. After listening to him, people wanted someone to take *action*, to ban the games. But the evidence is not what Grossman made it out to be. The U.S. Surgeon General did say some children are influenced by TV violence, and a few studies support that. But many others don't. And it turns out that many of the people who cite a link—cite *Grossman* as a source.

Even the Surgeon General's office told us: "The Marines use the game Doom to desensitize recruits." Where did they learn that? From *Grossman*. We called the Marines. They said the games are *not* used to desensitize Marines. They say they used a version of the software to teach eye/hand co-ordination and teamwork. Period.

And how do members of Congress know the games cause violence? They listen to "expert" witnesses. Senator Kay Bailey Hutchison (R-Texas) announced, "One of our witnesses today says that video games deliberately use the psychological techniques of desensitization used to teach soldiers how to kill in battle."

Who was that expert witness? *Lieutenant Colonel Grossman* again.

Do we, individual parents, get to decide for ourselves and our children, or will the government appoint some expert, maybe David Grossman, to decide for us? After all, he's the source of the "conventional wisdom" on the subject. Get out the shovel.

MYTH: Marrying a cousin is a bad idea, as is cousins having children.

TRUTH: Go ahead—marry and procreate.

I'd always thought marrying a blood relative as close as a cousin was in-cestuous, maybe even illegal, and certainly risky if you plan to have kids. Conventional wisdom says only primitive people who live in isolated places marry cousins. It leads to stupid children. A lot of "experts," politicians and clergymen, are dead set against it, and they've convinced most people that marrying a cousin is a bad thing to do.

But as is so often the case, what we think we know is wrong. If you have an eye on one of your cousins, read on happily:

Albert Einstein's parents were cousins, and Einstein married his cousin. So did Charles Darwin. Prince Albert and Queen Victoria were cousins. And

Rudolph Giuliani was briefly married to a second cousin. Worldwide, 20 percent of all married couples are cousins.

But in America, in half the states, marrying a first cousin is illegal. As with many of our laws, there is little reason for the ban. The laws date back hundreds of years to a time when the Catholic Church campaigned against cousin marriages because in the Bible, in Leviticus, it says, "None of you shall approach to any that is near of kin."

But a cousin isn't terribly "near." Just ask Brian and Caren Wagner.

Brian's dad and Caren's mom are brother and sister, so Brian and Caren spent a lot of time together at family functions. Eventually, they fell in love and decided to marry. This did not go over well with either of their parents, especially Caren's.

> **CAREN WAGNER** There was a phone call from my mother, to Brian's father, of, "What are we gonna do about this?"
>
> **PAT BRADFIELD, CAREN'S MOTHER** Kind of floored me a little bit.
>
> **DENNIS WAGNER, BRIAN'S FATHER** We said, "Well, we've got a couple of choices. Either we can say no, we don't want this to happen"—which, you know it wasn't our choice if this is what they were going to do. They're both over twenty-one. I said hey, we're not gonna lose you.
>
> **PAT BRADFIELD** That's the last thing that you want to do is to lose your kids.

The parents blessed the marriage. Then Caren and Brian wanted to have kids, but they were worried about birth defects and worried that their kids would be stupid. Now Brian and Caren have two sons, each of whom is at the top of his class in school.

That confounds the conventional wisdom. Novels like James Dickey's *Deliverance* and movies like *Brighton Beach Memoirs* (when Eugene professes his love for his cousin Nora, he is told, "You'll have a baby with nine heads!") reinforce the notion that cousin marriage will produce retarded children. But a groundbreaking study funded by the National Society of Genetic Counselors revealed that assumptions about cousin marriage are unfounded. The risks of birth defects or mental retardation, the study found, are 2 or 3 percent higher among married cousins. That sounds bad, but other parental risk factors are higher. Age, for example, increases the risk much more: There's a 6 to 8 percent chance that a woman over forty will give birth to a child with birth defects.

Before we leave the cousin myth, though, I should point out one real risk. Pat Bradfield, Caren Wagner's mother, had a warning about divorce: "You could divorce your husband," she told Caren, "but you can't divorce the whole family. Your father-in-law and your mother-in-law would still be your uncle and aunt."

Parents' expert perspective is often the best.

CHAPTER NINE

THE POWER OF BELIEF

L ike most people, I was brought up to respect science and scholarship. My father was an engineer. My brother is a scientist. I assumed everyone wanted to see evidence before they believed. I was wrong.

I have learned that many people simply believe what their religion teaches, what their political party believes, what their friends say, or what makes them feel good.

MYTH: Global warming will cause huge disruptions in climate, more storms, and the coasts will flood! America must sign the Kyoto Treaty!

TRUTH: This myth has to be broken into four pieces.

MYTH #1: The earth is warming!

TRUTH: The earth is warming.

It's true. The Intergovernmental Panel on Climate Change (IPCC) says the global average surface temperature increased about 0.6 degrees Celsius over the twentieth century.

> **MYTH #2:** The earth is warming because of us!
>
> **TRUTH:** Maybe.

If our fossil-fuel burning is responsible for the warming, something doesn't add up. Half of the global warming of the past century happened from 1900 to 1945. If man is responsible, why wasn't there much more warming in the second half of the century? We burned much more fuel during that time. What about that? Huh? You don't hear the environmental alarmists talking about it . . .

The planet is just in a gradual warming trend, coming out of what scientists call the "Little Ice Age," which ended in the 1800s. Our climate has always undergone changes, and it's presumptuous to think humans' impact matters so much in comparison to the frightening geologic history of the earth. A graph of temperatures over the last four thousand years shows today's warming isn't such a big deal.

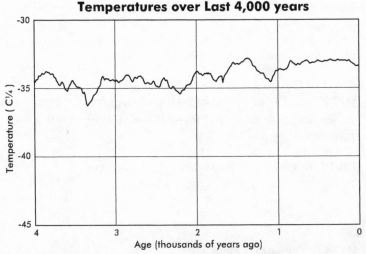

Temperatures over Last 4,000 years

Source: NOAA Paleoclimatology Program and World Data Center for Paleoclimatology, Boulder

> **MYTH #3:** There will be storms, flooded coasts, and huge disruptions in climate!
>
> **TRUTH:** Probably not.

Schoolchildren I've interviewed were convinced that America is "dying" in a sea of pollution and "cities will soon be under water!"

Lawyers from the Natural Resources Defense Council (another environmental group with more lawyers than scientists) warn that "sea levels will rise, flooding coastal areas. Heat waves will be more frequent and more intense. Droughts and wildfires will occur more often."

Wow.

But many scientists laugh at the panic.

Dr. John Christy, professor of Atmospheric Science at the University of Alabama at Huntsville says: "I remember as a college student at the first Earth Day being told it was a certainty that by the year 2000, the world would be starving and out of energy. Such doomsday prophecies grabbed headlines, but have proven to be completely false. Similar pronouncements today about catastrophes due to human-induced climate change sound all too familiar and all too exaggerated to me as someone who actually produces and analyzes climate information."

But the media like the exaggerated claims.

The Washington Post reported "The End Is Near!" because of melting ice caps and glaciers.

But Dr. Patrick Michaels, author of the Association of American Geographers' 2003 Climate Paper of the Year, points out that melting Arctic ice won't raise sea levels any more than the melting ice in your drink makes your glass overflow. "The Arctic ice cap is just floating ice . . . if it melted . . . it's not a land mass adding to water."

Of late, melting glaciers have become the issue. MSNBC and the BBC ran stories on the coming calamity from Greenland's melting glaciers. Unlike Arctic ice, say the alarmists, those melting glaciers *will* raise sea levels around the globe.

But only Greenland's southern glaciers are melting. The northern ones are not. And in October 2005, Norwegian, Russian, and American scientists issued a report that said Greenland's ice was thickening, not melting.

Most scary claims about heat waves and droughts are based on computer models that purport to predict future climates. But computer models are lousy at predicting climate because water vapor and cloud effects cause changes that computers fail to predict. In the mid-1970s, computer models told us we should prepare for global *cooling*.

Scientists tell reporters that computer models should "be viewed with great skepticism."

Well, why *aren't* they?

The fundamentalist doom mongers also ignore scientists who say the effects of global warming may be benign. Harvard astrophysicist Sallie Baliunas says added CO_2 in the atmosphere may actually benefit the world because more CO_2 *helps* plants grow. Warmer winters would give farmers a longer harvest season, and might end the droughts in the Sahara desert.

Why don't we hear about this part of the global warming argument?

"It's the money!" says Dr. Baliunas. "Twenty-five billion dollars in government funding has been spent since 1990 to research global warming. If scientists and researchers were coming out releasing reports that global warming has little to do with man, and most to do with just how the planet works, there wouldn't be as much money to study it."

MYTH #4: Signing the Kyoto Treaty would stop the warming.

TRUTH: Hardly.

In 1997, the United Nations met in Kyoto, Japan, and asked the developed nations of the world to cut CO_2 emission to below 1990 levels.

And even advocates of Kyoto admit that if all the nations signed the Kyoto agreement and obeyed it, global temperatures would still increase. The difference by 2050 would be less than a tenth of a degree! The fuss over Kyoto is so absurd. Even if Kyoto would have an impact, do you think all the signers are going to honor what they signed? China is predicted to out-emit us in five to ten years. India will soon follow. What incentive do they have to stop burning fossil fuels? Get the shovel.

The fundamentalist Greens imply if we just conserved energy, and switched from fossil fuels to wind and solar power (they rarely mention nuclear power—the most practical alternative), we would live in a non–global-warming fairyland of happiness. But their proposals are hopelessly impractical. Building solar panels burns energy, as does trucking them and installing them—then taking them down again to repair them.

To think that solar energy could stop the predicted temperature increase is absurd. EPCOT, a theme park with a solar energy ride, consumes about 395,000 kilowatt-hours per day. The Department of Energy says you'd need around a thousand acres of solar panels to generate that much electricity. EPCOT itself sits on only three hundred acres, so you'd have to triple the size of the park just to operate it!

Windmills are no panacea either. They are giant bird-killing Cuisinarts, and we'd have to build lots of them to produce significant energy.

In 2000, a group called Cape Wind proposed to erect 130 windmills in Nantucket Sound, off the coast of Massachusetts. I think the drawings make them look interesting, but—horrors!—they would be visible from the Kennedy family vacation compound in Hyannis Port. Robert Kennedy Jr., high poo-bah of the environmental zealotry movement, is leading a campaign to ban the windmills from Nantucket Sound. The group he leads, the Waterkeeper Alliance, says it supports wind farms—but Kennedy fights the one near his home. What a hypocrite.

Ninety percent of the world's energy comes from fossil fuels. Kyoto would decimate just about every Third World country's economy, and deliver a catastrophic blow to our own.

So what *should* we do about the threat of global warming?

First, calm down.

Second, if the world is warming, it is much more reasonable to adjust to it, rather than try to stop it: If sea levels rise, we can build dykes and move back from the coasts. It worked for Holland. Farmers can plant different crops or move north.

Russian farmers farmed northern Siberia for centuries. When the area became cold and desolate, the farmers moved south.

Far better to keep studying global warming, let the science develop, and adjust to it if it happens, rather than wreck life as we know it by trying to stop it.

Sorry to go on so long about global warming. I got carried away because the global warming myth-makers are so sanctimonious and insistent. On to simpler myths.

MYTH: More driving equals more pollution.

TRUTH: It's not how much you drive, it's *what* you drive.

One fringe of the environmental movement has been trying to rid the world of cars. It's all that driving, they say, that's polluting the air and destroying our lungs. They want everyone to take mass transit, walk, or ride bikes. That wouldn't change my life much. I usually ride my bike to work. But should everyone have to live the way I do?

Fortunately for you, no.

Cars are not evil. It's true that the more you drive, the more you pollute. But it's really just old, badly maintained cars that do most of the polluting. Because emissions technology has improved so much, today's new cars are 98% cleaner than cars built during the 1960s. Joe Norbeck, a U.C. Riverside environmental researcher, says emissions from dozens of current models are "almost below detection levels."

As a result, the air keeps getting cleaner, even as more people drive more. The Environmental Protection Agency has charted air pollution for more than 30 years. During that time, miles driven increased by 170%, but air pollution decreased by 54%.

Every time we junk our old car in favor of a more recent model, we are contributing to the decrease in pollution. So if you really want to help cut down on pollution, you don't need to bike to work. Just keep your car tuned or, better yet, buy a new one, and get Uncle Joe to junk his filthy old one.

> **MYTH:** Astrology must have some truth to it, or millions of people wouldn't believe.
>
> **TRUTH:** Millions of people believe ridiculous things.

Astrology is huge. Type the word into Google and more than eighty million sites appear. Big-time astrologers make thousands of dollars doing custom horoscopes. People swear by them—swear the astrologer knew things about them that "no one could have known!" Swear they predicted things that came true later. How can it be ridiculous if so many people believe?

Because some things are true about most everyone; for example, 95 percent of Americans believe they have "an above average sense of humor." When the astrologer says that, people think she's talking about them. Also, they make a thousand predictions about the future. People tend to forget the erroneous ones but remember the "hits." (See psychics, p. 209)

I once had an astrologer do a chart on Ed Kemper, the California serial killer and necrophile who murdered six female hitchhikers and his own mother. I then gave the twenty-five-page report to a class of college students, telling them it was their personal horoscope (I'd collected their birthdates previously). Most were impressed. A few were "amazed" that the astrologer could know so much about them. Some said they had been skeptical of astrology, but this detailed horoscope had made them total believers. Then I told them it wasn't their own horoscope, that all the horoscopes were identical. I told them who Kemper was. It was a good "TV moment."

I asked astrologer Susan Miller to do my horoscope. Miller writes astrology columns for magazines, and has a website that's viewed fifteen million times a month. The chart she gave me was twenty-two pages long, with observations like, "You have Jupiter in your Seventh House. So you do very well with partners, people who collaborate with you to help you . . ."

And on and on. When someone says stuff like that for twenty-two pages, they are bound to hit on things that will come true; then you say, "Oh, that really is me!" It is what is known in the craft as a "cold reading." They add plenty of flattery too, because we are happy to believe good things about ourselves.

> **SUSAN MILLER** You have Venus in the Tenth House, making you a very popular leader or personality. Do you want me to go on? (laughter)
>
> **STOSSEL** Go ahead.
>
> **SUSAN MILLER** In addition, those three planets in Pisces makes you very intuitive.
>
> **STOSSEL** This is silly. What you're saying about me, you could say about anybody. If you can predict this, why aren't you rich? Why aren't all astrologers rich?
>
> **SUSAN MILLER** Because I'm a Pisces, and I don't care about money. I give it all away.

Okay, Susan, give it all away. If it will help, I'll loan you my shovel.

> **MYTH:** Voodoo has real effects.
>
> **TRUTH:** Only if you think it does.

Voodoo is also taken seriously by millions of people. They pay voodoo priests to heal them, or to hurt others. And it works! It is a fact that voodoo priests have cursed people who have then promptly gotten sick and died. But it's not the voodoo. It's the power of suggestion. Just as there's a placebo affect, there's also something called a nocebo effect. It's the placebo's evil twin. Tell someone something bad will happen, and you may psych them into making it happen.

The voodoo priest says you'll get sick, and you do. Some say that's what Gulf War Syndrome's about. Thousands of veterans claim that serving in the first war in the Persian Gulf made them sick. They have real symptoms, headaches, allergies, lethargy, etc., but major studies have found no germ or pattern of chemicals that could explain how the war caused those symptoms. If, as claimed, they were caused by chemicals, you'd expect the soldiers closest to the action to be sickest. But people far from the chemicals also reported symptoms. Psychologists suspect that the publicity about Iraqi poison gas, environmental toxins, and testimony from other soldiers getting sick may be the cause of Gulf War Syndrome. If you truly believe that chemicals have poisoned you, or that a voodoo priest's curse has power, your body may just shut down.

Fortunately for me, one has to believe for the curse to work.

For a show we did titled "The Power of Belief," my depraved producers hired a voodoo priest named Elmer Glover to put a curse on me. "Break a bone," they suggested. Glover had us send him a sample of my hair and fingernails and an article of clothing I'd worn for a while. He then carved my name in a candle, which he brought to a New Orleans cemetery. He mixed in my hair and nails, and then, to call up the spirits of the dead, he sprayed some rum around, blew cigar smoke into a tree in the center of the graveyard, hung my clothing in the tree so the spirits could find me, shook a rattle, and then lit the candle and invited the spirits to hurt me. It was creepy to listen as he called down a curse upon me.

ELMER GLOVER　John Stossel! John Stossel! I ask the help [of] and pray to the voodoo spirits. I call upon all beings of voodoo being to assist me.

It's been several years—still no broken bones. If I do break a bone, I'll remember Elmer Glover, and wonder.

MYTH: If it happens in a hospital, it must be science.

TRUTH: Not necessarily.

Something that strikes me as very similar to voodoo is being practiced today in mainstream American hospitals. It's called "therapeutic touch."

In a Connecticut hospital, nurse Ann Minor let us watch as she "treated" a woman with leukemia. She held her hands three or four inches away from the patient, feeling for energy. "I can feel where the energy is balanced and where it's not balanced," she said.

Then, according to the theory, she channeled the "healing energy of the universe" through her hands to the patient. The patient told us that it didn't matter if there's no evidence that therapeutic touch works. "I don't need explanations because I have faith in the process," she said. "That's a really wonderful thing when you feel helpless, terrified."

It's hard to argue with satisfied patients. But several years ago, a nine-year-old girl in Colorado, for her fourth-grade science project, put therapeutic touch to the test. Her name is Emily Rosa, and her test was simple: She asked practitioners to feel the energy from her hand. But she used a towel to hide her hands from the practitioners' eyes. Emily didn't ask them to do any healing. Instead, she just asked the most basic question: "Tell me which of *your* hands you think *my* hand is over." Again and again, the touch therapists failed her test. They could have gotten 50 percent correct just by guessing, but the healers didn't even get to 50 percent.

> **STOSSEL** So were they embarrassed?
>
> **EMILY ROSA** No. Not really. Some thought if you got four out of ten right, they thought you'd pass. And obviously, they didn't know their statistics.

Obviously not. Emily's test was published in the prestigious *Journal of the American Medical Association*—but not with the negative effects you might imagine. Therapeutic Touch therapy now has more than a hundred thousand practitioners and is thriving.

People's wish to believe in the supernatural is very strong.

> **MYTH:** Police use psychics to search for bodies, so psychics must have special abilities.
>
> **TRUTH:** Police get suckered too.

If you are desperate, you'll try all kinds of things, including going to a psychic. Kathy Kupka went to several.

"I was a little out of my mind, you know, with desperation, and all I wanted to do was find her."

I understand why Kathy was upset: Her younger sister had disappeared.

She put up a huge billboard offering a $25,000 reward. Soon, psychics began calling her with messages from beyond—beyond the credible, that is. They said, "I know where your sister is." They sent her to location after location. She went, but found no trace of her sister.

Kupka was told to contact Sylvia Browne, one of America's most famous psychics. Browne's website said, "Visiting here explains the Meaning of Life."

She says she predicted Brad Pitt and Jennifer Aniston's marriage wouldn't last. Wow. What a gift of prophecy! How could anyone have expected that? Browne claims that she can talk to the dead, and the dead then tell her where they are. So Kupka managed to get on a TV show on a day when Browne was doing her stuff. "I was so super-hopeful," she said. "I was like, oh, that's it, we're definitely going to find her."

On the show, Browne quickly said Kupka's sister was dead in New Mexico—and communicating to Browne.

KATHY KUPKA Does she see us?

SYLVIA BROWNE Oh, sure. I mean, that's the only way I can get information.

Back in this world, police investigated Browne's lead. It was a phantom.

"It was so devastating," Kupka told me. "Desperation makes you do things that reasonable people don't do."

ABC News asked Browne to talk to us about this. She agreed but then backed out at the last minute. She had told us she solved thousands of cases. But several years ago, a magazine examined thirty-five of Brown's "cases." It couldn't find proof she'd solved any of them.

At least Browne didn't ask Kupka for money.

Michael Shermer, editor of *Skeptic* magazine, says that something a little less magical than psychic powers is responsible for some police officers' enchantment with psychics. "They simply are misremembering the hits and the misses," he told us.

"The psychics go to the police department," says Shermer. "They give lots and lots of statements. 'I see the body in a—body of woods, some water, a railroad track, and so on.' When the body is finally found, they retrofit the statement to see how it fits with what actually happened. So, 'Oh, yeah, that psychic said something about a railroad track.' Yeah, but the psychic also said something about a hundred other things." Often psychics say, the body is "near water," but water can mean an ocean, stream, puddle, bathroom, underground pipe, or most anyplace. If the body is found by a puddle, someone might say, "Wow, the psychic said 'near water.'"

ABC News went to another psychic, Kathlyn Rhea, who some police officers say has helped them find bodies.

Rhea claims she finds missing people all the time—sometimes three or four a week. The FBI maintains psychics have never helped solve a single missing-person case.

Rhea charges a fat fee. ABC News managed to get a special, bargain price: $1,800.

Rhea then told Kupka that Kristine had been murdered, and Rhea was confident that she knew where Kristine's body was: Go thirty miles north of Kristine's old neighborhood, look for a road that branches off like a Y, something that looks like a country church, and something with the letter S. We followed her instructions, using map companies, contacts with police, and numerous trips, but it turned out there were hundreds of Y's and V's in the road and all kinds of signs with S's. When I complained to Rhea about that, she said, "What do you want me to do, the legwork?" Facing yet another useless "psychic vision," Kathy collapsed into tears.

"My heart just fell," said Kupka. "I was like, she doesn't know."

Psychics don't know. But they do break hearts.

> **MYTH:** If you concentrate your mind, you can walk on hot coals without fear.
>
> **TRUTH:** Your mind has nothing to do with it.

You've heard all of that stuff about how mystics can use their minds to block out pain and accomplish impossible tasks, like walking on hot coals? Well, I can't vouch for the mystics and how they do it, but pass the word: *You* can walk on hot coals if you want to. I know because I did it.

For "The Power of Belief" TV special, I went to Johnstown, Pennsylvania, where "the world's longest fire walk" had been organized by David Willey. He's no mystic, he teaches physics at the University of Pittsburgh, and he invited us to walk on hot coals to demonstrate there was nothing at all mystical about it. He's heard the stories: that you have to concentrate, meditate, focus on God, focus on peace, etc.

DAVID WILLEY [They say] "If you lose your concentration, you're going to burn"—that the body is putting out some kind of field around you.

STOSSEL It's all bunk?

DAVID WILLEY Bunk is a word you might use, yeah.

Willey laid out 165 feet of lumber and set it aflame. As we waited for the lumber to turn into hot coals, he said that anyone can "fire-walk" in their bare feet, provided they keep moving, because when you touch burning wood or charcoal, the heat doesn't go instantly to your feet. You'd be burned if you walk on hot metal, but wood and charcoal don't conduct heat very well.

I wanted to believe him, but I was scared. I toasted a marshmallow over the coals.

STOSSEL Why am I not going to get burned? I mean, that's hot enough to roast a marshmallow.

DAVID WILLEY You're not going to get burned because wood is a poor thermal conductor.

STOSSEL What's the temperature now?

DAVID WILLEY About a thousand degrees Fahrenheit.

STOSSEL And I don't have to believe anything or chant anything?

DAVID WILLEY You don't. You don't have to believe anything. You don't have to chant anything. A nice, steady walk. You just walk across the fire.

I let him go first. When he didn't scream, I went. He was right. I wasn't burned, and neither were the fifteen people who set a world distance fire-walking record that day: 165 feet over hot coals.

> **MYTH:** Red cars attract police attention and cost more to insure.
>
> **TRUTH:** It's an urban myth.

Red cars are the Hester Prynnes of the automobile world, unfairly branded by their scarlet finishes. We've heard the bad rap for years: Red cars will get you pulled over by the police more quickly, and will cost you more in insurance premiums. Online insurance provider Esurance.com's website proclaims: "Drivers of flashier cars, especially red ones, are more likely to get cited for speeding and other violations."

But it's just urban gossip.

The Insurance Information Institute says red cars do not cost any more to insure than cars that are blue, black, green, or chartreuse. Even Esurance, when we called, said color doesn't matter. Premiums are based on data gleaned from previous experiences with millions of customers, like medical care and auto repair costs, a car's susceptibility to theft, the age and experience of the driver, and where the driver lives. One reason why New Jersey drivers pay more is because New Jersey has more lawyers per capita than any other state, and drivers there are more likely to enter into a lawsuit when they get into an accident.

Insurance companies will do just about anything to minimize risk. The fact that red cars cost nothing extra to insure shows that they are no more risky to drive.

Is it true that they are a more eye-catching target for police patrols? People believe that. An Internet bulletin board discussing the question has comments like: "Ever since I bought my red Saturn I have gotten a plethora of tickets. . . . I am so upset, I am ready to paint my car a different color."

We contacted six state police agencies, and each said there was no evidence, either anecdotal or scientific, that red cars get singled out for attention. Sergeant Bill Krumpton of the Kentucky State Police told us: "You always hear that. But it's absolutely not true—and this is on the record."

MYTH: Homeopathy is a good treatment for allergies and the flu.

TRUTH: Homeopathy is absurd.

Homeopathy is another form of alternative "natural" medicine that is very popular. "Doctors" of homeopathy claim they can cure illnesses by giving people minuscule doses of the substances that cause the illness. This, they say, will trigger your immune system to resist the flu, colds, allergies, and more.

Lots of people believe. Martina Navratilova uses homeopathic medicines. So does Cher. The Queen of England has her own homeopathic doctor. Trouble is, homeopathy makes no logical sense. The National Institutes of Health says a number of homeopathy's key concepts "do not follow the laws of science, particularly chemistry and physics."

Many homeopathic products are diluted to absurd degrees. One drop of medicine in 99 drops of water they call "1 C." But then they just keep diluting. At "12 C," it's like a drop in the entire Atlantic Ocean. At "16 C," it's like a drop in the oceans of a million earths. Yet the biggest seller, a remedy for the flu called Oscillococcinum, is diluted to 200 C.

I interviewed author Dana Ullman about homeopathy. He is its foremost spokesman, and has written seven books about it.

STOSSEL The more you dilute it, the stronger it gets?

DANA ULLMAN Not only does the medicine get stronger, but we need less doses of the medicines.

STOSSEL The FDA says some of these things have no molecules of the medicine left.

DANA ULLMAN In all probability, some of them don't have any molecules. But the water gets impregnated with the information or memory of the original substance.

STOSSEL The water remembers?

DANA ULLMAN Yes.

The water remembers! Does it remember where I left my shovel?

"Does water have emotions? Can it get sad?" was James Randi's wisecrack answer to Ullman's claim. Randi is a former magician turned professional skeptic. Unlike most believers in homeopathy, psychics, astrology, etc., he puts his money where his mouth is. His foundation offers one million dollars to anyone who can demonstrate that any paranormal or supernatural phenomenon works. A million dollars! With all those faith healers, astrologers, tarot card readers making all kinds of claims, I'd think they'd be clamoring to have Randi test them. But they rarely do—maybe they don't want a "scientific" test. He's offered the money since 1997, but no one has collected the million dollars yet.

Randi said he'd give me the million dollars if I could show that homeopathy works. I'm as greedy as the next guy, and Dana Ullman said that he knew a test that would prove homeopathy's powers, so I thought we'd give it a try. Ullman said we'd test white blood cells, and he was very confident: "Homeopathic doses of histamine would have a dramatic effect upon the white blood cells, these basophiles, and they would decrease in number."

So we set it up, in Europe, where similar tests claimed to find that kind of effect. Scientists at Guy's Hospital in London prepared samples of the type of histamines that Dana Ullman recommended. They'd test 400 samples and see their effect on the white blood cells. The test took a week to do. Three homeopaths made sure the dilutions were done properly. Finally, after five days of testing, J. Martin Bland, Professor of Medical Statistics, brought us the results. Did we show water has a memory? Do I win a million dollars?

"I guess not," said Dr. Bland. "There's no evidence at all that there's any difference between the tubes . . . Mr. Stossel can kiss his million dollars good-bye."

Sadly, Americans are already kissing many millions good-bye. Every year, companies sell hundreds of millions of dollars worth of homeopathic remedies.

MYTH: Medical hypnosis is another scam.

TRUTH: Hypnosis works—if you let it!

Just when my skeptic's antennae convince me I always know bunk when I see it, I get fooled. I assumed hypnosis in medicine was one more con game.

I'd seen those ads promising: "Hypnotherapy will help you lose weight!" C'mon, if it worked, there wouldn't be all those overweight people around. Hypnotists also claim they can help people stop smoking. That's plausible— I'd think if they can hypnotize people into clucking like chickens, as nightclub hypnotists do, they ought to be able to help people crave cigarettes less. So I used ABC's money to test half a dozen antismoking techniques. The smokers who went to the hypnotists did no better than people who tried other techniques, or quit cold turkey, and most of the hypnotized smokers were puffing away again within months.

When I was a young TV reporter in Portland, Oregon, hypnotists called me up to offer to cure my stuttering. That's a nice thing about being on TV— people come out of the woodwork and offer treatments. I tried two hypnotists who *promised* they could cure me. Both times I was left stuttering as much as ever. (What did finally help my speech was attending a three-week course at the Hollins Communications Research Institute.)

But another benefit of my line of work is that I get challenged on a regular basis. My opinion of hypnosis met its match in the person of an eighty-eight-pound woman named Kathy Platoni, of Dayton, Ohio, whom I watched undergoing painful surgery without *any* anesthesia.

Kathy was born with serious bone defects that she'd spent fifteen years trying to correct. The surgery we witnessed was a facial laser operation to literally burn off scars from previous surgeries. Kathy had endured a long series of operations over the years—this was her fiftieth operation—and had trouble getting over the effects of conventional anesthesia. "I've had great difficulty recovering from surgery," she told me, "and it takes me up to a year to recover all of my memory functions, and that's been devastating to me."

As a psychologist who occasionally used hypnosis with her own patients, Kathy believed that hypnosis could solve her problem. She persuaded her surgeon to do something he would never ordinarily do—perform the surgery without giving her local or general anesthesia. The doctor was skeptical, saying the operation would generate great pain. "It's as painful as taking and putting a match to your face," he said. "It hurts." He insisted on having an anesthesiologist on standby.

We watched as Kathy's hypnotherapist, John Baren, hypnotized her, telling her to anesthetize her hand by placing it in an imaginary bucket of ice. "Take your right hand and put it on your left cheek, completely and totally anesthetizing all areas," he told her soothingly, saying she would feel "a floating and drifting feeling, as though you were floating on a cloud, safe—secure."

She did. In the operating room, amid all kinds of scary sights and sounds—the laser was literally burning off several layers of skin—Kathy's mind was miles away. Toward the end of the operation a particularly deep cut briefly penetrated her trance. She started to feel pain, but John Baren led her back to Antarctica with word imagery: "Steely ice blue," he murmured, "like the Arctic Glaciers." Kathy escaped again; the pain retreated.

After the operation, she described her hypnotic refuge. "There's icebergs, and I'm standing on one that's very secure," she told me. "The sky is the same deep royal blue as the water. I'm seeing, oh, about a hundred penguins. And they approach me as if they are supposed to be there to help me through this."

She got through the surgery, depending solely on hypnosis.

I was still skeptical. Maybe it was some kind of setup (though I cannot imagine how). Would it still work if *we* picked the patient?

We chose Steve Norslinger, a New York dental patient. We picked him because he was extremely sensitive to pain. He had a deep cavity that needed lots of drilling and which, for Steve, would normally require lots of Novocain. We watched him go through the procedure without a twitch, guided by hypnotherapist Joyce Hanson.

STOSSEL How does it work? What does the mind do?

JOYCE HANSON What the mind is basically doing is altering its sense of awareness.

STOSSEL So, the pain that's happening to the nerve endings never gets to the part of the brain that tells him it hurts?

JOYCE HANSON That's right, because he's selectively thinking about something else. Maybe it's like the sunbeam coming out from behind the clouds, creating a wonderful sense of relaxation.

Hypnotists say that hypnosis is really *self*-hypnosis. They cannot get their subjects to do anything they really don't *want* to do. The hypnotists are basically guides who make a suggestion, but the subject has to have the desire for the suggestion to work. Maybe that's why the die-hard smokers and overeaters keep smoking and overeating. Autosuggestion is no substitute for conviction. And hypnotherapy doesn't work for everyone. Unfortunately, it doesn't work for me.

But once again, I learn that what I think I know—may not be so.

CHAPTER TEN

OUR HEALTH

D ebunking health myths is liberating. Once you know the truth, you don't have to bug your kids about eating sugar, or worry about them cracking their knuckles. I don't have to bundle up in the winter or feel guilty about eating a late-night snack. What freedom!

> **MYTH:** Being cold gives you a cold.
>
> **TRUTH:** It doesn't.

This old wives' tale is persuasive. I can't even convince my own wife that this one's a myth, even though tons of research has been done to disprove it. Once I went to a damp and dreary British "resort" where researchers get people to volunteer for medical testing by offering them a free two-week "vacation." Then scientists sprayed cold viruses into their noses and monitored them. Half of the group got to stay indoors in heated rooms, while the other half had to walk outside in the cold rain, and then sit shivering in unheated rooms. The chilled group got no more colds than anyone else. This wasn't a fun vacation for them, but at least the study participants taught us that being cold and wet made *no difference*.

We do get sick more often when the weather is cold, but that's only because we spend more time inside then, breathing on each other and passing viruses back and forth. Also, cold may cause your nose to run, but that has nothing to do with getting sick.

Knowing this made parenting easier for me. I was able to relax when the kids ran outside without a coat, and I didn't have to fight with them about what they wore. Moms in playgrounds would give me that you-are-neglecting-your-child stare, and I could confidently ignore them knowing I was doing nothing wrong. And the kids had more fun because they weren't nagged all the time.

Members of Polar Bear Clubs will happily tell you all about that. Every winter, these lunatics—I mean, swimmers—voluntarily jump into freezing lakes or oceans. One cold day in December, I interviewed a New York group that swims in the Atlantic every Sunday. As I approached them in my winter coat, they were sort of obnoxious about it:

> **POLAR BEAR CLUB MEMBER** You're overdressed, buddy. Come on, swim down here, shed that coat.
>
> **STOSSEL** All over America, a million mothers are telling their kids, "Don't go outside without a coat, you'll get sick."
>
> **POLAR BEAR CLUB MEMBER** I guess a million mothers are wrong.

They are.

Recently a new British study suggested that being cold *does* cause colds. The Common Cold Centre had ninety volunteers keep their bare feet in icy water for twenty minutes. 29 percent developed a cold, vs. 9 percent in a control group. That got front-page coverage in American newspapers and prominent play on the morning TV shows.

But "real" scientists will not reverse any theories based on that study, saying the subjects knew what was being studied. They were at the "Common Cold Centre," so they expected to get a cold because their feet had been wet, and that's what they then reported. To do the study properly, the scientists should use subjects who are "blind" to what is being studied, and take fluid samples to test for the presence of a cold virus. The Common Cold Centre didn't do that, the scientists said. Get the shovel.

MYTH: Cracking your knuckles is bad for you.

TRUTH: Crack away.

Parents tell kids that cracking their knuckles will make their knuckles big and ugly. Adults fear cracking will predispose them to arthritis. The Arthritis

Foundation says both fears are myths. The noise you hear when you crack your knuckles is the collapse of an air bubble that forms inside the joint when the joint is pulled apart. The air bubble doesn't do any damage to your hand and has nothing to do with arthritis. Maybe this old myth was started by a very irritated parent or teacher.

Annoying, yes. Arthritis, no.

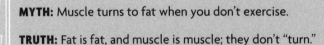

MYTH: Muscle turns to fat when you don't exercise.

TRUTH: Fat is fat, and muscle is muscle; they don't "turn."

Some people exercise out of fear: They work their muscles not only to keep them in shape (use them or lose them) but because they think that unused muscles will turn to fat.

There are a lot of good reasons to work out, but that's not one of them. Dr. Walter Thompson, professor of exercise science at Georgia State University and coauthor of a how-to book for the American College of Sports Medicine, told us that when you stop exercising, muscle becomes soft and nonfunctional, but "it's never going to become fat."

The body's fat cells and muscle cells are structurally different. "Muscle is muscle, fat is fat," fitness expert Donna Richardson Joyner added, "and you can't turn one into the other."

There is one connection between fat and muscle that's worth knowing: The more lean muscle you have, the more calories you burn off in a workout; burning more calories will get rid of the fat.

MYTH: If the label says 100 calories, a serving will give you 100 calories.

TRUTH: Some serving sizes are bizarre.

You wouldn't expect something called "Your Personal Pizza" to be a food you share, but the company that makes those little frozen pizzas claims it is meant to serve two. We took one to some New York City pizza parlors—and found a tough audience.

PIZZA MAKER 1 I don't think you could share this with anybody.

PIZZA MAKER 2 They'd throw it back in my face.

CUSTOMER 1 Where's the rest of it?

CUSTOMER 2 My cat could eat that.

Why care if the label has an odd concept of a serving size? Because we rely on labels to count calories, fat, and salt. You may think the amounts shown on the labels are calories per *package* but they are calories per *serving*—or, rather, what the company claims is a "serving." So if the serving size is ridiculously small, you eat two or three times as much fat/salt/whatever as you thought you ate.

We found a blueberry muffin that was basically a calorie bomb—645 calories. But the label said just 215 calories, because the company claimed a serving size was a third of a muffin. I couldn't find anyone who eats a third of a muffin.

STOSSEL They say this is for three people, three servings.

CONSUMER How small are these people?

You might ask, "Aren't there any rules governing serving sizes?" There are. In the early 1990s, government, in its wisdom, "solved" the problem of confusing food labels. They ordered the food industry to test, weigh, and measure 139 different types of food. The government then determined the amount of each we would customarily eat, and set a size for each "serving." A bureaucrat from the Department of Health and Human Services proudly announced that "the Tower of Babel in food labels has come down!"

As usual, the bureaucrats' "solution" created new problems: absurd serving sizes. It's a problem food companies probably like, because it lets them suggest their food is less fattening than it is.

None of the offending food companies would talk to us about this, which is too bad, because I'd love to know how America's Choice olives came up with 1½ olives as a serving size. Would you ever eat half an olive? Vlasic pickles claims a serving size is "three-quarters of a spear." Get the shovel!

> **MYTH:** Margarine is healthier than butter.
>
> **TRUTH:** It depends on the margarine.

For years we've been told: Butter is bad, margarine is better. The ads say it, and doctors used to say it, but it turns out that it's not the whole truth.

Manufacturers often solidify margarine to make it look like butter, in sticks. The process, called hydrogenation, creates something called "trans fats." Trans fats are as heart-unhealthy as saturated fat, that stuff in butter that raises the bad kind of cholesterol in our bodies.

So between butter with saturated fat or margarine with trans fats, what is the wise choice? "If I had to choose, I would choose the butter," Dr. David Katz told us. He is a nutrition expert at Yale University. He also said it's better to avoid both, and pick one of the new generation of margarines that are lower in trans fats.

The new spreads combine unsaturated oils with plant additives, and the combination can actually help bring down high cholesterol levels. Dr. Katz recommends products that contain only unsaturated oils, and that make health claims on the label indicating that the product can improve cholesterol or heart health (FDA approved). Many labels now say: no trans fats.

"Butter is better than the bad margarines," says Dr. Katz, "and the good margarines are better than butter."

In addition, tubs are generally better than sticks, because if the spread is softer, it's likely to have fewer risks from the solidifying process.

Deciding what to put on your toast is not so simple anymore.

> **MYTH:** Eating late at night makes you fat.
>
> **TRUTH:** It doesn't matter when you eat.

We hear this one all the time: Eat late at night, and you'll get fat, because you won't exercise the calories away.

But at the Oregon Health and Science University, scientists studied forty-seven female monkeys, keeping detailed records of precisely what they ate and when. The animals that ate their food at night were not the ones that gained the most weight. In fact, there was no correlation between eating at night and gaining weight.

But people do gain weight eating late at night. Not because we metabolize food differently then, but because many people save their higher fat snacks like ice cream, chips, and chocolate for the end of the day. I do that. I binge at night. People are appalled at how much popcorn, ice cream, and chocolate I can put away right before bedtime. I compensate by skipping breakfast. I'm not recommending this.

But the bottom line is that the researchers say midnight snacking won't make you fatter simply because you eat it late at night. What makes you fatter is taking in more calories than you burn.

A calorie is a calorie no matter *when* you eat it.

MYTH: Eating at home is safer than eating out.

TRUTH: Eating at home is more likely to make you sick.

Local news programs regularly do "sweeps week" reports on the local health department's "dirty restaurant list." They hype it: "Coming up . . . restaurants that can make you *sick!*" But in truth, you are more likely to make yourself sick cooking at home.

Restaurants have to be clean, not just because of the occasional health inspection, but because their business depends on customers returning. If they get a reputation for making customers sick, they go bankrupt. Over time, the restaurant business has learned the basics about keeping bacteria down.

But what about our very own kitchens? ABC's Don Dahler asked one couple who'd complained about restaurant cleanliness if they'd be open to having a health inspector take a look at their kitchen. They agreed. The inspector found far more health violations in their home than he'd ever found in a restaurant. The kitchen was crawling with bacteria. The sponge, which is the biggest bacteria breeder in most homes, was particularly nasty. It hadn't been cleaned for a month.

Dr. Philip Tierno, director of microbiology and immunology at the New York University School of Medicine, says there's much more danger lurking in your own kitchen than in a restaurant: "fifty to eighty percent of gastrointestinal infections, food-borne illnesses," he told us, "are caught within the home."

The FDA and Department of Agriculture agree—throw out those old sponges, or at least put them in the dishwasher when you do the dishes, and eat out with confidence.

MYTH: Chocolate is bad for you.

TRUTH: Not so fast, my sweet!

"If I could have one dream come true, it would be that chocolate would be good for me," one chocolate lover told my colleague Bob Brown when Bob reported on this myth. As it turns out, the dream is *already* partly true.

Chocolate recently underwent a series of scientific studies that revealed that chocolate has bona fide health benefits. The cocoa bean is rich in compounds called "flavonols," also found in red wine, green tea, apples, and onions, and flavonols are good for you.

"Chocolate can have very beneficial effects for your heart," says Katherine Tallmadge of the American Dietetic Association. She said the flavonols help people by "relaxing blood vessels, reducing blood clotting [an aspirin-like effect], and maybe reducing blood pressure. It also helps reduce inflammation, which is an emerging risk factor in heart disease."

It has to be the right chocolate, though. Flavonols are processed out of many chocolates because of their bitter taste. "You want the product that has as little processing as possible," says Ms. Tallmadge. "Look for the darkest chocolate you can find, and try to find a product that has a high level of cocoa and a low level of calories."

Despite this good news about possible benefits, chocolate is so high in sugar and fat that it's anything but a health food. I, however, have added dark chocolate to my binges. Soon you'll need a shovel for me.

MYTH: Sugar makes kids hyper.

TRUTH: Parties make kids hyper.

Parents are convinced that sugar drives kids crazy. Some of the kids believe it.

SIX-YEAR-OLD GIRL I go really nuts when I have candy.

TEENAGE GIRL You get really hyper!

TEENAGE BOY You can have like, one candy bar and be off the wall!

Books advocating the benefit of "natural food" claim refined sugar causes hyperactivity in children. But the research is very clear: sugar is *not* what makes a child hyperactive. Many studies have found that. One followed two groups of kids: one that was given foods with sugar and another that got foods with artificial sweeteners. To make sure preconceptions didn't influence the test results, neither the parents nor the researchers knew which group got the real sugar.

They monitored the kids for irritability and hyperactivity. They found no difference.

It's hard to believe, because I've seen kids go crazy at parties. Isn't that because of all the sugar they eat? Actually, no. The kids are hyper because they're excited, because there are twenty kids there, because it's a *party*. Food researchers say the only thing that might make kids hyper is the caffeine in chocolate and soda.

MYTH: Reading in low light hurts your eyes.

TRUTH: It won't.

This is another one my mom yelled at me about: "Stop that!" she'd say. "Reading in the dark will destroy your eyes. You want to wear glasses? You want to go blind?"

She was wrong, as she often was. Does it hurt your ears if you listen to a whisper? Nor will it damage your eyes if you read in the dark. In fact, before we had electric lights, most people read by candlelight or gaslight. It didn't hurt our ancestors' eyes, and it won't hurt ours.

Another worry: Sustained and/or close-up focusing, watching TV, computer use, or reading can overload the visual system and stress the muscles responsible for focusing!

Again, doctors say that's completely false. You may feel tired, but close-up focusing does *no* damage to your eyes.

Finally, some people say eyeglasses and contact lenses creates a dependency that makes your vision worse.

Again, this is totally false. Wearing glasses doesn't weaken your eyes in any way.

MYTH: Mouthwash cures bad breath.

TRUTH: Mouthwash often makes it worse.

Bad breath comes from bacteria in the mouth. Mouthwash does kill germs, but here's a dirty little secret: The alcohol in most mouthwashes reduces the bacterial count, but the alcohol dries out your mouth and leaves behind a beautiful home where bacteria grow even faster. So the mouthwash that briefly reduced the bad breath makes it *worse* later.

Doctors we consulted said keeping the mouth moist is the key to fresh breath. It's a reason babies don't have bad breath—they produce lots of saliva.

The companies that produce alcohol-based mouthwashes insist their products are effective. The makers of Scope and Lavoris told us their products have low amounts of alcohol. Listerine, which has up to 27 percent alcohol, sent us a statement saying they have a study proving that Listerine actually increases the flow of saliva. All that is counter to what doctors told us.

Everyone agreed, however, that the best remedy for bad breath is good oral hygiene: flossing, brushing your teeth for at least two minutes, and brushing your tongue. It also helps to keep your mouth moist by drinking lots of water. That also flushes some of the bacteria down.

MYTH: Laptop computers can reduce male fertility.

TRUTH: It does happen.

I assumed this was another urban myth. Laptops are bad for sperm count? C'mon!

The fact is, laptops produce heat. Heat is bad for sperm. "Anything that increases the temperature of the scrotum," Dr. Harry Fisch told us, "can adversely affect sperm production and fertility." Dr. Fisch is a sperm and male fertility expert, a professor of urology at Columbia University. "The testicles are outside the body," he said, "because they need to be cooler."

A 104-degree hot tub may be romantic, but it's a sperm killer, said Dr. Fisch, "and it may take four to six months for the sperm counts to recover."

Laptops, we discovered, produce even more heat than hot tubs. We measured temperatures of 107 degrees on a laptop that had been running for an hour. But there's a simple solution that probably has already come to your fertile mind: Don't put the machine in your lap. If more men put laptops on tables or counters, says Dr. Fisch, fewer couples will have trouble conceiving.

MYTH: Airplane air makes you sick.

TRUTH: Your seatmate makes you sick.

People get sick after flying, and many blame the air that blows out of those nozzles above your seat.

PASSENGER I definitely think that airplane air can make me feel sick. I often get a cold after I fly.

PASSENGER When I get off of the flights, I'm normally congested and have to use my inhalers. And I don't believe airplane air is conditioned the way it should be.

With all that recycled air blowing at you, it's logical to blame the air when you get sick. But filtration experts said cabin air filters are now so good that they capture 99 percent of bacteria and viruses. A 2002 medical study found that passengers flying in planes with recirculated air had no more colds than people on planes ventilated with fresh air.

So why did you catch a cold on the plane? Because you were sitting in a narrow aluminum cylinder crammed with people, some of whom had colds. You picked up their germs by breathing in what they exhaled, or by touching the armrests, pillows, and other things they touched and then touching your eyes or mouth.

Don't worry about that air blowing on you from those nozzles. It may even help keep you safe from some of those germs being coughed up all around you. Worry about washing your hands.

> **MYTH:** Washing with antibacterial soap helps keep you healthy.
>
> **TRUTH:** It's unlikely to make a difference.

For years, TV ads have told us that antibacterial is better.

The typical ad shows warm and fuzzy scenes of family home life, while a narrator ominously warns: "You got kids, you got germs! You need a soap that's made to kill germs."

It sounds logical, and people we interviewed were believers.

FIRST CONSUMER   During cold and flu season, I just like to make sure that I'm killing the bacteria.

SECOND CONSUMER   That's the whole purpose of it being antibacterial! It's supposed to work harder for you!

It is true that antibacterial soaps are thought to lower bacterial counts for a longer period of time, which is why they are used in hospitals. But they have no effect on viruses, and several studies have failed to find any evidence that antibacterial soap will reduce illness. Columbia University researchers once studied hundreds of households, some of which used antibacterial products, others which didn't. They found no difference in coughs, runny noses, sore throats, etc.

We tested some very dirty people: workers at New York's Staten Island Zoo. A microbiologist took bacteria samples from the workers' hands, and had some of them wash with antibacterial soap and some with regular. Then she took more bacterial samples. She found both kinds of soap did a good job killing bacteria. Other, more scientific tests, got similar results.

In other words, even if your workplace is a zoo, washing your hands well will kill the germs. *How* you wash makes more difference than what soap you use. The microbiologist said Americans need lessons in hand-washing technique. Lessons? But after watching her, I see her point: Most of us should wash longer than most of us do—at least thirty seconds, lather up plenty of soap, and rub *hard*—with lots of friction. It's the friction that pulls off the dead skin and dirt that harbors germs. After you dry your hands, be careful not to touch any part of the sink with your clean hands. This usually means using the paper towel to turn off the faucet.

That, said the microbiologists, is better than switching to antibacterial soap. In fact the FDA says it's possible that overuse of antibacterial soap breeds nastier bacteria that may cause more problems in the long run.

So use regular soap. Wash well.

Of course that raises the question, do most people wash at all? Many don't. A recent nationwide survey done in public arenas found that 10 percent of women don't wash their hands after using public restrooms. Men did worse: 25 percent didn't wash. Bad for them. Bad for everyone.

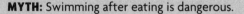

MYTH: Shaving makes hair grow back thicker.

TRUTH: It just seems to.

Little girls are told: Don't shave your legs. If you do, it will grow back quicker, thicker, and coarser.

It's not true. The hair just feels coarser as it first grows back, because the short hairs are stiffer, and that makes you think they're growing faster.

If shaving did increase hair growth, balding men would shave their heads.

Waxing hair off, however, does keep the hair away longer than shaving it does. That's because when you pull off the wax, you pull out hair from under the surface of the skin. It may be three to four weeks before the hair is noticeable again.

MYTH: Swimming after eating is dangerous.

TRUTH: Swim away.

It's another thing your mother nagged you about: If you swim on a full stomach, you may get a cramp—and drown.

The origin of this myth is probably comfort. It doesn't feel good to do *any* sort of strenuous exercise after eating a large meal. Your stomach diverts blood flow from exercising muscles during the digestion process, which leaves you weaker and more out of breath. If you try to work out vigorously, you may get a cramp, which sounds a little scary for swimmers trying to keep themselves afloat.

But the Red Cross says that getting a cramp in the deep end probably isn't life-threatening. As many doctors point out, the real threat to swimmers is alcohol, lack of safety gear on boats, and lack of attention to small children around pools.

For a *20/20* story, we fed Big Macs to a swim team right before practice. We had lifeguards standing by, but they all did fine.

> **MYTH:** A dog's mouth is cleaner than yours.
>
> **TRUTH:** You've got to be kidding.

Dog lovers believe it. They let their dogs lick their faces, and say things like "Dog mouths have nowhere near [as many] germs as live in people's mouths." One pet owner said, "Their saliva is much cleaner. And if you have a cut or anything, if they lick it, it helps heal the cut."

Are you kidding me? Think about where dogs put their mouths. Veterinarian Marty Becker, author of *Chicken Soup for the Dog Owner's Soul,* pointed out, "They lick their privates. They raid the garbage can. We give each other a peck on the cheek when we say hello. They give each other a peck on the rear end. I mean, all you got to do is look, watch, smell, and you'll realize that that is not true."

Maybe people believe dogs' mouths are clean because bacteria in a dog's mouth is usually species-specific—a staph or a strep infection in a dog is not transmissible to a human. You're more likely to get a serious illness by kissing a person than kissing a dog.

The other reason that people believe this myth is that they notice that after their pets lick a wound, the wound heals fast. But that's because the dog's tongue gets rid of the dead tissue, just like a surgeon does when he debrides a wound to get down to healthy tissue. The licking action also stimulates circulation.

But your dog's mouth is filthy.

> **MYTH:** Revenge is sweet.
>
> **TRUTH:** Forgiveness is sweeter.

What's the best thing to do for your health when you've been wronged? Get even? I would think so, because revenge is satisfying. It's why I like movies like *Kill Bill* and *Gladiator*. It feels good to see "justice" done. But it turns out scientists have actually studied revenge, and concluded that revenge is not the best answer.

"There's a lot of research on the negative effects of hostility," says Stanford University psychologist Fred Luskin, author of *Forgive for Good*. "It makes you much more likely to have heart disease. It increases your risk of stress-related disorders. It raises your blood pressure. Wanting to hurt somebody," Luskin told us, "is like pouring Drano into your own insides."

Eva Kor knows that feeling. She will never forget what happened to her and her twin sister sixty years ago. They were ten years old when the Nazis took their family to the concentration camp at Auschwitz. When they arrived, the SS said, "We're looking for twins." They pulled the girls away from their mother.

"We were crying, she was crying," Eva told me. "I remember looking back, seeing her arms stretched out in despair. As the years went by, I always wished that I would have had the courage to run back and say good-bye to her."

We found film in the ABC archives of the two girls at Auschwitz. The Kor sisters and other twins were used as guinea pigs for medical experiments conducted by the "angel of death," Dr. Josef Mengele.

Eva remembered disturbing details. "They took a lot of blood from my left arm. They wanted to know how much blood a person can lose and still live. Dr. Mengele stood by my bed and said I had only two weeks to live."

Somehow, she and her twin sister survived. The rest of their family was killed. But after years of hating the Nazis, Eva says she changed her life for the better simply by choosing to forgive them. I found that hard to understand.

STOSSEL You forgive this doctor?

EVA KOR I forgive everybody.

STOSSEL Why?

EVA KOR   A victim feels hurt, hopeless, helpless, and powerless. A victim never has any choice.

STOSSEL   You have a choice. You could be furious.

EVA KOR   Will that help me? Will it make my life better?

Instinctively, Eva figured out what the researchers had discovered: Letting go of hatred is better for our health and happiness.

CHAPTER ELEVEN

PERILS OF PARENTING

am so grateful that *20/20* assigned me to do parenting stories. I had no kids at the time, no plans to have them, and no interest in them. But I was the "medical psychology guy," and one day I found myself in a hospital nursery being taught how to hold a baby by Dr. T. Berry Brazelton: "Like you're cradling a football, but with the head safely in your hand . . ." I would have been helpless without the football analogy, and in the coming years I stumbled through other lessons.

When I finally married and had my own kids, what I had learned made me a better parent. A little knowledge makes so much difference.

MYTH: Parenting is an instinct.

TRUTH: Instinct is often wrong.

I had thought parenting was instinctive. People have done it for thousands of years. It didn't appear to be something that needed professional training.

My epiphany came while I was doing a report on "intergenerational" day care. Twenty-five-year-old PhD's from an Arizona child-welfare agency were telling retired people how to take care of kids at a day care center. I sat next to a grandmother on the edge of the kids' sandbox, waiting for the camera crew to do their endless lighting. The grandmother had raised a dozen kids and grandkids, and was taking the course only because it was required to get the job. "Aren't you insulted," I asked, "to have to listen to parenting advice from twenty-five-year-olds?" She gave me a surprised look and said, "No. I'm learning so many good new ideas, like, here in the sandbox, when a kid throws sand, instead of saying 'Don't throw the sand,' you tell the kids what *to* do with the sand."

It was my introduction to positive parenting. That, and a hundred other specialists I've been lucky enough to meet, taught me that kids learn best when we tell them what they're doing *right*. "Positive coaching" soccer clinics teach that kids improve most when the ratio of positive/negative comments is five to one. In other words, for every "not that way!" there should be five "good effort . . . nice using your left foot . . ." kinds of comments. This feels forced, but it gets easier, and it works. I know because it helped me with my kids at home.

"Catch your kids doing something right" is how one expert put it. It's not instinct to compliment a child merely for getting dressed on time, or for doing what she'd been told. It's more natural to say no, but when comments are positive, kids listen more. And kids crave attention; so if we don't speak up when they do something good, they'll get our attention by doing what we don't like.

Knowing this can make parenting *so much* easier. You've seen harried parents in the supermarket who constantly tell their kids no, don't do that. The parents who know to say, "Thank you for helping me find the milk" have more pleasant shopping trips. And happier kids.

> **MYTH:** Sparing the rod spoils the child.
>
> **TRUTH:** Other discipline works better.

The old woman in the shoe knew what to do: "She whipped them all soundly and put them to bed."

The Bible recommends beating your kids "with the rod."

Could hundreds of years of nursery rhymes, tradition, and the Bible be wrong? Today, almost every researcher we asked said, "Yes, they are wrong."

"It's probably the best-kept secret of American child psychology that spanking kids produces kids that are more trouble, more hassle for parents, and less well-behaved," sociologist Dr. Murray Straus told me. He spent twenty years studying parents' child-rearing techniques and concluded that parents who spank were more likely to have more trouble with their kids later.

Kids who were spanked frequently liked themselves less, had trouble making friends, and were more likely to be jailed. As adults, they were more likely to act violently, and perhaps because they had come to associate hitting with love, they were more likely to seek relationships with people who were abusive toward them.

The skeptic in me has to wonder: Were they troublesome kids first—and that led to the other problems and to the spankings? How could anyone know which came first? But nebulous as the research may be, the majority of American experts say: "Don't spank."

Few people follow this advice. A national survey found most parents spank their kids at least once every few months.

Dr. Straus and others we consulted recommend less physical forms of discipline: a time-out; taking away a privilege; a reprimand in a strong voice. That will work, they say, if you just *keep doing* it.

Linda and Steve Wursthorn told me, "Yes, it does work, but it's not enough." The Wursthorns and three other families agreed to let our cameras in their homes, so we could watch their lives for several days. (This became *20/20*'s technique for doing parenting stories: Get the cameras in the house so we can *see* it, rather than just hear the parent talk about it. Not only because it's interesting to watch, but because seeing is believing. Today's technology makes this easier: we mount motion-sensor cameras around the home.)

The Wursthorns and the other three families all believed in giving kids time-outs, but said that sometimes you just need to spank.

Linda and Steve have three daughters. We watched as three-year-old Lindsey would not stop tormenting her sister. After several warnings, Linda ordered Lindsey to go to her bed for a time-out. Lindsey wouldn't obey, and Linda spanked her. The spanking seemed to make a bigger impression, but didn't change Lindsey's behavior. The next day, she tormented her *other* sister. Her father gave her a time-out; Lindsey got mad and threw her shoe at him. Steve slapped her. That got her to obey.

Afterward, I sat down with them and told them what our consultants said after watching the tape.

> STOSSEL By hitting her, you're teaching her that violence *works*. This just encourages her to throw more shoes.
>
> LINDA WURSTHORN [getting mad] Well, the experts should be here around dinnertime, okay? Or like bath time, because, you know, I've read the

books. I know what they say. We're talking real life here! I don't think it's violent to spank a child on the bottom to show them, "I am in control here, not you."

STEVE WURSTHORN We're not spanking her to hurt her, we're spanking her to let her know that we're serious.

LINDA WURSTHORN You can't just all the time be sitting there and saying, "Please don't put your sister's head in the toilet bowl, 'cause she's going to drown." Okay? You just can't. If she does it, she's got to get a spanking.

Skeptical as they were, the Wursthorns agreed to meet with Dr. Straus and Dr. Peter Prevora, a psychologist who regularly works with families. The doctors complimented the Wursthorns for using time-outs and lectures, but criticized them for spanking Lindsey when she resisted the time-out. Steve pushed right back.

STEVE WURSTHORN It's not doing her any good if I say, "Yeah, go upstairs," and she doesn't go.

DR. STRAUS But the way to not tolerate it is not by doing just exactly what you're telling the child *not* to do, namely, hit someone. You're telling the child, "It's very wrong to hit other people," and then you *hit* her.

STOSSEL So what does he do about the shoe?

DR. STRAUS You do just what you did but without the hitting. Then when she gave you the other shoe, you reward her for that, and you say, "Oh, that's fantastic." Nothing works all the time, but the hitting doesn't work all the time either.

STEVE WURSTHORN How do we stop the child from running out into the street?

DR. STRAUS You run out, you grab the child, you say, "No!" you do everything you can. That message is communicated. You just leave out the hitting part.

The anxiety in your voice, they said, will spell it out as well as spanking. After two hours of debate, the Wursthorns left, saying they'd think about the methods of discipline the doctors recommended. Here are some of them:

First, talk to the kids. Kids hate lectures as much as spankings. If the child won't listen, demand a time-out, which means you take them away from where they want to be—where everyone's playing.

Second, reward good behavior (another version of the "catch your kid doing something right" advice). It's less natural to say "Thank you for not fighting with your sister," but it makes an impression.

Third, talk to the kids about what's expected of them before you do something with them, and when you're not angry with them. They don't listen well while you're mad.

In one story we did, a boy annoyed his parents by saying "I need to tinkle" whenever he got in the car. He wasn't faking it—it had just become a habit—getting in the car reminded him he had to pee. His parents kept telling him to "go before!" but it never stuck until, advised by a therapist, they had a family meeting. They'd been told: "Get him to look at you, then tell him what you want, and once he understands, have him repeat it back to you." So the father looked him in the eye and spoke to him.

FATHER We are going to have a new rule in the house.
CHILD Okay.
FATHER Every morning before you leave the house, you need to tinkle.
CHILD Okay.
FATHER Can you tell me what I said?
CHILD Yeah.
FATHER What did I say?
CHILD You said when I leave the house in the morning, I have to pee.
PARENTS Very good.

It worked. From then on they got into the car without interruption.

The Wursthorns? Six months later, they said the suggestions were working. Most effective, they said, was rewarding the kids for doing good things and preparing them before an event, away from the moment of frustration. Before she'd go to the supermarket, Linda would say, "Here's what I'd like you to do in the store." And if they did it, she'd praise them. She said that alone did a lot of good. They stopped spanking their kids.

> **MYTH:** Children should obey.
>
> **TRUTH:** Children should think.

Five-year-old Joseph was reluctant to obey. Sometimes, when Joseph's parents, Kristin and Joe Marquez, told him it was bath time, he'd just refuse, and throw a tantrum. Joe felt helpless. "I'll tell Joseph to do something and he turns around and says no to me, in my face."

Joseph's sister, three-year-old Victoria, was starting to copy her brother's behavior. Kristin and Joe told me they were desperate. They were fighting with their children all of the time, Kristin said, and she didn't like the people they'd become. "Every other word out of my mouth is 'Don't do that. Stop doing that. Play nice.' It's always something negative," she told me. "Spanking does not work. Time-outs don't work. I'm just searching my brain for ways to discipline him where it will stick in his mind."

> **KRISTIN MARQUEZ** Six forty-five in the morning it starts, the disobeying. You know, "No, I don't want to get out of bed. No, I don't want to brush my teeth. No, I don't want to wear that, I want to wear this." And battling.

> **JOE MARQUEZ** Every time I have to take him in the morning, my day's ruined and I get to work in the worst mood. I am always late, and he just drives me nuts . . . Sometimes I stop and I think, I'm just no good at being a parent.

> **KRISTIN MARQUEZ** I feel like nothing I do is gonna make anything better. I can't be a good mother, I can't be a good wife because I'm so, my gas is gone. I'm just, you know, I have no patience. I feel like I'm not connecting with my husband. My kids don't mind me. I'm just—emotionally, I'm done. I'm so done. I don't know what to do.

Mac Bledsoe said he knew what to do. Bledsoe is not the usual child care expert. He has no degree in child psychology. His expertise, he says, comes from twenty-nine years of teaching school and being a parent himself. He and his wife, Barbara, raised two successful sons. One is pro football quarterback Drew Bledsoe—famous not just for being an athlete, but for being a well-adjusted one.

Mac and Barbara Bledsoe developed a parenting course titled "Parenting With Dignity." What they and some other therapists teach may surprise you.

"*Obedience* as a tool for discipline is really, really dangerous," Bledsoe says. "It does not teach children to think for themselves, it teaches them to listen to an outside voice to find out how to act."

He said this after watching 20/20's tapes of Joe and Kristin fighting with Joseph. The disobedient behavior that drives Kristin and Joe crazy was a *good* thing, said Bledsoe. It meant Joseph is thinking for himself. "Roll the camera ahead," he said. "Junior high—some kid saying, 'Here's the drugs.' You're not there to say, 'Don't do that, Joseph, don't do that, don't do that.' The willful child that'll stand up to you and say, 'No, I won't do it,' will also stand up to the drug pusher at age sixteen and say, 'No, I'm not gonna do that either.'"

Instead of forcing children to obey, he says, parents should teach them how to make the right decision, and that starts with letting them make decisions—easy ones, where safety is not an issue. Like deciding what to wear.

Watching our videotapes, Bledsoe saw that Joe and Kristina picked out what they wanted Joseph to wear to school. One summer morning, Joseph wanted to wear pants, but because it was so hot, his mother kept giving him shorts. Joseph screamed, "Get the shorts away!"

"Why must Mommy make all the rules?" said Bledsoe. "Give decisions for them to make. Lots of them. Let the kids learn from their own mistakes. Let them experience the consequences." On that hot day, Joseph, in long pants, might be hot and sweaty, but so what? He would learn from his own mistake, said Bledsoe. "You teach a person to ride a bike by putting them on the seat; you teach a person to make decisions by giving them decisions."

Bledsoe thought Joe and Kristin said "no" too much, that what they viewed as disobedience was often just Joseph being a normal kid. Kristin stopped him from climbing into the trunk of their car.

"He's causing stress," said Kristin.

No, said Bledsoe, *Kristin* was causing the stress by stopping him from playing in the trunk for a minute. Because Kristin had so many rules, the kids just tuned her out—became "mother deaf" is how another therapist put it. Pick your battles, say parenting experts. If you don't have a million rules, it's much easier to enforce the important ones, like "Don't run into the street" and "Don't lock yourself in the trunk."

In addition, parents should use fewer words when they give instructions to their kids. Think "KISS"—it stands for "Keep It Simple, Stupid."

This was familiar advice. In story after story where we put cameras in people's homes and then let the experts watch, the experts have said the parents yammer at the kids, explain and justify too much, and so the kids become "parent deaf." "Keep it short," psychologists said. With young kids, you don't have to list the reasons why they should not hit their little sister. Just say, "Don't hit."

If you give fewer commands, the kids are more likely to listen when you have something important to say. We watched the tape of Joe trying to wrestle Joseph out of bed. "Joseph Alex, I have to leave!" Joe yelled. "I don't have time for this! Now I'm going to force you!" Joe was embarrassed that he got so angry. "I cringe looking at it," he said. Bledsoe saw a lesson in it.

> **MAC BLEDSOE** He's trained you to tell him when you really mean it. You don't mean it until you say, "Joseph Alex. I've had enough." Tell your children exactly what you want them to do.
>
> **STOSSEL** But they're *already* doing that. All of us are telling our kids, do this, do that.
>
> **MAC BLEDSOE** Watching the tapes, you're telling him what *not* to do. If I come to you and say, "Don't kick elephants," what are you thinking about right now?
>
> **KRISTIN MARQUEZ** (after a pause) Kicking elephants.

Put *good* images in your kids' heads, said Bledsoe, by telling them what *to* do. In the grocery store, Joseph wanted Kristin to buy him a toy. We videotaped Kristin as she argued with Joseph, saying, "You're *not* getting a toy."

That created the "kick elephants" problem: Joseph focused on the toy, and threw a tantrum. Bledsoe says Kristin should have said, instead, "That's a cool toy, put it back on the shelf and let's go find the popcorn." *Finding the popcorn* is the picture she wants in his mind.

The next step, says Bledsoe, is to teach kids that decisions have consequences. So in the store, Kristin should ask Joseph to help her shop and hope he decides to do it. "And if he doesn't do it," Bledsoe told her, "simply leave. *Say what you mean, mean what you say, do what you say you're going to do.*"

Leaving the store seems excessive and dramatic, but do it once, and the child begins to understand that "you mean what you say." It's not easy to do this if you are in a rush, as we so often are. Better to take the kids to the store when you have extra time, so you can "do what you say you're going to do."

Also, Bledsoe advised, rehearse the next activity. Sit the kids down before you go shopping, before the stress of the moment, and tell them what you expect of them, like, "Joseph, I'd like you to push the cart and help me find the popcorn. And I'd like you to tell me which size to buy." It's about teaching them to think for themselves, said Bledsoe, "so that when they're outside of my presence they can do it."

The Marquezes took home Bledsoe's parenting tapes, and two months later we came back with our cameras. Kristin showed us how trips to the grocery store had actually become "fun" since she started asking Joseph to help make the grocery list. And Joe says now that he lets his son make decisions, mornings are much easier.

> **JOE MARQUEZ** We're bumping heads a lot less. There's no arguments in the morning about what he's going to wear because he's involved in picking it out.
>
> **KRISTIN MARQUEZ** It's no longer "You do as I say." It's, "Well, why are you making that decision?"
>
> **JOE MARQUEZ** I feel good about him, and I'm really proud of him.

Joseph was so much calmer that his teacher commented on it. Best of all, Kristin says she and her husband rediscovered each other—with less stress over the kids, their marriage was better.

MYTH: Children of divorce are more likely to get divorced.

TRUTH: True. But there are ways to make divorce better for the kids.

I wish it were a myth that children of divorce feel more stress, have less emotional security, and are more likely to get divorced when they are adults, but it's all not a myth. When parents divorce, it violates a child's sense of security so much that children often carry the anxiety with them through life.

But there are better ways to ease children through it.

In Oakland, California, an unusual school called Kids' Turn offers a six-week course on coping with divorce. It's an odd course to observe: I watched a teacher say to a class of five-year-olds, "Spending time in two different homes can be confusing. You may feel pulled apart. Do you feel pulled apart?" One child volunteers that he does, saying, "Divorce is the worst part of a kid's life."

It's upsetting to hear that, but the kids seemed to like being there with other kids who were going through what they're going though. At first they were quiet, but they soon began to open up. One eight-year-old told me he'd come to terms with his custody arrangement. "I go to my dad's on Sundays and Wednesday nights," he said, "and this week is a special time, because I'm going to see him on Friday."

Benji and Lara Walklitt's parents had just gotten divorced, and Lara told me that at her school, even though many kids' parents were divorced, it was not okay to talk about divorce around her classmates.

STOSSEL What might they think?

LARA WALKLITT They might think I was weird, different.

BENJI WALKLITT When you talk about it, it makes you feel better.

STOSSEL Why couldn't you talk about it at home?

BENJI WALKLITT Because probably you would feel too sad.

By contrast, at Kids' Turn, they seemed happy to talk about it. Some kids talked about the day they found out about the divorce.

LARA WALKLITT My mom just said it. She didn't stall, she didn't explain it, she just said it and then she got in the car and drove away.

PATRICK My mom and dad took me into their bedroom and told me.

STOSSEL What were your thoughts?

PATRICK I didn't like it 'cause my mom promised that we wouldn't get a divorce and then we got one.

Today, almost a third of America's children live in homes where parents have divorced. Odds are that about five thousand kids will get the word this weekend. It will shake them up, and hurt them in school. Kids' Turn director Rosemarie Boland told me, "Often during the first year, children's grades drop. They have trouble concentrating in school if they're thinking about the divorce."

It's much harder for kids to recover if parents keep fighting. As part of Kids' Turn, kids get to talk to judges who specialize in divorce cases. Judges Roderic Duncan and Ina Gyemant got involved because they saw divorcing parents hurt their kids.

RODERIC DUNCAN The part that really eats you up is these fights that take place with the kids, a five-year-old sitting there watching his mom and dad scream and use horrible words at each other, maybe pick up dishes and throw them at each other, and you try to figure out some way to help them understand the corrosive effect this is having on the life of this little person that they've brought into the world. I've tried lecturing and it doesn't seem to work. I've tried begging them and I've tried putting them in jail.

STOSSEL That doesn't work either?

RODERIC DUNCAN In many cases, it doesn't work. They're back in court again.

STOSSEL Why would Kids' Turn make a difference if all this doesn't?

RODERIC DUNCAN When they sit down here with their kids in the other room and they see their kids talking to other kids who are going through divorce, it seems to get through to their brain.

INA GYEMANT There was one parent who said that he was going to move out of state and he was going to fight his former wife for custody of the child, and after going through the Kids' Turn program, he said, "I'm not going to put my child through that." He said, "I'm going to find a job here and I'm going to stay here."

At Kids' Turn, parents are told, even if you hate your spouse, shut up about it in front of the kids. Kids shouldn't have to take sides. Lara's mom, Karen Kaufman, had clearly gotten that message. "I make sure we include Daddy in their prayers," she said, "and Daddy's girlfriend and Daddy's girl-friend's kids and everything." *That* level of forgiveness is pretty extreme, but good for the kids.

Experts who study divorce say most kids think that somehow, the divorce was their fault. "Almost all kids believe it," Rosemarie Boland told me, that they were bad, that they didn't eat their vegetables, that they fought with their brothers or sisters. That's a big one. I've heard kids say several times, "If only we had gotten along better, Mom and Dad wouldn't have gotten divorced."

People assume older kids will handle divorce better because they are less dependent on their parents. But there's no evidence that older kids do better. They are less likely to blame themselves for the divorce, but more likely to carry their anger about it into other areas of their lives.

Talking about it helps, say the experts, because it teaches kids to accept what seems unacceptable, so they can get on with the business of living their own lives. By week four at Kids' Turn, many kids seemed quite sophisticated about divorce. "At the beginning, it's going to be really, really shocking," Lara Walklitt told me, sounding wise beyond her years, "but after time, it will get better, even though it seems like the world was ending right at that moment."

> **MYTH:** Try for Perfection.
>
> **TRUTH:** Try for Good.

We all want to be perfect. Why wouldn't we? Everywhere we look we're told perfection is the goal. The media applauds the perfect score—the perfect dive, the perfect ten. But one can have too much of a good thing.

Ten-year-old Carly Minder told me, "You have to look perfect. You have to be thin. . . . You have to write perfect, you have to do everything perfect."

For a while, her perfectionism worked for her. She did so well in school that she was moved into a gifted program. When I met her, she was writing at a fourteen-year-old level. But her perfectionism had become tough on people around her. She had lost most of her friends.

> **CARLY MINDER** I think that they were too imperfect. I know that sounds really mean, but—
>
> **STOSSEL** I assume I'm not perfect. What's imperfect about me?
>
> **CARLY MINDER** Just the way your hair is and your eyebrows and . . .
>
> **STOSSEL** What about it?
>
> **CARLY MINDER** It annoys me.

I annoy myself sometimes, but give me a break. I didn't know if Carly was a perfectionist or had obsessive-compulsive disorder, but what she said sounded very much like what I'd heard from kids in Ohio who attended psychologist Sylvia Rimm's class for gifted kids. Rimm showed us tests she uses to separate healthy ambition from unhealthy perfectionism.

For one test, she asks kids to draw something. Some gifted kids were so self-critical that they erased more than they drew. Balls of crumpled paper were hitting wastebaskets all over the room. I watched ten-year-old Caleb look scornfully at his picture. "It makes me feel really weird if I don't have it done exactly right," he said. This perfectionism is not a good thing, says Dr. Rimm, because it makes kids so afraid to fail, that they don't try. "Perfection means there are no mistakes. Kids have to *learn* how to make mistakes."

Carly started having that problem in school. She didn't hand in her work because it was never good enough. She started calling her perfectionism "Mr. P." "I would just get in her face and say, 'Knock it off,'" said Carly's mother. "You know, it's enough already with this Mr. P! Put him to sleep, you know, *euthanize* him!"

Carly said she grieves for her old life, when she was a champion swimmer.

> **CARLY MINDER** I made top ten. I was doing everything.
>
> **STOSSEL** You just gave it up?
>
> **CARLY MINDER** Yeah. I can swim perfectly. I can do my flip turns perfectly [but] I couldn't score the perfect time.
>
> **STOSSEL** It sounds like you're missing out on a lot of what happy little girls have.
>
> **CARLY MINDER** I'm, I'm not happy anymore.

So what should you parents do if you suspect your child has these tendencies? Dr. Rimm says, make it clear to kids that you don't expect perfection. "You want to say, 'You're a kind kid, you're a sensitive kid, you're a strong kid, you're a smart kid, you're a good thinker, you have good ideas,'" she told me. "You're avoiding the kinds of words that put them under pressure to feel like they have to be perfect people."

"Good work" is better than "You're the best!" "That's smart . . ." and "Creative idea" are better than "Genius," "Brilliant," "Albert Einstein."

It's good to remember this when following the "catch your kids doing something right" advice—don't overdo the compliments: "Nice pass" is better than "Perfect pass." Keep it real.

MYTH: Having kids is good for the marriage.

TRUTH: Having kids wrecks some marriages.

Marjorie Johnson had a fantasy of what family life would be. "'Goo goo. Oh, look at the cute little baby. Aren't we going to have a good time?' You know, I had this picture in my mind, one of those hazy sort of Ivory Snow commercial sort of things. Wrong!"

Her child, Lawrence, was not quite two when I met Marjorie and her husband, Stewart. Before Lawrence was born, Stewart and Marjorie shared everything—conversation, romance, even the chores. Lawrence's presence turned out to be something of a shock. They found themselves bickering over proper parenting, and felt less close than they were before their child was born.

STOSSEL What about sex?

MARJORIE JOHNSON What's that?

STEWART JOHNSON We used to be very physically close constantly. We were always all over each other.

MARJORIE JOHNSON Walk down the street, holding—arms around each other, holding hands.

STOSSEL You miss that?

MARJORIE JOHNSON I miss that a lot.

Marjorie said her disappointment with Stewart's parenting killed her affection toward him. "I just didn't want to be touched," she told me.

Doctors Carolyn and Phil Cowan, psychologists married to each other, say marriages often disintegrate after the children are born. "The natural tendency once couples have babies," Carolyn told me, "is for them to feel somewhat more distant from each other, to have more conflict."

"They don't expect to get into conflict with each other," added her husband. "They don't expect that something's going to happen to the relationship that wasn't there before."

But "something" does happen to the relationship. Often it is tension over the sharing of the work. Marjorie chose to be a full-time mother. She spent all day with Lawrence, and felt tied down. Yet when Stewart offered to take Lawrence, Marjorie balked. She said she didn't like the way Stewart handled him. "Marjorie has a way that she does things, and I don't do it the same exact way," Stewart told me. "I feel that my way is probably every bit as good, but sometimes Marjorie would prefer it to be done her way. And that is a source of tension."

Corey and Robbin Weiner were also having trouble with that. Corey helped with the kids, but Robbin said the kids were her responsibility, and she felt overwhelmed. Watching her, I saw why she felt overwhelmed.

She worked about thirty hours a week as an accountant, and when she was home, worked even harder, attending to the details of the kids' lives. Yes, Corey did pitch in. But somehow all the little stuff that has to be done— the schedule, cooking the kids' meals, cleaning and buying their clothes, breaking up fights—the family knew those were things they counted on Robbin to do.

STOSSEL It's kind of like she's the parent and you're the assistant parent?

ROBBIN WEINER It's a good way to put it.

COREY WEINER It's a good way to put it.

Why didn't Corey do more? The same reason Stewart didn't: Their wives don't like the way they do it. We watched Corey help his son with his math, and then watched Robbin complain that Corey let him use a pen instead of a pencil. "He's not allowed to use a pen!" Robbin shouted.

Like Stewart, Corey clearly was not a coparent—he was more the bumbling assistant. Robbin says if she weren't the boss at home, things wouldn't get done "right." "When he serves dinner, it's a hot dog, and I'll say, 'Oh, what did they eat with it?' And he'll say, 'Nothing.'"

Corey just shrugged.

What's going on? Corey's not normally a lazy guy. He is a radiologist who works hard at the office. Yet at home he backs off, and leaves the parenting to Robbin.

Psychologist Ron Taffel runs workshops for parents. He says the conflict over who does how much work at home is such a common problem that a simple test illuminates it. Taffel asks fathers and mothers to make a list of what they do for the kids. First he reads a list from one of the more involved fathers, something like, "I talk to the kids, try to find out how school was, put the dishes in the dishwasher, set up for dinner . . ."

Many women say, "I wish my husband did that much." Then Taffel pulls out the women's lists. Everyone laughs at how much longer they are. One woman's list was on a scroll that dropped all the way to the floor. The "endless list," Taffel calls it, and said, "Every woman watching knows what I mean when I say the 'endless list.' They just get it, they know."

They get it because despite today's supposedly egalitarian relationships, women still do the vast majority of the housework and child raising. To illustrate how unequal the work is, Taffel quizzes the parents:

Do you know your child's shoe size?

Do you know their teachers' names?

Who chooses the pediatrician? The babysitter?

Who organizes birthday parties?

It's almost always mothers who raise their hands. It's why Robbin said she was "the boss," and Corey the "assistant parent."

STOSSEL You supervise him?

ROBBIN WEINER Well, it needs to be done. Sometimes I wish I didn't need to.

STOSSEL And how do you feel when she talks to you that way?

COREY WEINER Like I got to answer to the boss of the house, at least as far as the kids are concerned.

Taffel says when fathers feel supervised and judged, they take on even fewer responsibilities. He tells mothers, if you want your husband to do more, relinquish control. "The biggest single thing that mothers can do," he said, is to "not comment, criticize, or monitor when your husband does stuff around the house with the kids." Let them do it 'wrong.' Your husband won't kill your child if he does it his way, and if you cut him some slack, he'll do more parenting."

It made sense to Robbin, who said, "I didn't realize that I kind of perpetuated a lot of my problems." Once Robbin backed off, Corey started doing more. When we returned a month later, his relationship with their daughter was better, and Corey and Robbin's relationship had improved enough that she could laugh at how controlling she had been.

ROBBIN WEINER He fed them, I think, two nights this past week, and I never even asked him what he fed them.

COREY WEINER They're still alive.

ROBBIN WEINER [smiling] Right.

Dr. Phil Cowan had other advice: "A couple should sit down every day for five minutes—not for an hour, not even going out for a long dinner—and kind of check in and say, 'How are you? How are you doing?'" he told us. "Just check in with each other. That tends to get left out in a busy day."

Many marriage counselors tell couples five minutes is good, but you should also have one real "date" a week—even if it's just dinner at home without the kids. Get friends, grandparents, whomever, to babysit, but spend some time alone. The goal is to remind yourself why you got married in the first place: You are husband and wife, not just parents.

For months, the Johnsons couldn't do that.

STEWART JOHNSON We wouldn't say anything to each other. And we were walking around, there was this—this tension. You could slice the air with a knife.

STOSSEL What broke that?

STEWART JOHNSON Marjorie finally said something to me.

MARJORIE JOHNSON We were driving in the car, and I just started to cry. I remember looking out the window and just feeling so bleak. I was so miserable and so sick inside. I just said, "I can't be married to you anymore if we don't do something about this."

They started to talk about it. That was the therapists' other advice: Make yourselves talk about it. In the Johnsons' case, it led to those "dates" and still more talk. "I guess it's like any problem in that regard," Stewart told me. "You know, the first step is acknowledging that it's there."

Finding ways to talk about it, it turns out, is key to improving many family relationships.

> **MYTH:** Boys won't talk about their feelings.
>
> **TRUTH:** Boys talk, if you know how to ask.

In 1986, baseball player Lee Mazzilli helped the New York Mets win the World Series. After retiring from the big leagues, he took a job in Florida, managing a minor league team. His kids missed him. His daughters, Lacey and Jenna, let their feelings pour out. They regularly wrote letters saying, "Daddy, I love you and miss you." They spent hours talking to him on the phone. We eavesdropped.

JENNA MAZZILLI I love you too. And Daddy, before you go, can you talk to me one more time?
LEE MAZZILLI Okay, babe.
JENNA MAZZILLI Okay, I love you.

By contrast, Lee's son, LJ, said he didn't want to talk to his father on the phone; he'd rather go outside to play. You might say there's nothing wrong with this. Boys will be boys. But LJ had begun acting out in school and at home. It upset his mom.

DANI MAZZILLI LJ went sort of off the wall.
STOSSEL Off the wall how?
DANI MAZZILLI Well, he's just more aggressive, more quick to a temper than he usually is, picking fights all the time with the girls.

LEE MAZZILLI Instigator at times.

DANI MAZZILLI Disruptive, not listening to me at all.

LEE MAZZILLI I think sometimes my wife likes to get too analytical about a lot of things, just all the time. She gets to that deep stuff. I look at it as normal.

STOSSEL That it's because he's a boy?

LEE MAZZILLI That's what I feel.

While Lee said LJ's behavior was just normal "boy stuff," Harvard psychologist William Pollack said it is not normal, and not good for boys. Boys stifle their emotions because people tell them to "act like a man," he said, and by age six, boys have learned to keep their feelings to themselves.

At the University of Connecticut, Professor Ross Buck hooks men and women up to a polygraph machine that registers nervousness. Then he shows them slides—some pleasant, others threatening. Women visibly react to the slides, but men are stone-faced. It's not that they don't react. They just hide it. Their polygraph readings show they feel lots of emotion.

While six-year-olds might deny that they're hiding anything, the twelve- and thirteen-year-olds I interviewed at West Middle School in Andover, Massachusetts, admitted it. They told me it's bad to show weakness. Jeff Schmidt was once hit by a baseball in gym class, and he cried.

JEFF SCHMIDT, THIRTEEN I will be teased about it for the rest of the year. And maybe it will even continue throughout the summer. Because it's not normal. Not normal for a boy to cry.

OLIVER GREGORY, THIRTEEN Also, when a guy has a problem, especially if, like, another guy is making fun of you at school. If you were to tell your parents about it and then someone were to find out, you will be made fun of for the rest of your life. That's wussy. That's like a mama's boy. So you, like, *never* want to do that.

JEFF KANE, TWELVE It's really difficult to go up to people and say, you know, "I have a problem." Even though there's guidance counselors and there's teachers and parents and stuff, I personally feel uncomfortable going to people with a problem.

Girls told us they'd have no trouble saying that they have a problem. Nor would they shrink from "acting like a boy." Girls can move out of the "girl" stereotype and be tomboys. A boy, however, cannot be a "tom girl"—or a "jane boy"—there isn't even a name for it. Dr. Pollack told me this pressure to be "manly" is not good for boys.

"If we were to say to four- or five-year-old girls, 'Be on your own. Don't express your feelings. Don't cry, you're being a baby,' we would say, 'Oh, my God, we can't do that to her,'" Dr. Pollack said. "But we do it with boys, not because we don't love them, but because we think that's what will make them real men. It doesn't work that way."

When I asked Lee Mazzilli's daughters if they missed him, the girls immediately said they did, and that they sometimes cry for Daddy. But LJ told me he never cries.

L J MAZZILLI Not me.

STOSSEL So [your sisters] cry, but you don't?

L J MAZZILLI Nope.

STOSSEL How come you don't cry?

L J MAZZILLI I don't know. *[I looked at him until he broke the silence.]* Because I'm a boy and I'm not a girl.

That, anyway, is what he told me. But Dr. Pollack says the way to learn the truth from a boy is to *do* something with him—some activity, anything he likes—in LJ's case, building a truck out of Legos. While building trucks, LJ told Dr. Pollack the truth, which was the opposite of what he'd told me.

DR. WILLIAM POLLACK Do you ever cry when you feel sad?

L J MAZZILLI Yeah.

DR. WILLIAM POLLACK Do you think people know that you're crying?

L J MAZZILLI No.

DR. WILLIAM POLLACK You're not supposed to show them?

L J MAZZILLI Nope.

I asked Pollack why L J didn't say that to me. I thought his answer was enlightening. "Boys are almost phobic of being ashamed," he said. "When I talked to him, I did three things that were different. I put him in a safe space in which there weren't other people or at least a lot of other people watching. I engaged in action—because it's so important to engage in action play with boys when we talk. And I let him lead the talking. And once that started, I did one other thing. I shared my own feelings with him. I told him about my own childhood, how my own father had been away for a while. And all of a sudden his sadness just opened wide up."

DR. WILLIAM POLLACK It must be really hard not having your dad at home.

L J MAZZILLI Yeah, it is.

DR. WILLIAM POLLACK So what do you do about that?

L J MAZZILLI I do my homework in his office where he does his work.

DR. WILLIAM POLLACK In the same place where he would do his work?

L J MAZZILLI Yeah.

DR. WILLIAM POLLACK So it's almost like you're right where he would be, huh?

L J MAZZILLI Yeah.

DR. WILLIAM POLLACK Do you ever pretend like you're being him?

L J MAZZILLI Yep.

Pollack says parents should learn that their sons probably won't respond to direct questioning as well as their daughters. Girls volunteer more, and the more we say, the more they say.

DR. WILLIAM POLLACK The typical example is the little girl rushes home from school, bursts in the door, is almost always in tears and says, "Mommy, Julie wouldn't let me play with her, and she said these bad things . . ." And Mom sits down and says, "Oh, let's talk about it." And they talk for hours and hours and hours. And she says, "Oh, Mom, you really helped me." Johnny comes home. He has a scowl on his face. He's lost a soccer game. Mom, in her gut, knows something's going wrong. He says, "Nothing, Mom. I'm fine." He goes to his room.

STOSSEL What should a parent do?

DR. WILLIAM POLLACK Don't push him. Give him space to save face. And then he'll come out of that room, and he'll give a signal. It won't be one that's easy to know. You have to learn about that. He might say, "When's dinner going to be ready?" or "When's Dad going to be home?" That's his signal, without knowing it, for saying, "I need some help." I had one mother who talks about what she called "car therapy." Her son would do this kind of thing after a soccer game or a difficult time at school. And she'd wait for that moment, and he'd come out and he'd say, "When's dinner ready?" And she'd say, "You know, let's not do dinner right now. Let's go for a ride and get some ice cream." And his eyes would light up. And they'd get in the car.

And they'd go for the ride. But it wasn't the ice cream, it was the action and the safe space with Mom. And on the way there, she'd say, "You know, you seem a little upset." And tears would come to his eyes. And he'd talk about his feelings.

Over the next few months, Dani Mazzilli tried out Dr. Pollack's advice. When Dani sensed something might be bothering LJ, she gave him time to be alone and then offered to play basketball with him. While playing the game, LJ suddenly started talking. Dani calls it "basketball talk." And it's worked. LJ stopped acting out in school, and he's happier at home.

> **MYTH:** Parents should teach boys and girls the same things.
>
> **TRUTH:** Boys and girls need some different lessons.

Each sex negotiates the world a little differently. Men tend to just say what they want. Women often pepper their requests with "please," "thank you," or "would you mind?"

Think I'm being sexist? Check out the experiment that child development expert Cam Leaper persuaded me to do: We made some lemonade, but instead of putting in sugar, we put in lots of salt. Then I gave it to some boys and girls, ages eight to twelve. The boys made faces, rudely spat it out, and said it tasted terrible.

I assumed the girls would do the same things, but was I ever wrong. They politely drank it, although some looked as if they were choking.

STOSSEL How is that lemonade?

FIRST GIRL It's good.

SECOND GIRL Good.

STOSSEL Is it really? [Only when I pushed her, did she shake her head and make a face.] How come you didn't tell me it was bad?

FIRST GIRL 'Cause I didn't want to be rude to you.

THIRD GIRL I just didn't want to make anyone feel bad that they made this so sour.

Most boys didn't worry about making the lemonade maker feel bad. We tried another test. We brought brightly wrapped gifts into the room, and told the kids they could pick one. Following Dr. Leaper's advice, we had filled each box with a truly disappointing gift: socks and a pencil. Again, the girls were so polite.

STOSSEL So what do you think of that as a gift?
FIRST GIRL Good.
STOSSEL Come on, isn't this kind of a lousy gift?
SECOND GIRL Ooh.
STOSSEL Ooh? Ooh, what?
SECOND GIRL Just what I needed, socks and a pencil.

These girls obviously had social skills I lack. Anyone who gives them a gift is going to feel good about it. The boys were not about to make me feel good.

FIRST BOY What? Socks and a pencil? Rip-off!
SECOND BOY Who needs socks? I got plenty of socks at home.

Susan Witt, who teaches childhood development at the University of Akron, told me boys and girls respond differently in situations like that because we parent them differently. We teach boys to be assertive, and girls to please others. These differences came out when we asked the kids to describe themselves. Almost all the girls used the word "nice" or "nice person." Boys rarely said "nice."

STOSSEL Drew, he's . . .
FIRST BOY Talented.
SECOND BOY I am smart.
THIRD BOY I'm very good at math.
FOURTH BOY I'm funny a lot.

Both funny and nice are good qualities, but many girls are too eager to be nice, and boys too direct, says Dr. Witt, and it's up to parents to teach them differently. I suggested that maybe boys and girls are different because we're born different.

"We're born different," she told me. "We've got, you know, boys are X-Y's and girls are X-X's. But, by and large, John, it is primarily socialization and I believe that right down to my socks."

Psychologist Phyllis Katz found evidence of that in her famous "Baby X" study. She asked adults to play with a baby: "We said, 'This is Johnny, just play with Johnny any way that you'd like,' or 'This is Jane, just play with Jane any way that you'd like. Here's some toys.'"

It was always the same baby. But when adults thought they were holding "Jane," they held the baby gently, and gave it dolls. When they thought the baby was Johnny, they were rougher, and offered toys like footballs. That can change the way a child thinks.

We tried a "bitter lemonade" test on university students too. Again the women lied.

FIRST WOMAN Did you make this yourself? It's really good.
SECOND WOMAN I do like it.
THIRD WOMAN It's good.

The college men were not as rude as the little boys, but they were honest. They made faces.

FIRST MAN Rather tart.
SECOND MAN Very tangy lemonade.

Georgetown University linguist Deborah Tannen did the adult test for us. She's written best sellers about gender differences, and argues that these experiments suggest both sexes have room for improvement. Research in the workplace shows men's careers are hurt when men are too blunt, and women achieve less when they're too nice. Each sex, she says, would benefit by adopting some of the opposite sex's traits.

DEBORAH TANNEN For the men, it might mean backing off, toning down, or just saying a few words to show that they're cognizant of the other person's feelings.
STOSSEL But men dominate the workplace. So maybe being honest or brutally obnoxious works?
DEBORAH TANNEN It's going to work with some people and not with others. Guys who didn't get promoted or hired because they were called "arrogant," as I encountered in my own research, those guys might have done better if they'd come across as less assertive.

So how do we teach the girls to be more assertive, and teach the boys people skills? As usual, we asked some families from our experiments to let us put cameras in their homes. Then we showed the tapes to Dr. Witt. She noticed that at the home of the girls who were very nice, the word *nice* was used a lot, as in "You're so nice . . . be nice to your sister." When the girls got aggressive, their parents repeatedly reined them in.

"The parent is constantly telling the little girl to 'be nice, be careful, cool it,'" Dr. Witt told me. "It gets in the way of them being assertive and making decisions for themselves."

Witt also pointed out parents of girls tended to do things for their kids—lift things for them—help them open a box that's hard to open. This can make girls feel helpless, less confident, explained Witt. The moral: "Challenge daughters, don't step in and rescue them every time they have a problem." She gave the same advice I'd heard dozens of times for other parenting issues: Whenever you can, let little girls make choices—even if it's just picking out what to eat.

"The girl who knows how to make a decision or starts making decisions when she's little," said Witt, "is going to be one of those girls who's better able to make decisions and assert herself as she gets older."

And what about those obnoxious boys? At home, the tapes showed they were given lots of room to "act like boys." Too much, said Witt. One boy yelled for a glass of milk. Watching his mother on tape, Witt said, "When he's screaming for the drink, she could walk out of the room and say, 'I'm not going to respond to you when you behave that way.'"

Her point: Teach better behavior by withdrawing attention—save the attention for a time when he politely asks for the milk (catch him "doing something right"). Then, says Witt, "Give the child a hug, a pat, some kind words." Do those things, she says, and both boys and girls will be better for it.

MYTH: Teenagers do foolish things.

TRUTH: Teenagers do foolish things.

In some ways, teenagers are superior to adults. Their minds are open to ideas adults miss. Teenage chess prodigies Bobby Fischer and Garry Kasparov found strategies their elders never conceived of. Jaron Lanier was fifteen when he invented the computer simulation virtual reality. Picasso was just fourteen when he painted masterpieces. Mozart . . . You get the point.

And yet teens do stupid and reckless things. How can they be smart and stupid? Do their brains work differently? Yes, say researchers at Harvard Medical School's Brain Imaging Center. By using MRI machines to scan the brains of teenagers and people my age, doctors can see just how substantial these differences are.

The doctor in charge, Deborah Yurgelun-Todd, told me that when adults answer questions, the MRI scans show that we use our prefrontal cortex—the rational, thinking part of our brain. Teens, by contrast, rely on the amygdala, the instinctual part of their brain. This may be why teens are creative. "Some of our better creative works occur during this time of life," she said, "because there's not that sense of 'I shouldn't do this' or 'I can't do this.' "

Unfortunately, working the amygdala also means teens do less critical thinking. The amygdala is the gut-reaction part of the brain, and "going with their gut" is a reason teens do foolish things: Their gut isn't very smart. As part of the Harvard test, they had us look at pictures of faces and asked, "What expression are these faces making?"

The facial expressions seemed clear to me: Shocked. Angry. Sad. Happy. But teens don't read the faces very well. Yurgelun-Todd says this is why teens often exercise bad judgment. They just are not aware that the teacher is mad or that their girlfriend is hurt. "Their brains aren't adult or mature," she said, "and they don't yet have the wherewithal to do everything we expect them to do."

So they do dumb things. And then they lie about it. On anonymous surveys, about 90 percent of high schoolers said they lie to their parents. A group of teens laughed and nodded when I read them that 90 percent statistic. "I lie all the time!" one told me unapologetically. "It doesn't matter if it's to my mom or to a teacher. You lie to get your ass out of trouble."

Lori Bloom knows her daughter, Ashley, lies to her. We were taping in their home in Bath, Maine, when Lori figured out that Ashley had hidden a bad test result.

ASHLEY BLOOM I forgot. I'm sorry.

LORI BLOOM I don't think you forgot. I just— I don't trust that you're going to tell me the truth. I don't trust that you tell me that you're going to go somewhere and that you're going to be there.

Ashley told us she and her friends *have* to lie because parents go crazy if they tell them the truth.

ASHLEY BLOOM   That terrifies us. We don't know how they're going to react, if they're going to scream, if they're going to cry, if they're just going to storm off and say, "Get out of the house!"

The advice from many family therapists was similar to the advice we got
about younger kids: The more rules you have, the tougher it is to parent, and
with a teen, the more you get lied to. Our cameras were rolling in the home
of Francine Wenzel, a single mom in Haskell, New Jersey, who tried to maintain control of her kids by having *very* strict rules, like a 9:30 weekend curfew
for her fifteen-year-old son, Matt.

FRANCINE WENZEL   If you were home more often, you could sit and talk to
me. One night a week, I don't work, Saturday night. Why don't you
just try to stay home?

MATT WENZEL   Yeah, right, Saturday night. Now, you, you're smoking crack.

FRANCINE WENZEL   You've lied to me on several occasions. [Even a 9:30] curfew is a privilege which you don't deserve.

MATT WENZEL   Nine thirty, I'm fifteen. Come on now.

FRANCINE WENZEL   What time do you want it to be?

MATT WENZEL   Mom—people don't go out till eight thirty!

FRANCINE WENZEL   You're still children! There are crazy people out there.
You know this! But I forgot, you're Jesus Christ. Nothing happens to
you, right? You're invincible, right?

Here Francine made a mistake I often make. Sarcasm is my favorite form
of humor, and sometimes I use it when dealing with my kids. But experts told
us, as parents, sarcasm *hurts* our cause. Little kids may think we're serious,
and with teens, sarcasm creates a "kicking elephant" problem. It puts the
wrong image in their brains.

When we showed our tapes to family therapists Dr. Charles Foster and
Mira Kirshenbaum, their first comment was about Francine's strict rules.

MIRA KIRSHENBAUM   She wants to spend more time with him. Please! One
night a week. And she can't get him to do it. Well, of course not. What
do they do when they spend time together? They fight!

DR. CHARLES FOSTER   She says, "You don't make good decisions. You don't
have good judgment. You're a child. You're a mess." She might as well
just build a fire and then pour gasoline on it. Because she's saying, "I
don't care what you say. You're just a kid." It's that attitude, which is

perfectly appropriate to a five-year-old, [that] means that she's struggling now that her kid is fifteen. She should be saying to him, "I know you're not a kid anymore."

MIRA KIRSHENBAUM To have a self, to know who you are is an enormous task. And in the five thousand days of adolescence, every teenager is trying to leave home. And the only way she can leave home is if she accomplishes that. But if you're going to try to control her, then you're making it a battle between listening to you or listening to herself.

MYTH: Be your kid's friend.

TRUTH: Be a parent.

Some parents think they are supposed to try to be their teens' friends. But Dr. Foster said that's a bad idea, and anyway, he joked, "Why would you want to be your kid's friend? They don't know anything, and their music's lousy." Instead, he said, be an ally—someone who offers help, but doesn't try to control.

Parents want to impose rules to control their kids because they want to protect them, but with teens that's almost impossible. Just enforcing rules is tough enough, because parents are not with their teenagers for most of the day.

MIRA KIRSHENBAUM Eighty-five percent of the time, kids are alone or with their friends.

DR. CHARLES FOSTER Why would you have a rule that you can't enforce, you can't police, and you can't monitor? What are you going to do? Tell him what to do until he's what, twenty-five, thirty-five?

MIRA KIRSHENBAUM And then what? This is a human being who has not learned to listen to himself. What is he going to do? If you've been controlling your kid, then you have created someone who doesn't know how to navigate.

STOSSEL So you have to let your fourteen-year-old daughter date? And what if she comes home with a guy whose tongue is pierced and has something gross printed on his T-shirt? You say, "Welcome, kids"?

DR. CHARLES FOSTER If you're a smart parent, when she comes home with this guy with the disgusting message on his T-shirt and his tongue is pierced and he has an arrow through his head or whatever, you say, "Hey, Scar, welcome to our family."

STOSSEL   I don't like this kid in my house.

MIRA KIRSHENBAUM   You're setting up a Romeo and Juliet scenario, because then she goes underground with it and she falls more and more deeply involved with him.

DR. CHARLES FOSTER   It's not a problem that you have values. It's good that you communicate your values. The problem enters when you have a bunch of little rules that poison your relationship with your teenager.

Fighting over small stuff isn't worth it, the experts told us. Get off your kid's back. Instead, focus on a few important rules—don't drive drunk, call when you're late, don't cheat—whatever's important to you.

MYTH: Teens need their parents less.

TRUTH: Teens need parents just as much.

Many parents pull away when their teenage kids grow quiet, or moody, and act like they don't need us. The moodiness comes as a shock because when they were preteens, the kids were so attached to us. Now they often act as if they don't care if we're alive or dead. Part of us understands that this is a necessary breaking away, a separation from parents that has to happen during adolescence for the teen to become an independent adult. But it is hard to watch. I liked how Dr. Foster framed it. He said, "Why put it in terms of rebellion? Why not put it in terms of a transition from listening to you, the parent, to listening to *himself*, as the adult?"

It's no longer enough for us to tell them the stove is hot; now they have to touch it themselves. I grew up in the 1960s, when we rebelled in all kinds of ways that bugged our parents. In the '50s, there was rock and roll. Now teens may dye their hair, pierce their tongues. It's the rite of passage, the need to try out new personalities, and become a separate person. If it appalls parents, so much the better—because that reassures the teen that he is achieving a degree of independence.

But teens do need rules, and they need *us,* reminded the experts. Some of us parents feel that, by the time our kids are teens, we no longer have any influence, because the only people teens will really listen to are their peers. But that's not true.

Every psychologist we consulted told us teenagers may act as if they don't like our questions, but they do hear them, and they would be sad if we stopped asking. "You have an enormous amount of influence," Dr. Foster told me. "Deep down, your kid is feeling unloved and scared."

Interviewing teens, I was surprised at how often I heard that.

FIRST MALE TEEN I've always been so scared of, you know, what am I going to do with my life?

SECOND MALE TEEN I really wish I was, like, a lot closer with my dad especially, because he, like, gets home from work at, like, five or six o'clock and then he goes into his room and watches basketball and football or whatever season it is.

FIRST MALE TEEN You know, sometimes I wish that they would be more strict, like, you know, set a little more rules. I know I'm going to regret [saying it on TV].

STOSSEL Why would you want them to be more strict? That would take away your freedom.

FIRST MALE TEEN Because if they're more strict, then, like, they participate more in my life.

Teenagers may not show it, but they do want our interest and want us to set limits. It makes them feel safe and loved. Research actually shows the current teen generation feels unusually close to their parents. I thought their heroes were rock stars, professional athletes, and friends, but the researchers said, "No, go ask them and you'll see." So I did.

STOSSEL Who would you say are the people in your lives that are the most important to you?

FIRST MALE TEEN My parents.

SECOND MALE TEEN Mostly my father.

THIRD MALE TEEN Both my parents.

So it went. We are still very important to them.

But they are hard to talk to. To maintain communication, the therapists advised, don't lecture. Instead, said Mira Kirshenbaum, "Ask questions. Listen, listen, listen!"

"If you ask your kid questions about how she felt and why she did it and what it meant," said Dr. Foster, "she's going to feel that you are a safe person to tell things to. Then you can say, 'Can I tell you how I feel?' You've earned the right now to talk about how you feel because she's opened up first," he explained. "That's how parents who really do have influence with their kids get influence, by listening to their teenagers talk first."

Only after you listen should you say what you would do. The teens may not act like they hear it, but the experts say it will make a difference later. After all, surveys show most young adults eventually do adopt their parents' values.

For many parents, what worries them most during the teen years is the sexual experimentation. By the end of high school, about half the teens in America say they've had sex. It's always tough for parents to talk to kids about sex, especially when the kids roll their eyes and act like they don't want to talk to you about anything. But they do.

MYTH: Talking to your kids about sex will make them want to have sex.

TRUTH: They're already thinking about it.

I understand why people hesitate to talk to teens about sex. It's logical to think that if we parents bring it up, our kids will think, "Oh, I guess it's time for us to do it."

Yet there's a lot the kids should know. Not talking about sex leaves room for so much ignorance. Years ago, there was so little sex talk that even adults were ignorant. That's actually why we now have products like Kellogg's Corn Flakes and graham crackers. People thought spicy foods would lead kids to have sex—Dr. Justin Richardson, author of *Everything You Never Wanted Your Kids to Know About Sex, But Were Afraid They'd Ask*, explained that those bland foods were designed to avoid "inflaming the sexual appetite." Today we know more about sex, and parents are told, "Don't wait for the kids to ask, *you* bring it up." I spoke to Dr. Richardson.

STOSSEL Couldn't bringing up the subject backfire? If you tell a twelve-year-old kid about sex, they're going to want to go have sex.

DR. JUSTIN RICHARDSON That's the myth and it's a really common fear. But the research says the answer is no.

STOSSEL And how can that be? I mean I would think the twelve-year-old, the fourteen-year-old says, "Gee, if everybody is talking about it, I should check this stuff out." He might have never thought about it before then.

DR. JUSTIN RICHARDSON You may not be going there as a parent. But believe me, their friends are going there! And the media is going there. They're hearing about sex. What you want to do is lend your voice to the chorus. It's important to make sure that somebody is talking to your kid about sex other than their best buddy or a character on a television show.

Twenty-eight studies of school sex education programs, regardless of whether they teach abstinence or condoms, found no suggestion that early sex discussions lead to earlier experimentation. Nine studies concluded it made the kids wait longer to have sex. Of course sex ed isn't the same as parents ed (there are no controlled studies on parents talking to children), but every expert we asked said: *Talk* to your kids.

Susan's daughter, Emily, was twelve when Susan decided to have The Talk.

SUSAN I said, the best time to do this is in the car.

EMILY She locked the doors, wouldn't let me get out. *[Emily was so uncomfortable, she wouldn't look at her mother.]* I looked at my feet, the floor, out the window. Anywhere else but at my mom.

But she said the talk itself was comforting, and her mother was glad she did it. "I think it relieved some of the things that were going on in her head about the other kids in school. And I think it gave her what she needed."

MYTH: You can't watch your kids too closely.

TRUTH: You can get too close for comfort.

In this era of two-paycheck families, kids are often left unsupervised for large portions of the day. How is a parent to cope? Technology is one answer: More parents are spying on their kids.

Spying is suddenly much easier than ever before. Many stores sell surveillance cameras right alongside the home video models, and these days they are tiny and relatively cheap—as little as seventy dollars. Linda Puzino's job kept her away from home until seven p.m., but her thirteen-year-old son, Derrick, got home at three; in any parent's mind, that's a four-hour window for trouble.

Derrick told his mother he'd spend the time alone in his room, doing homework. She decided to be sure: She had a camera installed in his room. From any computer at the office, she is able to monitor what he is doing. Even out of the office, she could watch him on her handheld PDA.

> **LINDA PUZINO** He doesn't know when I'm looking at him. So it really is being a detective of sorts.
>
> **STOSSEL** And how often do you watch?
>
> **LINDA PUZINO** I watch, I don't know, probably every ten minutes or so. The camera acts as a cop in the corner.
>
> **STOSSEL** What message does this say to his friends when they come over?
>
> **LINDA PUZINO** Your mom loves you. And she's watching out for you the best that she can.

Linda at least told Derrick about the camera; some parents install equipment secretly—and it can be very hard to spot.

We found cameras available that were hidden in smoke detectors, teddy bears, pencil sharpeners, and phone jacks. We viewed home videos that confirmed some parents' worst fears: kids stealing money, drinking liquor, getting drunk and throwing up.

One man selling this equipment told us that confronting your kids with taped evidence is the best way to get everyone to admit there's a problem and move toward solving it: "You're doing it because you love them," he said. "You want to make sure that they are on the straight and narrow."

Louis Gonzalez and Patricia Quiceno told me they spied on their kids because they believed it would help keep them safe. "We do feel a little bit badly because we took a little bit of their privacy," Louis said. But he and Patricia worked two jobs, and they worried about leaving their kids home alone. So they bought a camera and hid it in their living room.

Mostly they saw the kids doing homework and watching TV. But one day, the camera captured twelve-year-old Cynthia and eleven-year-old Jesse hosting a "spin the bottle" party with three other friends. It's not the spin the bottle I knew as a kid. In this game, if the bottle points to you, you take off your shirt or—as Jesse did—take a swig from a bottle of beer.

"What really surprised me the most was seeing my son grabbing the beer and drinking it," Louis said. "And then kissing this little girl and dancing and acting all weird," Patricia added. "I never imagined that they could do something like that at home."

Louis and Patricia confronted the kids, who at first tried to bluster that it wasn't they who were on the tape. We watched with our own cameras as the kids finally fessed up, seemingly contrite. "I was disgusted by my own behavior," Jesse said. "What we did was wrong," said Cynthia, "and hopefully those people that see this video will want to buy the surveillance cameras."

It sounded too pat to me, so I put the matter before a jury of Jesse's and Cynthia's peers—a group of teenagers who had also been snooped on by their parents. I played back the contrite statements about "never doing it again," and watched the kids snicker.

ARIEL ASTRACHAN He's a liar. They'll do it again.

STOSSEL Why would he lie to us?

ARIEL ASTRACHAN Because they're kids. They don't want to embarrass their family. They have to say those things.

ASHLEY KEELOR My parents don't trust me now. But they lied to me also, so I don't trust them as much.

JOHN MCDEVITT There's just a lack of respect now. The only thing that my parents have achieved is that I don't talk to them.

Loss of trust is the reason that every teen expert we consulted told us spying is a bad idea. "All spying does is tell a kid that the reason for doing the right thing is because you're being watched," psychologist Dr. Neil Bernstein told me. "That doesn't instill any values." Then how do we parents find out what our kids are doing? "*Ask* them, for goodness sakes," Dr. Bernstein said. "If you have a relationship, he may not lie to you. Call other parents, talk to friends, talk to teachers, talk to the school."

The teenagers agreed. Don't spy, they said, just talk to us.

STOSSEL Can you learn as much by talking?

ARIEL ASTRACHAN Yeah.

STOSSEL But you might lie.

ARIEL ASTRACHAN So? When you were younger, your parents didn't have this technology.

STOSSEL And I lied to them.

ARIEL ASTRACHAN Exactly. So why can't we just continue that? I mean, I think you turned out fine.

That remains to be seen.

One final thought. No matter what you tell your kids, every expert said they're more influenced by what you *do* than what you *say*. They look up to you. Even when you don't think they're paying attention, they notice all kinds of things about you. Later they imitate what you do.

So if you're a good person, you give a good message to your kids.

CHAPTER TWELVE

THE PURSUIT OF HAPPINESS

We take the pursuit of happiness seriously. We spend millions on therapy, self-help books, and keeping up with the Joneses. Being happy is such an ingrained goal that it's shocking to discover that it is a relatively new idea. Through most of history, life was so nasty that happiness never even occurred to most people.

"People lived in shacks with dirt floors," says Princeton University history professor Robert Darnton. "They were hungry. They were happy to get two meals a day. And those meals often were the same thing, which you can hear if you listen to the old-fashioned nursery rhymes, you know, 'Pease porridge hot, pease porridge cold,' and that's what the family ate for breakfast, for dinner, maybe for seven days."

Work was brutal, and life was short. Few people had time to worry about pursuing happiness. The concept of happiness was associated only with the afterlife: People struggled through a vale of tears on earth, in hopes of earning salvation—and happiness—in heaven. Only when living conditions improved—as technology made life less brutal, as vaccines saved children—did it occur to most people that happiness might be possible on earth.

Today we take pursuit of happiness for granted, Professor Darnton told me, so much so that we've forgotten that we've even changed the endings of children's stories. "The original 'Little Red Riding Hood,' as told in the fifteenth, sixteenth, seventeenth centuries, ends with the wolf simply eating Little Red Riding Hood. Today, you have to have a happy ending."

When Thomas Jefferson said we have a right to pursue happiness, that was a radical idea, said Darnton. Actually, Aristotle talked about happiness years before, but by the time the Declaration of Independence was written, more people were in a position to pursue it. "The key moment is, indeed, when Jefferson grabs his quill pen and writes, 'Life, liberty, and the pursuit of happiness.' People will feel not simply that happiness is a desirable state of being, but that it's a right. And if they're deprived of that right, they should raise hell. They should kick out the politicians. They should kick out the husband or the wife. They should move to California. They should change their lives."

But will that make them happy?

MYTH: Money buys happiness.

TRUTH: Not for long.

Americans are increasingly convinced that money can buy happiness. Thirty-five years ago, when college students were asked what's important, most said "Family" or "Developing a meaningful life philosophy." "Today," says Dr. David Myers, a psychologist who wrote *The Pursuit of Happiness* "most students say being very well-off financially."

But *how* well-off? If you don't have life's necessities, if you're hungry or scared that your children won't have food or clothing, it's hard to experience joy. International studies found that the least-happy people live in the poorest countries. Money would help them, says psychologist Ed Diener of the University of Illinois. They are so consumed with their quest for necessities that they have little time to consider their own happiness. "When we ask people in China and India to fill out a scale, how happy they are, we get a pretty high percentage of people who say, 'I've never thought about that before.' In America, you get virtually nobody who says that."

In America, most people say they are fairly happy, but that they'd be happier if they had more money. Would more money really do it?

I interviewed two lottery winners: Curtis Sharpe won five million dollars, Sherry Gagliardi won twenty-six million dollars.

CURTIS SHARPE For a time, it seemed like I was in a dream world, you know?

STOSSEL Did you come down to earth?

CURTIS SHARPE Oh, yes, I came down, you know. I came down to earth. I got divorced from my first wife and married my second wife, and I spent a lot of money on the wedding, you know.

STOSSEL A hundred thousand dollars on a grand wedding.

CURTIS SHARPE Yes, that didn't last five years. You know what I'm saying?

SHERRY GAGLIARDI I was numb for three years.

STOSSEL But you must have been happy?

SHERRY GAGLIARDI Yes and no. I got a divorce two years after we had won. People have a misconception about having money. You go out and you go, "Oh, that's what I want, I'll buy it." Well, a couple weeks later, it's like, you know, that emptiness comes back. Then what?

CURTIS SHARPE I mean, how many suits can I wear? How many hats can I wear? You know what I'm saying?

Dr. Myers, who spent six years examining hundreds of studies on happiness for his book, says once you are past poverty, money often doesn't help, no matter how much stuff you buy. "Clearly, the stockpiles of CDs, the closets full of clothes, the big-screen stereo TV systems don't do it."

One reason more money doesn't make us happier is because people adapt. "Having achieved that level of wealth," said Dr. Myers, people get used to it, "and it takes new increments—a faster computer, a bigger TV screen, or whatever—to rejuice the joy."

"To rejuice the joy" is a concept you see even in babies. Give a baby a mobile with two objects, and most like it. But researchers at St. John's University in New York discovered that when kids were given a ten-object mobile, and then later returned to the two-object mobile, they lost interest. Some cried.

Were they "spoiled"? That word comes to mind when we think about adults and money. No matter how many things some people acquire, their joy runs out of juice. The U.N. Development Report (1998) shows that the income needed "to fulfill consumption aspirations" *doubled* in the U.S. between 1986 and 1994.

Are the very wealthy more content than the rest of us? Evidence varies. One survey found that the top fifth of income earners are about 50 percent more likely to call themselves "very happy." But a survey of the people on the Forbes richest list found that they rated themselves no happier than anyone else.

But for most of us, says Dr. Myers, "with double the incomes and double

what money buys for us, we're no happier than we were forty years ago."
Then Dr. Myers put me to the test, on camera.

DR. DAVID MYERS   I mean, just look at the "lifestyles of the rich and famous."
Don't they look happy? Wouldn't you like to be like them?
STOSSEL   Yes. I am. I'm on TV.
DR. DAVID MYERS   So are you very happy?
STOSSEL   No.

That was embarrassing.

I have money, and I have achieved success in a glamorous field. When I
was twenty, if someone told me that I would someday have what I have now,
I would have predicted that I'd be deliriously happy. But I don't wake up
happy, eager to go work. Instead, I wake up worrying: "What will I do on
20/20 this week? Is my story good enough? Interesting enough? I fear it isn't.
What if I don't have time to fix it?" And so on. I'm a worrier.

I'm also a skeptic. It's probably why I do a TV segment titled "Give Me a
Break."

I was skeptical of the whole concept of "happiness research." How do
these scientists know what makes for a happy life? You can't measure happiness the way we measure blood pressure. What the researchers do—and
there really are people at universities who work full-time trying to analyze
happiness—is simply ask people, "How'd you feel this year? Rate yourself
from one to nine. Are you unhappy? Neutral? Very happy?" Since the circumstances of the moment might change your answer, some researchers
have subjects spend a month wearing beepers. When the beeper goes off,
they write down how they feel right then.

Other researchers show these faces and ask, "Which is you?"

When I gave this test to Barbara Walters, she chose what I chose: we
went back and forth between these two faces.

Charlie Gibson immediately picked this one:

I envy him. Okay, this is not precise science, and it may seem silly, but over the years, the researchers have surveyed more than a million people in America, Asia, and Europe, and they found some clear patterns.

> **MYTH:** Some people are just born happy.
>
> **TRUTH:** Apparently so.

Barbara Herbert and Daphne Goodship are absurdly happy. They were guinea pigs in a big psychological study, where researchers were fascinated by their good cheer. So were we. Our camera crew couldn't believe how these two women would smile about *everything*.

Barbara and Daphne are identical twins. You might explain their happiness as the result of a good childhood or their influence on each other—except that as kids, they never knew each other. They were born twelve minutes apart and were immediately given up for adoption. Barbara didn't even know she had a twin until she was thirty, when she found her sister with the help of newspaper reporters.

Dr. Thomas Bouchard, a psychologist at the University of Minnesota, thought Barbara and Daphne would be good candidates for his groundbreaking study of twins raised apart. "When they got here, they really shook us up in terms of a remarkable similarity," he told me. "They had a tendency to break out in laughter and giggle." The lab named them the "giggle twins."

For Barbara, there was no doubt as to whether the cause of their good mood was nature or nurture. "It's definitely nature," she said. "I don't think the environment or anything else has affected us, it's just what we are like." Science bears her out: The outlooks of twins—sunny or not—tend to be remarkably similar, the Minnesota study found, whether they are raised together or apart. "If *only* environment shaped our personality, identical twins reared apart would have no similarity," said Dr. Bouchard, "and yet they're every bit as similar as identical twins reared together."

Studies at the University of Maryland found that some children are literally *born* happy or unhappy. Scientists there used electrodes to monitor babies' brain activity when they smiled: Babies who smiled a lot had more measurable activity in their left frontal lobes.

"There are certain brains that are more predisposed to experience happiness compared to other brains," Dr. Richard Davidson told me. "You're just born with it."

Or not. I wasn't born with it, apparently. I sat down in Dr. Davidson's lab, and let him wire me up to measure my brain activity.

> **DR. RICHARD DAVIDSON** Your data, John, shows less left-sided frontal activation than the average person. It's not extreme, but it's certainly less than we see in the average.

Damn. That left-sided frontal activation! If only I had more . . .

I'm also a pessimist. Damn again. Optimists tend to be happier than the rest of us. If you simply expect good things to happen, say the people who study such things, you will be happier.

Senator John McCain (R-AZ) is an optimist. He told me it was his natural optimism that kept him going during the horrific five years he spent as a prisoner of war in North Vietnam. His captors tortured him. They put him in solitary confinement for more than two years. But all that time, he said, he was buoyed by his positive outlook.

> **SEN. JOHN MCCAIN** A fundamental belief that things in the end were going to be okay.
>
> **STOSSEL** You didn't know that things were going to be okay.
>
> **SEN. JOHN MCCAIN** No, but you had to believe that. You had to believe that.
>
> **STOSSEL** There were times you would say you were happy?
>
> **SEN. JOHN MCCAIN** Many times. They were times when I would laugh at the Vietnamese, the guards, and the interrogators. And I could tell you the reason why so many of us were able to come out of that experience with a very good mental condition was because we were happy a lot.

That's a good attitude to have. I wouldn't have been happy in the North Vietnamese prison.

But there is hope for people like me. While biology has a significant impact upon our happiness, our choices have a big influence too.

> **MYTH:** If I could just turn all these decisions over to someone else, life would be better.
>
> **TRUTH:** Control makes us happier.

A few years ago, when Chrysler was concerned about morale on its assembly line, company management tried something radical—it gave the workers more control. Workers were allowed to help redesign a major plant in St. Louis, and change the order in which some work was performed. The assembly line workers decided it would be better if they could put in the seats before the doors, and if they could stop the line whenever they saw a problem.

Employee attitudes improved significantly. "Ten years ago, it wasn't a very happy place that you wanted to come to every day," one told us. "Now, you get up, and it's a very happy place to come to."

It is now routine to consult assembly line workers about changes in factories in order to improve morale by giving them some measure of control over their environment.

The connection between control and happiness begins in the cradle. At Rutgers University, researchers tied a string around a baby's wrist. When the string was pulled, a picture appeared. Eventually the babies figured that out, and liked that; pulling the string and making pictures appear made them smile.

But then the researchers took the baby's control away. The pictures didn't appear, or appeared randomly. The children soon withdrew, or cried. When they gave them the control back, the babies were smiling again.

"If we think of ourselves as victims," says psychologist David Myers, "if we think that our life is out of control, we live with less joy." This may be why people in authoritarian countries rate lower on the happiness scale. Studies conducted in Hungary in the Communist 1980s show that the people there rated themselves as less happy than folks in any industrialized country. And poverty wasn't the sole reason for their misery: Countries like India, Bangladesh, and Turkey were just as poor but reported far higher levels of well-being.

The data from around the world is consistent. As Dr. Myers says: "People that live in nations where people are empowered—in West Germany as opposed to East Germany during the 1980s, for example—report greater satisfaction and just visibly look happier than people living under conditions where they feel very little control over their lives."

> **MYTH:** Religious people are happier.
>
> **TRUTH:** Religious people are happier.

People who say they're actively religious are more likely to also report that they're very happy. Many religious people say happiness comes from the sense of purpose that serving God gives them: a sense of commitment to something bigger than themselves. And church may persuade you to be more charitable. Charity-givers are forty percent more likely to say they are "very happy" than non-givers.

Belief in God also correlates with happiness. According to a Gallup survey, the closer people feel to God, the better they feel about themselves and other people. One of the most comprehensive social surveys found that more than 48 percent of adults who are both married and weekly churchgoers reported that they are very happy, compared to just 20 percent of unmarried adults who don't attend church.

Of course, going to church, temple, or the mosque may also aid happiness because it leads you to spend more time with other people. That alone increases the odds of being happy.

> **MYTH:** Leave me alone, and I'll be happy.
>
> **TRUTH:** Close relationships make people happier.

Married people rate themselves as happier than singles, but it's not just marriage that makes the difference, say psychologists; all kinds of relationships help. This is probably why extroverts rate themselves happier. So do people who say that they have a friend to call when something goes wrong. Research suggests that after a divorce, women recover emotionally sooner than men. Women typically say they have five or six friends with whom they have intimate conversations; men often say they have one—their ex-wife.

The psychologist David Myers says, "Close, supportive, connected relationships make for happiness, and we have fewer of those relationships today in the United States. Three times as many of us today live alone as lived alone a half century ago."

When we asked the happiness researchers "Are there some people you'd think more likely to be happy?" several referred us to the Amish, a small religious order that shuns most of the conveniences of the modern world. Although the Amish spend long hours doing what most of us would consider tedious work, sociology professor Donald Kraybill says they benefit from having a clear purpose in life. "The roots of their happiness are tied to their communal values. They talk about cooperation. They talk about self-denial. They talk about giving up things for the sake of the community."

Are they really happy? They don't look very happy in their black clothes and old-fashioned black buggies. For one of my TV specials, we persuaded a few dozen Amish people to take a test, designed by university researchers, that rates happiness on a sliding scale. All rated themselves "happy" or "extremely happy." They scored above the American average (even though some rated themselves less happy than they were, they said, because it is not polite to brag). One woman said if we'd point our camera away, she'd tell us why they're so happy. Here is what she had to say.

> **AMISH WOMAN** Our home is heaven. You have lots of cousins, maybe 100 or 150, that would always be there to take care of you if you have a need. It's a security we probably take for granted. I guess we all like material things, but doing without something you've never had is not a sacrifice. You don't know better. It takes so little to excite an Amish child. Just going for a walk is as exciting to them, probably, as your children maybe going to Hawaii.

Perhaps that's why 85–90 percent of the Amish children choose to reject the temptations of the modern world and stay in the Amish community. As Donald Kraybill put it, "The Amish way of life torments the modern soul, because the tourists come, curious about the Amish, and they leave tormented that maybe the Amish are happier than they are."

> **MYTH:** Disability brings years of unhappiness.
>
> **TRUTH:** The disabled are as happy as anyone else.

A disabling handicap or injury is devastating . . . for a while. But just as lottery winners find that, within a year, they are as unhappy as they were before, the disabled often find that once they get over the shock of their injury, they are as happy as they were before.

Dennis Heaphy was paralyzed from the neck down in a diving accident, but he says he is a happy man. He counsels cancer victims, and spends time at a homeless shelter teaching people to read.

> **STOSSEL** Some people would say, how can you be happy? You have to have help getting dressed. You can't feed yourself.
>
> **DENNIS HEAPHY** It sucks, but you do what you have to do with it. And I'm very grateful, because I have so much.
>
> **STOSSEL** Teaching homeless people sounds difficult. I would think happiness would be in doing fun things—going to the movies, watching TV. This is work.
>
> **DENNIS HEAPHY** It's not work. It's, again, finding where you're at. I'm not someone whose joy is sitting watching TV. There's no human interaction there. It's the relational aspect, I think, that makes me happy. It's so much fun to sit in the classroom and to be with other folks and just laugh when someone else laughs. That's happiness. That's what gives me kicks.

> **MYTH:** Happiness decreases with age.
>
> **TRUTH:** The old are as happy as the young.

The fountain of youth is portrayed as a route to happiness. David Myers pointed out that there are good reasons to believe we lose opportunity for happiness as we age.

> **DAVID MYERS** Your income is waning, your health is fading, your friends are dying month by month. It must be a pretty unhappy time of life, so most people suppose.

STOSSEL Is it?

DAVID MYERS Clearly it is not. People at every age are about, on average, equally happy.

The surveys are so similar that the graph is boring. People in all age groups report the same levels of happiness.

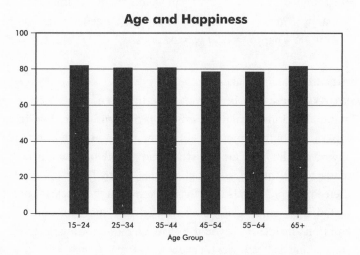

I interviewed my ninety-one-year-old father about it.

STOSSEL People my age fear that by the time I'm your age, it's just much harder to be happy. There's less to be happy about.

OTTO STOSSEL No, that's not the case at all. The feeling of happiness does not necessarily go down just because your circumstances are not what they used to be.

STOSSEL But how can they not? You're less healthy. You have less to look forward to.

OTTO STOSSEL Yes, but I know that with increasing age, there is no choice. This just has to be the way I live right now.

As we age, say the researchers, our highs do become less high, but the good news is the lows also become less low, because we learn to accept what we can't change. Older people often describe their lives as hard, but say that they feel less stress. That's why older people report happiness levels that are just as high as those of the young.

> **MYTH:** You can't fake happiness.
>
> **TRUTH:** Fake it until you make it!

What about those of us born without those happy genes that blessed the giggle twins, and those who are not optimistic, religious, gregarious, married, or surrounded by friends, etc.? Can we do anything simple to help ourselves be happy? "Yes," says David Myers. "People actually do feel happier when they put on a happy face." I was skeptical.

STOSSEL *Acting* happy makes you happy?

DAVID MYERS There have been many experiments now in which people are manipulated into making a smiling facial expression, told to turn up the corners of their mouth as instruments are attached, and they actually do feel happier. Or one study had people bite on a pencil, which tends to activate the smiling muscles, or to [just] hold it between their lips, which tends to activate the frowning muscles. That manipulated their emotions. Going through the motions can trigger the emotions inside. So if you'd like to be more optimistic or outgoing, start acting as if you were. Fake it.

STOSSEL How do you fake being outgoing?

DAVID MYERS You start talking to people in the theater line. I mean, you can actually be given homework assignments.

STOSSEL Just do it.

DAVID MYERS Just do it, absolutely.

STOSSEL This would make me unhappy.

DAVID MYERS Well, if you want to change some of your traits, the way not to change them is to sit on your duff just waiting for change to strike you from within. The way to change is to get up out of that chair and begin acting as if you were the person you'd like to be.

> **MYTH:** More leisure time would make us happier.
>
> **TRUTH:** Busier people are happier.

Some people say they'd be happy if they just had more time to relax. No way, say the experts. Inactivity is a curse. Happiness comes when we test our skills through some meaningful activity. David Myers says, "People who get in the *flow* of life, whose work experiences and recreation challenge their skills and engage them, in other words, people who become caught up in what they're doing, live with greater joy."

People often find flow in jobs. It doesn't have to be a high-paying job, just one that makes you feel useful. Others find happiness losing themselves in hobbies and sports, or volunteering for a charity. Their happiness comes not from pursuing happiness, say the researchers. While pursuing other things, happiness just happens.

Happiness is a side effect of doing other things, says David Myers. "People who are passive, who are vegetating—dare I say watching television—are less likely to report themselves happy than people who are actively doing things."

So put this book away. Turn off *20/20*. Get out there and *do* something!

CONCLUSION

PEOPLE CALL ME A CONSERVATIVE.

I understand why. The publisher of my last book called me the "Scourge of the Liberal Media" on the cover. Liberal writers call me "that conservative on ABC." Not that they actually know what the word means—to many in the mainstream media, "conservative" seems to mean anyone they don't trust or don't like. They even call extreme leftists, like Soviet and Chinese Communists, "hard-line conservatives."

In New York City, where I live, "conservative" is a terrible thing to be. Conservatives are reviled as stuffy, narrow-minded bullies who want an authoritarian government that will police the world, police your bedroom, and force everyone to become Fundamentalist Christians.

The stereotypes above are a smear on conservatism, but there is also some truth behind the smear. Many conservatives believe that American troops are very capable of "nation building." Some are uncomfortable with people who fall outside social "norms." Many want the government to pass laws against behavior they consider immoral.

These are some of the reasons that in 1960, the philosopher F. A. Hayek wrote an essay entitled "Why I Am Not a Conservative." He said, "The conservative position rests on the belief that in any society there are recognizably superior persons whose inherited standards and values and position ought to be protected and who should have a greater influence on public affairs than others."

His words came to life as I watched "fiscally conservative Republicans" expand government even faster than Bill Clinton did. Suddenly, they didn't mind that government was growing, as long as it grew in the ways that *they* liked.

On the campaign trail, President Bush repeatedly said, "Prosperity must have a purpose," suggesting that it was government's job to figure out that purpose and fund it. But I don't want *government* telling me what the purpose of profit is; in a thousand different ways, private individuals and companies are better at figuring that out for themselves.

As I write this, Republicans are attacking oil companies for price "gouging," they're trying to amend the Constitution to ban gays from marrying, and they just created a new Medicare entitlement. If that's conservatism today, then it holds little appeal for me.

The way that today's liberals define themselves doesn't hold much appeal for me either. The Democrats push destructive policies on behalf of unions, trial lawyers, and other special-interest groups that feed them money. Liberalism has come to mean spending more on everything—speech police, failed poverty programs that reward dependency, a bigger nanny state telling us we cannot eat fatty foods, workplace rules that stifle opportunity, and absurd environmental regulations.

I like the idea of personal *freedom* that is often put forward by the Democrats, but they never seem to connect that with personal *responsibility*.

The big government they seek is something I thought Democrats and other professed "friends of the little guy" would fear. Once you say to government, "You must take care of me," you invite the government to come in and tell you how to live, who to marry, what lyrics are permissible, and how you can have sex.

I want government to leave people alone. I think people should be free to do anything they want—as long as they don't hurt anyone else. I may disagree with their choices, but I don't think The State should take their choices away. If you want to put drugs in your body, burn a flag, or rent yourself out for sexual use, you should be free to do that. If people want to buy or sell a kidney, I say, let them. If a man wants to have sex with another man, that should be his choice.

These are not conservative ideas.

Yet conservatives are at least willing to talk about them. I am continually amazed at how generous conservatives are in debate. Even those who disagree with my ideas welcome me warmly at their conferences. The supposedly "narrow-minded" social conservatives politely hear me out. The liberals, by contrast, don't want to talk at all.

When I wrote my last book, *Give Me a Break*, I assumed the high poobahs of the leftist media would be eager to debate my ideas, if only to demonstrate how foolish my arguments were, or to discredit the reporting of their misguided colleague who had gone "over to the dark side," as one TV writer put it.

I was wrong.

The conservatives were eager to have me; I got to discuss my ideas with dozens of talk-radio hosts and the stars of the Fox News Channel. They made *Give Me a Break* a best-seller. But the liberal media—CNN, NPR, and the *New York Times*—basically held their noses and ignored me. Where was the "open debate" the liberals always praise? Mostly on the *conservative* broadcasts. Few conservatives wanted to spend much time debating drug laws (Sean Hannity did), but at least they heard me out.

Liberals wouldn't.

There were a few exceptions: Robert Redford, of all people, flew me out to his Sundance book festival. Alan Colmes grilled me on his radio program. Larry King eventually had me on; it was only his weekend show, but he said he'd have me back on a weekday. I'm still waiting.

I thought I'd have a shot at a fair debate with Al Franken because we're acquaintances; our kids went to school together. No such luck. He invited me to his studio, but he ranted so much about what he claimed was a "lie" on page 305 that I could barely explain why he was missing the point.

There wasn't much openness in the "open-minded" liberal media. I found it talking to conservatives.

But that doesn't make me one of them.

So if I'm not a liberal and not a conservative, what can I call myself? The word that comes closest is "libertarian."

It's not a great word. People don't know what it means, or think it means "libertine." Hayek thought the word "libertarian" was too "manufactured," and wished he had a "word which describes the party of life, the party that favors free growth and spontaneous evolution." Me too. Those ideas, embodied in the writings of John Locke, John Stuart Mill, and Adam Smith, are what was once called "liberalism." It's why many libertarians refer to themselves as "classical liberals." But most people don't know what "classical liberal" means either. What are my other choices? "Volunteerist?" "Consensualist?" "Live-and-let-live-ist?"

I want the word "liberal" back! Today's liberals stole it and perverted it. They've changed it into a philosophy that advocates health police, high taxes, and speech codes and despises the creative liberalism of free markets. "Liberal" doesn't mean liberal anymore.

In the eighteenth century, libertarianism, or liberalism, was a reaction against monarchy, the aristocracy, and established religion. The limits on state power embodied in the Declaration and the Constitution offered a liberal alternative to the dictatorship of the central planners. It affirmed that we had "unalienable rights."

The Founders' vision of limited government encouraged Americans to voluntarily join with others to help their communities and themselves. It led us to create a nation that is prosperous, free, and peaceful. We have done it not because we were compelled, but because we were free to do so.

I believe that the best thing about America is free people exercising the unalienable rights that the Founding Fathers affirmed: having families, forming communities, and working together—mostly *without* government.

It's a very old, very *liberal* idea.

ENDNOTES

IT'S A NEW WORLD and we're experimenting: ABC News Internet mavens Michael Clemente and Mark Cardwell have put additional information and resources for this book on the web. We will make it a "living" document, adding to the list as more information becomes available, and correcting the record (tell us if you find a mistake).

For schoolteachers, there is also a link to help you bring some of these ideas to your students—free. Just download the video.

Please join us at *www.abcnews.com/2020*. I'd like to keep a conversation about liberty going.

CHAPTER 1: CLUELESS MEDIA

Page 4: Natural radiation levels: American Nuclear Society, "Radiation Dose Chart," *www.ans.org.*

Page 6: Lives that irradiation could save: Robert V. Tauxe, "Food Safety and Irradiation: Protecting the Public from Foodborne Infections," Conference Presentation, Centers for Disease Control and Prevention, June 2001. Since Tauxe is assuming that 50 percent of processed meat would be irradiated, he also assumes that this meat would be the source of 50 percent of foodborne *E. coli* O157, *Campylobacter, Salmonella, Listeria,* and *Taxoplasma* infections.

Page 7: Graph: Surveillance, Epidemiology, and End Results (SEER) Program, National Cancer Institute, "Annual Age-adjusted Cancer Incidence Rates Among Males and Females for Select Cancers, U.S., 1975–2002," 2005. Rates are age-adjusted to the 2000 U.S. standard population and adjusted for delays in reporting, with the exception of melanoma.

Page 9: no surge in cancer due to DDT: Edmund Sweeney, EPA Hearing Examiner's recommendations and findings concerning DDT hearings, April 25, 1972. J. Higginson, "DDT: Epidemiological Evidence," IARC Scientific Publications, 1985.

Page 17: Death risks and school violence: National Center for Health Statistics, Centers for Disease Control and Prevention, "Annual Mortality Report," 2002. Bureau of Justice Statistics and the National Center for Education Statistics, "Indicators of School Crime and Safety," 2002.

Page 17: Drop in school violence, 1992–2002: U.S. Departments of Education and Justice, "Indicators of School Crime and Safety," 2005.

Page 17: Kids are twice as likely to become victims of violence away from school rather than in school: Bureau of Justice Statistics and the National Center for Education Statistics, "Indicators of School Crime and Safety," 2002.

Page 21: Nielsen Media Research, "Nielsen Reports Americans Watch TV at Record Levels," September 2005.

Page 22: ABC News, *20/20*, "Hurricane Rita: State of Emergency," September 23, 2005. Take a look at this piece at *www.abcnews.com/2020/*.

Page 22: Gas prices: Energy Information Administration, *www.eia.doe.gov*. Historical gas price info: Energy Information Administration, "Short Term Energy Outlook: Real Petroleum Prices," November 2005.

Page 22: Fuel taxes: American Petroleum Institute, "Nationwide and State-By-State Motor Fuel Taxes," November 2004.

Page 24: Full moon: ABC News, *20/20*, "Strange Things Happen During a Full Moon," March 22, 2004. Check this story out at *www.abcnews.com/2020/*.

Page 25: America's garbage for the next five hundred years: A. Clark Wiseman, "U.S. Wastepaper Recycling Policies: Issues and Effects," Discussion Paper ENR 90-14, Resources for the Future, August 1990.

Page 27: Babies born before this book is finished: The World Health Organization, *www.who.int*. According to WHO, 15,514 children are born every hour across the globe, and we estimate around 8 hours of reading-time for this book.

CHAPTER 2: HE AND SHE

Pages 31–32: I think their arguments are absurd, but if you want to read more about alleged gender bias in the tests, read away at *www.fairtest.org*.

Page 34: Most teachers, psychologists, pharmacists, and real estate agents are women: Bureau of Labor Statistics, U.S. Department of Labor, *www.bls.gov*.

Pages 36–39: Sex discrimination and sports: ABC News, *20/20*, "The Losing Team," May 29, 1998. Check out this story at *www.abcnews.com/2020/*. For more information on Title IX, visit the U.S. Department of Education's website at *www.ed.gov/pubs/TitleIX/index.html*.

Page 40: Wage gap statistics: The Bureau of Labor Statistics and the U.S. Census Bureau, "Current Population Survey," 2002.

Page 42–43: Male vs. female drivers: Social Issues Research Center, "Sex Differences in Driving and Insurance Risk," August 2004.

Page 42: Decrease in fatal crashes for both men and women: Insurance Institute for Highway Safety, "Fatality Facts 2004: General," 2005. The rate of motor vehicle crashes per 100,000 people has declined by 30 percent since 1975.

Page 43: Men more aggressive than women: Department of Gender and Women's Health, World Health Organization, "Gender and Road Traffic Injuries," 2002. World Health Organization, "Injury: A leading cause of global burden of disease," 1999.

Page 46: Infidelity statistics: Edward Laumann, et al. *Sex in America: A Definitive Survey,* CSG Enterprises, Inc., 1994.

CHAPTER 3: BASHING BUSINESS

Pages 55–57: Drug development statistics: Standard & Poor's Industry Survey, "Healthcare: Pharmaceuticals," July 21, 2005.

Page 56: Cost of developing a new drug: J. DiMasi, R. Hansen, and H. Grabowski, "The Price of Innovation: New Estimates of Drug Development Costs," *Journal of Health Economics,* 2003. In this study, the cost of compounds abandoned during testing was linked to the cost of compounds that obtained marketing approval.

Page 56: Minority of drugs earn back R&D costs: H. Grabowski, J. Vernon, and J. DiMasi, "Returns on Research and Development for 1990s New Drug Introductions," *Pharmacoeconomics,* 2002.

Page 57: Advertising and R&D budgets for the private pharmaceutical industry: Pharmaceutical Research and Manufacturers of America (PhRMA), *www.phrma.org.*

Page 57: Public approval of price regulation on drugs: Kaiser Family Foundation, "Americans Value the Health Benefits of Prescription Drugs, But Say Drug Makers Put Profits First," February 25, 2005.

Page 58: The vast majority of new drugs come from private industry: The National Institutes of Health, U.S. Department of Health and Human Services, "A Plan to Ensure Taxpayers' Interests are Protected," July 2001.

Page 58: NIH funding of HIV/AIDS drugs: Pharmaceutical Research and Manufacturers of America (PhRMA), "How Government and the Rx Industry Cooperate for the Benefit of Patients," 2002, *http://www.phrma.org.*

Page 61: Florida called the "Blue Roof State": Abby Goodnough, "Long After Florida Storms, a Whirlwind for Roofers," *The San Diego Tribune,* February 27, 2005.

Page 63: About 3% of workforce earns minimum wage: Bureau of Labor Statistics, U.S. Department of Labor, *www.bls.gov.*

Page 63: Living-wage ordinances across the country: Association of Community Organizations for Reform Now (ACORN). Paul K. Sonn, "Citywide Minimum Wage Laws," *Brennan Center for Justice, Economic Policy Brief No. 1,* June 2005.

Pages 64–65: Outsourcing jobs: ABC News, *20/20,* "Outsourcing is Bad," January 28, 2005. Take a look at this story at *www.abcnews.com/2020/.*

Pages 65–66: Clothing, toy, TV prices: Bureau of Labor Statistics, U.S. Department of Labor, *www.bls.gov.*

Page 66: 500,000 jobs outsourced since 2000: TechsUnite, a project of the Communications Workers of America, AFL-CIO, *www.techsunite.org.*

Page 68: Jobs lost and gained: Bureau of Labor Statistics, U.S. Department of Labor, "Private Sector gross job gains and job losses, seasonally adjusted," November 18, 2005.

Page 68: Companies that outsource double jobs at home: Matthew J. Slaughter, "Globalization and Employment by U.S. Multinationals: A Framework and Facts," *Daily Tax Report,* March 26, 2004.

Page 68: Average American wage increase: Bureau of Labor Statistics, U.S. Department of Labor, "Employment Cost Index," October 28, 2005.

Page 68: Fastest growing occupations: Bureau of Labor Statistics, U.S. Department of Labor, "Occupational Employment Projections to 2012," December 2002.

Page 69: Percentage of Americans who work on farms: Alan Olmstead and Paul Rhode, "The Transformation of Northern Agriculture 1910–1990," in Stanley Engerman and Robert Gallman (eds.), *The Cambridge Economic History of the United States, Volume III, The Twentieth Century,* Cambridge University Press, 2000.

Page 70: Wages in sweatshops: Aaron Lukas, "WTO Report Card III: Globalization and Developing Countries," Center for Trade Policy Studies, Cato Institute, June 20, 2000. Cato, at *www.cato.org,* is America's foremost libertarian think tank.

Pages 74–75: Sixty thousand people wait for a kidney, deaths while waiting for organ transplants: National Kidney Foundation, *www.kidney.org.* United Network for Organ Sharing, *www.unos.org.* The number of patients waiting for kidneys does not include those who are also waiting for a pancreatic transplant.

CHAPTER 4: MONSTER GOVERNMENT

Page 79: Ronald Coase, "Advertising and Free Speech," *The Journal of Legal Studies,* January 1997.

Page 81: Government spending increases: Office of Management and Budget, Executive Office of the President of the United States, "The Budget for Fiscal Year 2007, Historical Tables," 2006.

Page 83: Employees fired by the US government: Chris Edwards, *Downsizing the Federal Government,* Cato Institute, 2005.

Page 85: Farm subsidies to Ted Turner, Ken Lay, and David Rockefeller: Environmental Working Group (a deceitful activist organization, but I think they are right about farm subsidies).

Page 86: Crops not subsidized: Farm Service Agency, U.S. Department of Agriculture, "Commodity Estimates Book for FY2006 President's Budget," February 7, 2005, *www.fsa.usda.gov.*

Page 87: American farms, USDA employees, 1900 and 2005: National Agricultural Statistics Service, U.S. Department of Agriculture, *www.nass.usda.gov.* USDA employees, 2005: U.S. Office of Personnel Management, *www.opm.gov.* USDA employees, around 1900: Centennial Committee, U.S. Department of Agriculture, "Century of Service," 1963.

Pages 87–88: Two of my producers object to my including President Bush's claim that "the United States is ready to eliminate all tariffs." They say those are "weasel words" because Bush knew there was no chance other countries would accept. I chose to believe that the President was sincere.

Page 88: PBS viewers are 44% more likely to earn more than $150,000: William Schulz, Corporation for Public Broadcasting, "The Assault on Public Broadcasting," September 13, 2005.

Page 88: 15% of PBS is government funded: David Boaz, Executive Vice President of Cato Institute, "Ending Taxpayer Funding for Public Broadcasting," Statement to Committee on Appropriations, Subcommittee on Labor, Health and Human Services, Education, and Related Agencies, United States Senate, July 11, 2005.

Page 91: Hidden taxes: Chris Edwards, *Downsizing the Federal Government*, Cato Institute, 2005.

Pages 91–92: Percentage of Nebraska cell phone bill that goes to taxes: "The Excessive State and Local Tax Burden on Wireless Telecommunications Service," Kimbell Sherman Ellis, July 2005.

Page 92: Local, state, and federal taxes add 8 to 34 percent to your local phone bill: "Effective State, Local & Federal Telecommunications Taxes by State, 2004," The Tax Foundation, May 25, 2005.

Pages 92–95: The *Congressional Record*: ABC News, *20/20*, "Your Tax Dollars At Work," December 3, 1993. See this story at *www.abcnews.com/2020/*. Per-page cost of the Congressional Record: The Government Printing Office, *www.gpo.gov*.

Pages 97–98: Cocaine and marijuana use: Substance Abuse and Mental Health Services Administration, U.S. Department of Health and Human Services, "National Survey on Drug Use and Health," 2004.

Page 98: Drug arrest statistics: "Crime in the United States, 2004," FBI Uniform Crime Reporting Program, 2004.

Pages 101–103: Endangered species: ABC News, *20/20*, "Government Protects Wildlife at Expense of Humans," August 2, 2002. Check out this story at *www.abcnews.com/2020/*.

Page 103–104: Laws against artificial lawns and household repairs on Sundays: *Reason Magazine, www.reason.com. Reason,* by the way, is a great magazine. It celebrates free minds and free markets, making me laugh or cry at the excesses of the regulatory state.

CHAPTER 5: STUPID SCHOOLS

Pages 108–109: International test administered to 4th graders: Trends in International Mathematics and Science Study (TIMSS), International Association for the Evaluation of Education Achievement, 2003. **International test administered to 15-year olds:** Program for International Student Assessment (PISA), OECD Programme for International Student Assessment, 2003.

Page 110: Jan De Groof and Charles Glenn, *Balancing Freedom, Autonomy, and Accountability in Education,* Wolf Legal Publishers, 2000.

Page 111: American parents satisfied with their child's public school: National Household Education Surveys Program, National Center for Education Statistics, U.S. Department of Education, *http://nces.ed.gov/nhes*.

Page 111: Jay P. Greene, *Education Myths*, Rowman & Littlefield Publishers, Inc., September 25, 2005.

Page 111: The school-zone detective "busting" non-resident students: ABC News Special Report, "Stupid in America: How We Cheat Our Kids," January 13, 2006. The transcript is available on the Web at *www.abcnews.com/2020/*. If you would like to purchase the DVD for this special, go to *www.ABCNewsStore.com*, or dial 800-505-6139. A copy of John's shows can also be purchased from Laissez Faire Books at 800-326-0996 or on the web at *http://www.laissezfairebooks.com*.

Page 115: Defense and education spending: Congressional Budget Office, "The Budget and Economic Outlook: Fiscal Years 2006–2015," 2005, *www.cbo.gov*.

Page 115: American education spending vs. other countries: Organization for Economic Cooperation and Development, "Education at a Glance 2005," 2005.

Pages 116–117: Graphs: National Center for Education Statistics, U.S. Department of Education, "Digest of Education Statistics," 2004, *www.nces.ed.gov*.

Pages 118–119: Student-teacher ratio figures: National Center for Education Statistics, U.S. Department of Education, "Digest of Education Statistics," 2004.

Page 119: Catholic school performance vs. government school performance: National Assessment of Education Progress (NAEP), National Center for Education Statistics, U.S. Department of Education, "The Nation's Report Card," 2005.

Page 127: Cost of teachers in "Rubber Rooms" in New York City: Dan Weisberg, Executive Director of Labor Relations, New York City Department of Education.

Page 127: Twenty thousand teachers rally at Madison Square Garden: ABC News Special Report, "Stupid in America: How We Cheat Our Kids," January 13, 2006. The transcript is available at *www.abcnews.com/2020/*.

Pages 128–131: Steps required to fire a teacher: Common Good, "How Do I Fire an Inept Teacher," 2005, *www.cgood.org*.

Page 133: Wage rates: Bureau of Labor Statistics, U.S. Department of Labor, "National Compensation Survey: Occupational Wages in the United States," July 2004.

Pages 133–134: Missouri teacher applicants: Michael Podgursky, "Is Teacher Pay 'Adequate'?" Presented at a conference given by the Program on Education Policy and Governance, Kennedy School of Government, Harvard University, October, 2005.

Pages 135–136: Effects of vouchers on public schools: Caroline Hoxby, "Rising Tide: New Evidence on Competition and the Public Schools," *Education Next*, 2001.

CHAPTER 6: CONSUMER CONS

Page 141–142: Consumer rating of store brand products: The Gallup Organization, 2001.

Pages 143–145: Bottled water: ABC News, *20/20*, "Too Good to Be True—Bottled Water vs. Tap," May 6, 2005. Check out this story at *www.abcnews.com/2020/*.

Page 149: Visible food makes people eat more: P. Chandon and B. Wansink, "When Are Stockpiled Products Consumed Faster? A Convenience-Salience Framework of Post-Purchase Consumption Incidence and Quantity," *Journal of Marketing Research,* 2002.

Page 150: Identity theft: Javelin Strategy & Research, "Identity Fraud Survey Report," 2005.

Pages 153–154: Cars that require high-octane gas: Alliance of Automobile Manufacturers, *www.autoalliance.org.*

Page 157: Price of hair transplant surgery and procedures required: American Society of Plastic Surgeons, *www.plasticsurgery.org.*

Pages 159–161: Funeral scams: ABC News, *20/20,* "R.I.P. Off—Funeral Parlor Scams," November 3, 1995. See this report at *www.abcnews.com/2020/.* Average price for funeral and burial services: National Funeral Directors Association, *www.nfds.org.* Many organizations offer more information about savings on funeral services, such as the Funeral Consumers Alliance, *www.funerals.org* and the International Cemetery and Funeral Association, *www.icfa.org.*

Page 162: Efficiency of Halliburton vs. soldiers: Congressional Budget Office, "Logistics Support for Deployed Military Forces," October 2005.

CHAPTER 7: THE LAWSUIT RACKET

Page 164: Hyper-defensive medicine: U.S. Department of Health and Human Services, "Confronting the New Health Care Crisis: Improving Health Care Quality and Lowering Costs by Fixing Our Medical Liability System," July 24, 2002.

Pages 164–165: Most lawsuit winners are not malpractice victims: A. Russell Localio, et al. "Relation between malpractice claims and adverse events due to negligence," *New England Journal of Medicine,* July 25, 1991.

Page 165: Four companies make the flu vaccine: Centers for Disease Control and Prevention, *www.cdc.gov.*

Page 165: The cost of lawsuits on vaccine research: Paul A. Offit, *The Cutter Incident: How America's First Polio Vaccine Led to the Growing Vaccine Crisis,* Yale University Press, 2005.

Page 166: No link between Thimerosol and autism: Institute of Medicine, "Immunization Safety Review: Thimerosol-Containing Vaccines and Neuro-developmental Disorders," October 1, 2001.

Page 166: Lyme disease vaccine: Division of Vector-Born Infectious Diseases, The Centers for Disease Control, *www.cdc.gov.*

Page 166: Contraceptive research: Steven B. Hantler, "The Seven Myths of Highly Effective Plaintiffs' Lawyers," *Civil Justice Forum,* The Manhattan Institute, April 2004.

Page 166: Silicone and Lawsuits: "Product-Liability Law Scares Silicone Firms Out of Market," *The Nikkei Weekly,* August 28, 1995.

Page 166: Bendectin and birth defects: L. Miklovich and B. van den Berg, "An Evaluation of the Teratogenicity of Certain Antinauseant Drugs," *American Journal of Obstetricians and Gynecologists,* May 15, 1976.

Page 167: Obstetricians sued: The American College of Obstetricians and Gynecologists, "Medical Liability Survey Reaffirms More Ob-Gyns Are Quitting Obstetrics," July 16, 2004, *www.acog.org.*

Page 168: C-section data: National Center of Health Statistics, *www.cdc.gov/nchs.*

Page 168: Cerebral palsy rates have not declined: Center for Disease Control, National Center on Birth Defects and Developmental Disabilities, "Cerebral Palsy," August 2004.

Page 169: Causes of cerebral palsy: American College of Obstetricians and Gynecologists and the American Academy of Pediatrics, "Neonatal Encephalopathy and Cerebral Palsy: Defining the Pathogenesis and Pathophysiology," January 31, 2003.

Page 169: Doctors conceal mistakes: Office of the Assistant Secretary for Planning and Evaluation, U.S. Department of Health and Human Services, "Confronting the New Health Care Crisis: Improving Health Care Quality and Lowering Costs by Fixing Our Medical Liability System," July 24, 2002.

Pages 170–172: Teachers falsely accused: ABC News, *20/20,* "Teach But Don't Touch—False Accusations of Sex Abuse," March 17, 1995. See this report at *www. abcnews.com/2020/.*

Page 174: Class-action lawsuits and Big Tobacco: Walter Olson, *The Rule of Lawyers,* St. Martin's Griffin, 2004.

Page 177: Campaign donations in Madison County: American Tort Reform Association, "Justice for Sale," October 3, 2002.

Pages 178–179: ABC News, *20/20,* "Panhandlers Sue the City," December 17, 2004. Check out this story on the web at *www.abcnews.com/2020/.*

CHAPTER 8: EXPERTS FOR EVERYTHING

Pages 185–188: Exodus Ministries: ABC News, *20/20,* "Can Homosexuals Change and Become Straight?" March 2, 2001. To view this story, go to *www.abcnews. com/2020/.*

Pages 190–191: Stock information: Morningstar, *www.morningstar.com.*

Pages 192–196: Pediatric chiropractors: ABC News, *20/20,* "Handle With Care," February 4, 1994. See this story on the web at *www.abcnews.com/2020/.*

Pages 196–198: Violent video games and children: D. Scott, "The Effect of Video Games on Feelings of Aggression," *Journal of Psychology,* March 1995. Dmitri Williams, et al. "Internet Fantasy Violence: A Test of Aggression in an Online Game," *Communication Monographs,* June 2005.

Pages 198–200: Married couples that are cousins worldwide: Robin Fox, Professor of Social Theory, Rutgers University. Fox is the author of *Kinship and Marriage,* a widely used anthropology textbook.

Page 198: Legality of cousin marriage: National Conference of State Legislators, *www.ncsl.org.*

Page 199: Cousins and birth defects: RL Bennett, et al. "Genetic Counseling and Screening of Consanguineous Couples and Their Offspring," *Journal of Genetic Counseling,* April 2002.

CHAPTER 9: THE POWER OF BELIEF

Page 202: Global warming between 1900 and 1945: Dr. William H. Schlesinger, Dean of the Nicholas School of the Environment and Earth Sciences at Duke University. Dr. Sallie Baliunas, Harvard-Smithsonian Center for Astrophysics. This statement was based on data from the Intergovernmental Panel on Climate Change.

Page 202: Global warming graph: NOAA Paleoclimatology Program and World Data Center for Paleoclimatology. Glaciologist Richard B. Alley provided the data shown following his analysis of ice cores taken from central Greenland glaciers.

Page 203: Greenland's ice thickening: Ola Johannessen, et al. "Climate Change," *Science,* November 2005.

Page 204: Potential benefit of Kyoto implementation: T.M.L. Wigley, "The Kyoto Protocol: CO2, CH4, and climate implications," *Geophysical Research Letter,* July 1, 1998.

Page 204: Energy from solar panels: National Renewable Energy Laboratory, U.S. Department of Energy, *www.nrel.gov.*

Page 206: Today's new cars 98% cleaner: U.S. Department of Energy, *Transportation Energy Data Book,* 2004.

Page 206: Car emissions "below detection levels": Ted Balaker, "Air Quality: Winner for Best Gaseous Emissions," *Reason Magazine,* February 25, 2005.

Page 206: Miles driven and air pollution: Environmental Protection Agency, "National Air Quality and Emissions Trends Report," 2003. This pollution-level decrease was based on emissions of the six principal air pollutants.

Page 208: Gulf War Syndrome: Phil Brown, et al. "A Gulf of Difference: Disputes Over Gulf War–Related Illnesses," *Journal of Health and Social Behavior,* September 2000. Charles C. Engel, "Post-War Syndromes: Illustrating the Impact of the Social Psyche on Notions of Risk, Responsibility, Reason, and Remedy," *Journal of the American Academy of Psychoanalysis and Dynamic Psychiatry,* 2004.

Page 209: Therapeutic touch and Emily Rosa: Emily Rosa, et al. "Close Look at Therapeutic Touch," *Journal of the American Medical Association,* April 1, 1998.

Pages 209–211: Psychics and the FBI: Joseph Gomes, "Prophet Motive," *Brill's Content,* November 27, 2000.

Pages 211–212: Walking on coals: ABC News, *20/20,* "The Power of Belief," October 6, 1998. Watch this story at *www.abcnews.com/2020/.*

Page 213: New Jersey has more lawyers per capita than any other state: "Justice Expenditure and Employment in the United States 2001," Bureau of Justice Statistics, May 2004.

Page 214: James Randi's one million dollar prize is still up for grabs! *www.randi.org.*

CHAPTER 10: OUR HEALTH

Pages 218–219: ABC News, *20/20,* "Getting Cold Will Give You A Cold," January 23, 2004. Viewable at *www.abcnews.com/2020/.*

Page 220: American College of Sports Medicine, *ACSM Fitness Book,* Human Kinetics Publishers, 2003.

Pages 222–223: Monkeys that eat at night: Judy L. Cameron, et al. Oregon National Primate Research Center, Oregon Health and Science University, Society of Neuroscience meeting, November 2003.

Pages 223–224: Most foodborne illnesses caught in the home: U.S. Department of Agriculture, "Changing Attitudes—Changing Behavior: What Food Safety Communicators Need to Know," Panel Discussion, June 12–13, 1997. Most meals are eaten at home, so that skews the data, but microbiologists say restaurants are safer.

Pages 224–225: Kids and sugar: Mark Wolraich, et al. "Effects of Diets High in Sucrose or Aspartame on the Behavior and Cognitive Performance of Children," *The New England Journal of Medicine,* February 1994.

Pages 228–229: Antibacterial soap: ABC News, *20/20,* February 18, 2005. Check out this story at *www.abcnews.com/2020/.* Elaine Larson, et al. "Effect of antibacterial home cleaning and hand washing products on infectious disease symptoms: A similar randomized, double-blind trial," *Annals of Internal Medicine,* March 2, 2004.

Page 229: American Society for Microbiology and The Soap Detergent Association, "2005 Hand Hygiene Survey," August 2005.

Pages 231–232: Hostility and health: K. Raikkonen, et al. "Effects of hostility on ambulatory blood pressure and mood during daily living in healthy adults," *Health Psychology,* January 1999. D. Shapiro, et al. "Effects of anger/hostility, defensiveness, gender, and family history of hypertension on cardiovascular reactivity," *Psychophysiology,* September 1995.

CHAPTER 11: PERILS OF PARENTING

Pages 234–235: Effects of spanking: Murray Straus, "Corporal Punishment and Primary Prevention of Physical Abuse," *Child Abuse and Neglect,* September 2000. Murray Straus and Glenda Kaufman Kantor, "Corporal Punishment of Adolescents by Parents," *Adolescence,* Fall 1994.

Page 235: Most parents spank their children: "What Grown-Ups Understand about Child Development: A National Benchmark Survey," DYG, Inc. sponsored by ZERO TO THREE, CIVITAS, and BRIO Corporation, 2000.

Pages 238–240: More parenting advice from Mac Bledsoe at *www.parentingwith dignity.com.*

Pages 241–243: Effects of divorce on children: Divorce Statistics Collection, *http:// www.divorcereform.org/stats.html.*

Pages 249–253: ABC News, *20/20,* "The Secret Life of Boys," January 24, 1999. Check out this story at *www.abcnews.com/2020/.* Study of facial reactions from girls vs. boys: Ross Buck, et al. "Sex, Personality, and Physiological Variables in the Communication of Affect Via Facial Expression," *Journal of Personality and Social Psychology,* October 1974.

Page 254: Parenting and gender roles: Susan Witt, "Parental Influence on Children's Socialization to Gender Roles," *Adolescence,* Summer 1997.

Pages 254–255: Adults treated baby differently: Phyllis Katz, et al. "Baby X—The Effect of Gender Labels on Adult Responses to Infants," *Sex Roles,* 1975.

Page 257: Teens' brains: Deborah Yurgelun-Todd, et al. "Functional Magnetic Resonance Imaging of Facial Affect Recognition in Children and Adolescents," *Journal of the American Academy of Child and Adolescent Psychiatry,* 1999.

Page 257: Around 90% of kids lie to their parents: Josephson Institute of Ethics, "2004 Report Card Press Release and Data Summary: The Ethics of American Youth," 2004.

Page 259: Five thousand days of adolescence: Even though this number seems pretty high, Kirshenbaum believes that "adolescence" covers the ages between 10 and 23.

Page 261: Children feel close with their parents: Kristin A. Moore, et al. "Parent-Teen Relationships and Interactions: Far More Positive than Not," Child Trends Research Brief, December 2004.

Page 262: High school students having sex: Kaiser Family Foundation, "U.S. Teen Sexual Activity," January 2005, *www.kff.org.*

Page 263: Early sex discussions don't lead to experimentation: Three more prominent referenced studies include:

- Marion Howard and Judith Blamey McCabe, "Helping Teenagers Postpone Sexual Involvement," *Family Planning Perspectives,* 1990.
- Betty M. Hubbard, et al. "A Replication Study of Reducing the Risk," *The Journal of School Health,* August 1998.
- Douglas Kirby, "The impact of schools and school programs upon adolescent sexual behavior," *The Journal of Sex Research,* February 2002.

Pages 263–266: ABC News, *20/20,* "Snooping Parents, Broken Trust?" May 30, 2003. See this story at *www.abcnews.com/2020/.*

CHAPTER 12: THE PURSUIT OF HAPPINESS

Page 268: Money and young people: Alexander Astin, et al. "The American freshman: Thirty year trends, 1966–1996," Higher Education Research Institute, University of California, 1997.

Page 268: Happiness and poor countries: Ed Diener and Robert Biswas-Diener, "Will Money Increase Subjective Well-Being?" *Social Indicators Research,* February 2002.

Pages 268–269: Unfulfilled lottery winners: ABC News Special Report, "The Mystery of Happiness," January 22, 1998. Check out this story at *www. abcnews.com/2020/*.

Page 269: Change in income needed to "fulfill consumption aspirations," 1986–1994: United Nations Development Programme, *Human Development Report 1998*, Oxford University Press, 1998.

Page 269: Top fifth of income earners call themselves "very happy": National Opinion Research Center, University of Chicago, *General Social Survey*, 1992–2002.

Page 269: Forbes wealthiest people no happier: Ed Diener, et al. "Happiness of the Very Wealthy," *Social Indicators Research*, April 1985.

Pages 270–271: Happy faces scale: F. M. Andrews and S. B. Withey, *Social Indicators of Well-Being: Americans' Perceptions of Life Quality*, Plenum Press, 1976.

Page 271: Twins separated at birth: ABC News Special Report, "The Mystery of Happiness," January 22, 1998, *www.abcnews.com/2020/*. Thomas J. Bouchard Jr., et al. "Sources of Human Psychological Differences: The Minnesota Study of Twins Reared Apart," *Science*, October 1990.

Page 273: Babies in control: Developmental Psychology, "Violation of Expectancy, Loss of Control, and Anger in Young Infants," September 1990. Child Development, "Infant Emotional and Cortisol Responses to Goal Blockage," March 2005.

Page 273: People who live in authoritarian states: Ronald Inglehart and Hans-Dieter Klingemann, "Genes, Culture, Democracy, and Happiness," in Ed Diener and Eunkook Suh (eds.), *Culture and Subjective Well-Being*, MIT Press, 2000.

Page 274: Charitable people, married people, religious people and happiness: National Opinion Research Center, University of Chicago, *General Social Survey*, 1992–2002. Chris Wilson and Andrew Oswald, "How Does Marriage Affect Physical and Psychological Health? A Survey of the Longitudinal Evidence," *IZA Discussion Paper No. 1619*, June 2005.

Page 274: Spiritual people feel better about themselves: The Gallup Organization, 1986, 1988.

Pages 276–277: Older people's highs become less high, lows become less low: Martin Pinquart, et al. "Age differences in perceived positive affect, negative affect, and affect balance in middle and old age," *Journal of Happiness Studies*, 2001.

Page 277: Age and happiness graph: Ronald Inglehart, *Culture Shift in Advanced Industrial Society*, Princeton University Press, 1990.

INDEX